Seasons Such As These

SOCIAL PROBLEMS AND SOCIAL ISSUES

An Aldine de Gruyter Series of Texts and Monographs

SERIES EDITOR

Joel Best, *University of Delaware*

David L. Altheide, **Creating Fear: News and the Construction of Crisis**

Ronald J. Berger, **Fathoming the Holocaust: A Social Problems Approach**

Joel Best (ed.), **Images of Issues: Typifying Contemporary Social Problems** (Second Edition)

Joel Best (ed.), **How Claims Spread: Cross-National Diffusion of Social Problems**

Joel Best (ed.), **Troubling Children: Studies of Children and Social Problems**

Cynthia J. Bogard, **Seasons Such As These: How Homelessness Took Shape in America**

James J. Chriss (ed.), **Counseling and the Therapeutic State**

Donatella della Porta and Alberto Vanucci, **Corrupt Exchanges: Actors, Resources, and Mechanisms of Political Corruption**

Jennifer L. Dunn, **Courting Disaster: Intimate Stalking, Culture, and Criminal Justice**

Jeff Ferrell and Neil Websdale (eds.), **Making Trouble: Cultural Constructions of Crime, Deviance, and Control**

Anne E. Figert, **Women and the Ownership of PMS: The Structuring of a Psychiatric Disorder**

Mark Fishman and Gray Cavender (eds.), **Entertaining Crime: Television Reality Programs**

James A. Holstein, **Court-Ordered Insanity: Interpretive Practice and Involuntary Commitment**

James A. Holstein and Gale Miller, **Challenges and Choices: Constructionist Perspectives on Social Problems**

Philip Jenkins, **Images of Terror: What We Can and Can't Know about Terrorism**

Philip Jenkins, **Using Murder: The Social Construction of Serial Homicide**

Valerie Jenness and Kendall Broad, **Hate Crimes: New Social Movements and the Politics of Violence**

Stuart A. Kirk and Herb Kutchins, **The Selling of DSM: The Rhetoric of Science in Psychiatry**

John Lofland, **Social Movement Organizations: Guide to Research of Insurgent Realities**

Donileen R. Loseke, **Thinking about Social Problems: An Introduction to Constructionist Perspectives** (Second Edition)

Donileen R. Loseke and Joel Best (eds.), **Social Problems: Constructionist Readings**

Ellie Lee: **Abortion, Motherhood, and Mental Health: Medicalizing Reproduction in the US and Great Britain**

Leslie Margolin, **Goodness Personified: The Emergence of Gifted Children**

Donna Maurer and Jeffrey Sobal (eds.), **Eating Agendas: Food and Nutrition as Social Problems**

Gale Miller, **Becoming Miracle Workers: Language and Meaning in Brief Therapy**

Elizabeth Murphy and Robert Dingwall, **Qualitative Methods and Health Policy Research**

James L. Nolan, Jr. (ed.), **Drug Courts: In Theory and in Practice**

Bernard Paillard, **Notes of the Plague Years: AIDS in Marseilles**

Dorothy Pawluch, **The New Pediatrics: A Profession in Transition**

Erdwin H. Pfuhl and Stuart Henry, **The Deviance Process** (Third Edition)

Theodore Sasson, **Crime Talk: How Citizens Construct a Social Problem**

Wilbur J. Scott and Sandra Carson Stanley (eds.), **Gays and Lesbians in the Military: Issues, Concerns, and Contrasts**

Jeffrey Sobal and Donna Maurer (eds.), **Weighty Issues: Fatness and Thinness as Social Problems**

Jeffrey Sobal and Donna Maurer (eds.), **Interpreting Weight: The Social Management of Fatness and Thinness**

Carolyn L. Wiener, **The Elusive Quest: Accountability in Hospitals**

Rhys Williams (ed.), **Cultural Wars in American Politics: Critical Reviews of a Popular Myth**

Mark Wolfson, **The Fight Against Big Tobacco: The Movement, the State, and the Public's Health**

Seasons Such As These

How Homelessness Took Shape in America

Cynthia J. Bogard

ALDINE DE GRUYTER
New York

About the Author

Cynthia J. Bogard
Associate Professor of Sociology at Hofstra University

Copyright ©2003 Walter de Gruyter, Inc., New York

ALDINE DE GRUYTER
A division of Walter de Gruyter, Inc.
200 Saw Mill River Road
Hawthorne, New York 10532

This publication is printed on acid free paper

Parts of Chapter 2 have appeared in a somewhat different version in *Symbolic Interaction* 24:425–454. © 2001 by the Society for the Study of Symbolic Interaction.

Library of Congress Cataloging-in-Publication Data

Bogard, Cynthia J.
  Seasons such as these : how homelessness took shape in America / Cynthia J. Bogard.
        p. cm.—(Social problems and social issues)
Includes bibliographical references and index.
  ISBN 0-202-30724-7 (alk. paper)—ISBN 0-202-30675-5 (pbk : alk. paper)
  1. Homelessness—United States. 2. Homelessness—New York (State)—New York. 3. Homelessness—Washington (D.C.) 4. Social problems—United States. 5. United States—Social policy—1980–1993. I. Title. II. Series.
  HV4505.B6 2003
  362.5'5'09730904—dc21

                                                                      2003002638

Manufactured in the United States of America

10 9 8 7 6 5 4 3 2 1

To the CCNV past and present

May we all pursue our
calling with such dedication

Poor naked wretches, whereso'er you are,
That bide the pelting of this pitiless storm,
How shall your houseless heads and unfed sides,
Your loop'd and window'd raggedness, defend you
From seasons such as these?

—William Shakespeare, *King Lear,* Act III, Scene iv

Contents

Preface

Many books, including this one, are written because of the author's need to answer some pressing questions to her own satisfaction. In this case, I came to have two sets of pressing questions, one having to do with how sociologists examine social problems, the other having to do with "my" particular social problem, American homelessness. I began researching homelessness as a social condition in 1989 when, as a social welfare master's student, I conducted a small study concerning the educational needs of homeless children. Later, as a graduate student in sociology I was a member of a research group that involved itself in a number of projects concerning homelessness. In several studies we explored the lives of homeless people living on the streets of suburban Long Island, New York, just east of New York City. Two Long Island townships also hired us to enumerate the homeless people in their area. Most importantly, our group was part of a team hired to evaluate a shelter for homeless families operated by H.E.L.P., an organization founded by Andrew Cuomo, who would later become our nation's "housing czar" and still later our secretary of Housing and Urban Development in the Clinton administration. That particular project grew into a three-year examination of the family shelter system and its inhabitants in all of Westchester County, New York, the county just north of New York City. During the years I worked on these various studies, interviewing homeless people, collecting statistics about them, and observing the enactment of social policy aimed at them, a sense of moral outrage grew in me as it does in many people who have contact with those who are homeless. It seemed to me that the one problem that homeless people (who are a very diverse lot) shared was the lack of regular housing that was appropriate, available, and affordable for them. Some merely needed less costly housing, some needed safer housing, some needed flexible housing arrangements, some needed stabilized arrangements, and some needed supervised housing. But so little of homeless social policy had to do with housing and so much of it had to do with the presumed individual deficiencies of homeless people. So few of the resources America spent on homelessness went toward the provision

of permanent and accessible housing, while so many went toward study-
ing homeless people's characteristics, "rehabilitating" homeless people
from their deficits, or warehousing them in shelters that are both costly
and temporary. Homelessness had become a social problem that was
primarily *not* about solving the nation's housing crisis. My first pressing
question became: How (and why) did homelessness become the social
problem that it did become, one that was only tangentially related to the
problem of inappropriate or insufficient housing? Why, when people demanded that something be done about homelessness, did they get this
policy, these outcomes? Somehow, the shorthand answers of "conservative politics bred conservative policies" or "American individualism pre-
cludes government investment in housing" did not explain it sufficiently,
especially given all the advocacy and research that had occurred in the
1980s and 1990s.

Trying to understand why homelessness became defined by the characteristics of those who are homeless rather than the characteristics (particularly the lack of appropriate housing) of the wealthy society that
failed to house some of its members led me to the constructionist approach to social problems. Constructionists view social problems as the
activities of some members of society as they try to convince others of
their view of a social problem and its "solution." This focus on people
who make claims about a social problem rather than on its conditions is
the distinctive methodological stance of constructionism. The constructionist view helped me to see how the social conditions I observed as a
researcher of homelessness could be framed in various ways depending
on the agenda of the person who spoke about them. This stance, though
it backgrounds "the facts" about homelessness as a condition, is undertaken, at least in this work, in an effort to understand how social change
proceeds so that people with social justice ends in mind can pursue their
claimsmaking strategies more effectively. In this sense, distancing oneself
from "the facts" of homelessness and adopting the constructionist analytical stance might help us to better understand why documenting social
conditions is so often unpersuasive as politics.

Examining these "claimsmaking activities," as constructionists call
them, sociologically, however, is a daunting task because the activities
engaged in by people in the attempt to persuade others are fluid, subtle,
and complicated as are the responses to these social actions. My second
set of pressing questions revolved around this central problem: How can
we adequately represent and sociologically examine this very complicated human activity of social problems construction?

My answer to these questions is a book that can be read two ways.
For those who are interested in the story of the career of homelessness
as a social problem in America's two "national" cities, the book should

be read from the beginning through the conclusion. The technical matter in the appendix can be ignored. For those readers with an interest in social problems constructionism, however, this book is meant as a "cookbook" of sorts. Each chapter emphasizes a feature of constructionism, such as an important group of claimsmakers or an important aspect of the claimsmaking process. The appendix describes the theoretical commitments behind this presentation of homelessness as a constructed social problem, and the ontology, epistemology, and methodology growing out of those commitments. To these readers, I suggest that the appendix be read following the introductory chapter, and before returning to the extended exemplar of my method.

Acknowledgments

I do not know the names of the people I most need to acknowledge. First, I thank the many homeless people who have shared their stories and lives with me over the years, thus enriching my understanding of what it means to be poor in America. Second, I thank the CCNV members and supporters who collected, catalogued and archived materials pertaining to homelessness and the CCNV. Your diligence made this book possible.

I also thank the fund for the Advancement of the Discipline sponsored by American Sociological Association and the National Science Foundation and Hofstra University for their financial support of my research.

The current staff of the CCNV also has my deepest gratitude. They invited me to live in their shelter, allowed me unfettered access to their archives and their xerox machine. I especially want to thank Smitty, Larry and Fred for their help, Executive Director Terry Bishop for her time and her acceptance and Victor Aderele for taking me on a tour of the CCNV and the sites in Washington where the CCNV worked and protested.

Thanks also to the people who have commented on drafts of this book and related articles. Here I must especially thank Margaret Abraham and Anna Linders for their constant support and last-minute reviews. Many others have contributed with their comments on earlier work that wound up in this book, including Leon Anderson, Joel Blau, Kathy Charmez, Jim Holstein, Kim Hopper, Peter Ibarra, and Harry Murray.

The staff at de Gruyter, including Amy Odum and Mike Sola deserve lots of credit for quickly taking this work from manuscript to publication and I thank my editors Joel Best and Richard Koffler for their encouragement.

I want to thank my friends and family for putting up with my absences during the time I was writing this book. Finally, my love and gratitude to my partner in life, Michael Strebe, who continues to offer me unwavering encouragement and support.

Introduction

This book is a study of the career homelessness had as a social problem in America's two "national cities"—New York and Washington, D.C., during the pivotal years between 1977 and 1987. For a social problem to become institutionalized as a "real" public issue "about which something should be done" (Miller 1993:4), some social actors must persuade important others of the issue's importance. Members of four sectors of society are central to this process—sectors Joel Best has termed the "iron quadrangle" of social problems work (1999:63): the media, activists, government, and experts. Here I analyze members of this iron quadrangle as they engaged in claimsmaking activities around homelessness during the time this issue reemerged as a social problem in the late 1970s until the passage of the Stewart B. McKinney (later known as McKinney-Vento) Homeless Assistance Act in 1987. Because it focuses on analyzing claimsmakers as they attempted to influence public perception of a social problem, this is a work about homelessness as a social *construction* rather than a social *condition*.

This is not to say that claimsmakers constructed the social problem of homelessness out of "thin air" (Fine 1997). Every attempt at counting homeless people in the past few decades, regardless of methodology, and regardless of the definition of homelessness used, has found significant numbers of inhabitants of the nation's streets and, later, homeless shelters (Bogard 2001; Burt and Cohen 1989; Wright 1992). Indeed, the common observation that homelessness seemed to be on the rise, especially in urban areas led, by the early 1980s, to efforts to define and enumerate the population affected (Appelbaum 1987, 1990; Hombs and Snyder 1982; Horowitz 1989; Wright and Devine 1992; Salo and Campanelli 1991; Rossi, Wright, Fisher, and Willis 1987). The rise of homelessness during the Reagan era, its seriousness as a social problem, and one unconscionable in such a wealthy nation are grounding assumptions of this work and the engendering motivation behind it. The methodological stance taken in this work, however, backgrounds concern with the extent, characteristics, and causes of homelessness as a social condition because what is of analytical interest here is the social process of claimsmaking activities around these social conditions.

Homelessness has been much studied as a social condition in recent decades. An objectivist account of this social problem, guided by the findings of social science, would conclude that homelessness increased quite dramatically beginning with the recession that marked the Carter administration. It also can be stated firmly that a "new" type of homelessness emerged during the 1980s (Hoch and Slayton 1989; Wright, Rubin, and Devine 1998). By this, scholars generally mean that the types of people who became homeless changed as well as the reasons behind their homeless state. Prior to the 1970s, the homeless population was comparatively small and confined primarily to "skid row" areas of some of the nation's major cities. Homeless people were mostly white middle-aged males, many of whom had drinking problems (Bahr 1973). In fact, even most of these men were not literally homeless. Instead they lived in "flophouses" or, more formally, single-room-occupancy hotels (SROs) that charged minimal daily or weekly rates for a minimum of comfort and privacy (Rossi 1989). Some were also housed in missions, jails, and municipal lodging houses, institutions that appeared with the rising numbers of "unaccommodated men" that marked the Great Depression (Hopper and Hamberg 1984).

In the last few decades of the twentieth century, the homeless population, as well as what was meant by the term "homeless," dramatically changed. First, the people finding themselves homeless more and more were young urban men of color, particularly African-Americans, who were in their prime working years—their twenties and thirties (Burt and Cohen 1989). As we look back, it is clear that many of these men suffered from the severe changes in the structure of the economy we now refer to as "globalization." Most of the fathers of these men had been employed in the trades and manufacturing sector; their sons, though they were as a group better educated, found this option markedly reduced as entire sectors became automated, moved to suburban areas, and/or moved overseas (Bluestone and Harrison 1982). Second, these men did not live in flophouses primarily but engaged in a desperate scramble for resources that Hopper, Susser, and Conover have referred to as "economies of makeshift" (1985). Their strategy for housing included staying for short periods with lovers, friends, and relatives, hoarding the good will of these network members by interspersing nights spent indoors with them with nights spent literally "on the streets." Many of these men could not afford the few dollars needed for an SRO; others had no access to such cheap lodgings as many of these hotels converted to upscale housing for professionals during the 1980s (Brower 1989). When crack cocaine hit the streets in the mid-1980s these were the men who were most vulnerable to becoming addicted to it, and some did.

The severe recession of the early 1980s, though, affected more than young, would-be blue-collar working men of color. In some cities, especially cities like New York, wide swaths of the poor were losing their housing due mostly to unaffordability. The proportion of housing affordable to the poor and, because of race-based housing segregation, realistically available to low-income people of color, shrank markedly during the 1980s (Massey and Denton 1993). This was caused, in turn, by local policies favoring gentrification as big-city mayors tried to beat the recession by trying to get in front of the globalization curve. In New York, in particular, this involved upgrading the housing stock to make it appealing to the white-collar employees of leading financial institutions—one important sector that New York officials tried to lure to the city to help it rebound from a fiscal crisis spawned by global economic upheaval (Blau 1992). Many of the people who were priced out of the housing market as a consequence were women of color, again disproportionately African-Americans, with young children (Knickman and Weitzman 1989; Shinn and Gillespie 1994). Family homelessness and that of single women also grew tremendously in the late 1980s (Burt 1992).

A final group, the mentally ill, constituted yet another portion of those who were homeless—the most visible portion. Much has been made of the deinstitutionalization of psychiatric patients from state hospitals and the possible effect this had on the homeless population. I tend to side with those who think the closing of state psychiatric hospitals had only a small effect on the total homeless population. It was a visible one, however, because severely mentally ill people are often very noticeable in ways that other homeless people are not (Blau 1992; Snow, Baker, and Anderson 1986). It is also probably true that certain cities, among them New York, were disproportionately affected by deinstitionalization. The significance of psychiatric patients as homeless people, however, was as much a political reality as a demographic one.

"New" homeless people are not easy to lump together because there are various reasons for their homelessness and the condition affects a demographically diverse group. When speaking of the "new" homeless though, most scholars mean that they are a much younger group than the "skid row" men of earlier decades, that they are disproportionately African-Americans, and that many more women and children find themselves homeless than previously (Wright, Rubin, and Devine 1998). In addition, many scholars (including myself) would insist that the "new" homeless people are homeless in different ways and for different reasons than the "skid row" men of mid-twentieth-century America. Literal homelessness became more common in the Reagan era, that is, people sleeping in public places, or, to quote Rossi "not having customary and regular access to a conventional dwelling" (1989). And the seismic economic shifts that shook the nation were directly responsible for the homelessness of many in a way that had not been the case previously, at least not since our last huge economic upheaval, the Great Depression.

Looking back at the Reagan era from the vantage point of twenty years time, that is the social scientific story I would tell about "new" homelessness as a social *condition*.

The story I would tell about homelessness as a social *construction*, however, has a different plot, with different underlying presumptions, and somewhat different social actors. And my goals in relating it are quite different. What I start with here is the idea that social conditions (such as homelessness) do not present themselves as "facts" about which there is unilateral agreement. "What to make" of a set of social conditions takes work, what constructionists refer to as "social problems work" (Holstein and Miller 1993). By now, "everybody knows" that homelessness is a serious social problem in America. But just how did we come to something resembling a consensus, or at least a dominant opinion, about what homelessness is and what should be done about it during the 1980s? Who did this social problems work? What exactly did they do? What effects did these claimsmaking activities have? Who won the conflict over what we as a public should conclude about the set of social conditions called homelessness? Why did one version of "the facts" and "the solution" regarding homelessness become dominant instead of another? These are the types of questions that I ask and try to answer here.

Claimsmaking activities (Spector and Kitsuse 1977) are the actions taken by some people in an attempt to persuade others of their view of a social problem and what should be done about it. Holstein and Miller (1993) use the term "social problems work" to describe these interactive processes and define it as "any and all activity implicated in the recognition, identification, interpretation, and definition of conditions that are called 'social problems' " (ibid.:134). "Claimsmaking activities" conceptually casts a wide net. It is intended to capture the public strategic actions of the iron quadrangle (Best 1999:63) of social actors that typically construct and reinforce social problems. But it also refers to "the hard work of nonpublicly formulating putatively objectionable conditions into problems" (Gubrium 1993:59). The nonpublic side of social problems work has to do with what happens behind the scenes to construct a social problem. These types of activities include meetings, letter writing and other communication between claimsmaking groups, and private negotiations.

Whether privately or publicly conducted, all claimsmaking activities attempt to typify to others the social problem of interest. Typification

(Schutz 1962) can be defined as an effort on the part of a person or persons to interpret and represent some aspect of reality to others. In a general sense, typification is what people do when they experience, then interpret their world. In regards to social problems, typification is what claimsmakers do when they convince others that some putative social condition is problematic and that it is so in a certain way.

The successful construction of a social problem occurs when claims-makers are able to establish a dominant view of a social problem by convincing others to see a set of social conditions as a problem, and one about which "something must be done."

My version of constructionism necessitates a close and comparative examination of who said and did what about homelessness as events unfolded over time, a reconstructed history of claimsmaking activities. Multiple sources of data are essential to the reconstruction process. Archival data, a range of print media, televised media, scholarly publications, and commentary by key informants are used in this study in an attempt to reconstruct a sense of context, claimsmaking activities, their interpretations, and their interplay as they emerged over time. Particular attention is paid to the dominant print media in each city, the *New York Times* (*NYT*) and the *Washington Post* (*WP*), in their coverage of homelessness because these two dominant papers primarily represent the views of the power elite in their respective cities. They are widely read by those most likely to emerge as local claimsmakers and those who are likely to respond to claims as well as by others among the educated voting public. In addition, the *New York Times* is often cited as "America's paper of record" while the *Washington Post* makes in-depth coverage of national politics its primary concern. Thus each of these papers is an important producer and arbiter of what becomes influential public knowledge about social problems at a national level. In this sense these two papers are a good reflection of public discourse, as Gamson (1992) argues more generally about the media.

Obviously, in making decisions about what to cover and how, editors themselves act as claimsmakers. Newspapers and all media cannot be treated as though they merely supply objective historical material about a public issue such as homelessness (Johnson 1995:17; Best 1990). I employ them here because as dominant and elite voices in the public conversation about a social problem, these media sources are important sites of reality construction. Thus they offer *relevant* accounts of typification efforts by others and often, such as in editorials, try to typify a social problem themselves.

To counterbalance the claims and coverage of these elite newspapers as sources of data, this analysis also employs archival material and secondary news coverage as well as works and commentary from activists and scholars who were involved in this issue during the stipulated time period. The data from all these sources are reconstructed and presented in chronological order so that a sense of "events as they happened" can be gained in what Ian Hacking (1999) has termed a "history of building" constructionist method. A broad definition of "claimsmaking activities" ensures that a variety of "social problems work" is examined.

Of course, social life is too complex to be reconstructed exactly and analytic decisions still have to be made. For example in the next chapter I focus on one campaign and then another, though they happened simultaneously. There are also pivotal moments when the trajectory of a constructed problem takes shape and these receive more attention. Often the early, emergent phases of a social construction process set the direction for later claimsmaking, so these are important to examine in detail. Claimsmaking sometimes focuses on the problem itself, while at other times more attention is paid to typifying the people who suffer from the problem (Spencer 1996) or setting the emotional or moral response to the problem (Loseke 1999). These different emphases are also often worth distinguishing. The analytic decisions that must be made make the narrative reconstruction something less than an "exact reproduction" of reality. But the history of building method I employ is used to emphasize that social life and social problem construction are ongoing, fluid, and interactive processes. By presenting claimsmaking activities mostly as they happened I employ an "open epistemology" that allows the reader to better follow my analytic practices.

In addition, I take seriously the context in which these activities are set. All meaning-making activities occur within a context. Context, as I employ the term, is meant to evoke a notion of the "world as it is" (Schutz 1962) or the "conditions of action" (Schwalbe et al. 2000:440)— the circumstances claimsmakers must confront, use, and change if they are to successfully pursue their projects. In interactionist terms, the social context is not a fixed or objective entity. Instead, context, as I view it and employ it here, is defined as sedimented, or previously typified, systems of power/knowledge as these systems are reinvigorated by current social actors, a fluid and reflexive sense of the larger social arena in which claimsmaking takes place (Schutz 1962). Gubrium and Holstein refer to this sense of context as "discourses-in-use" (2000; Foucault 1972). It is context that provides material and symbolic resources to claimsmakers and those with whom they interact, the claimsmaking audience. In order to understand *why* claimsmaking activities took shape as they did, were reacted to as they were, had the outcomes they had, it is necessary to delineate the important elements of context as they shaped and were shaped by claimsmaking activities.

The analytic goal of constructionism, as I view it, is to examine the interplay of claimsmaking activities and the context in which they are embedded in order to both richly describe how claimsmaking activities constructed a social problem such as homelessness and why it was constructed as it was. But of course, claimsmaking activities and the interactive context in which they operate elaborate *one another*. Examining their interplay enables us to cautiously answer the question of why social life proceeds as it does and not in some other way (Archer 1995). Examining the typification process is best accomplished, first, by strategically and artificially separating claimsmaking from context, a tactic Archer refers to as analytic dualism (1995, 1996) and is further enhanced by using a comparative design when possible.

In each chapter I first build a narrative about the development of homelessness as a social problem by detailing relevant claimsmaking activities as they occurred. An analytical segment that examines the salient elements of context and their interplay with claimsmaking activities follows the narrative. Through this process I attempt to build a case about why the career homelessness as a social problem unfolded the way it did unfold.

I argue that the "formative years" of homelessness as a national social problem are best discerned by examining how the problem emerged in New York and Washington, D.C., because these are America's two "national cities." Although homelessness was emerging as a social problem in other, especially urban, areas during this time period, New York and Washington are uniquely situated as national centers of politics, intellectual activity, and public opinion formation. As such, initial local efforts at typifying an emergent social problem such as homelessness take on added importance, in large part because what is termed of national interest is often synonymous with what news is covered by the press in these two cities.

In each chapter I emphasize either a member of the iron quadrangle or an important feature of social problems construction. Obviously, this is an analytical tactic and not meant to imply that a certain claimsmaker group or feature was only relevant during the time period covered by that chapter.

Chapter 1 examines the emergence of homelessness as a social problem and how activists fostered that emergence. It also explicates "context" as I use the term throughout this volume. Chapter 2 focuses on government officials and their roles as claimsmakers. In Chapter 3 I take up the media in their complex role as both the context in which the claims of others are publicized and as claimsmakers in their own right. Chapter 4 discusses the interaction of government, the media, and activists as the construction of homelessness continues. This chapter also takes up how claimsmaking around the problem of hunger helped to enhance and solidify the position of homelessness as a social problem. Chapter 5 takes up the fourth member of the iron quadrangle—social science experts—and specifically examines what role they played in the construction of one important "fact" about homelessness—the size of the problem. Chapter 6 calls attention to moral activities and how these solidified homelessness as a social problem. Chapter 7 notes a distinctive group of claimsmakers who fall somewhat outside the iron quadrangle—film, music, and television celebrities—and examines how their participation in homelessness claimsmaking led to the strange glamorization of the issue. The chapter also explores the outcomes of homelessness as a social problem, how these were achieved, and what was accomplished. Chapter 8 looks back from the present and examines the ironic outcomes, silenced issues, and unintended consequences of claimsmaking during the age of Reagan.

1

Activists and the Emergence of Homelessness as a Social Problem in Washington, D.C.

INTRODUCTION

Homelessness as a constructed social problem got its start in Washington, D.C., in the late 1970s. Oftentimes, it is activists who first bring attention to some feature of social life and define it as problematic, and such was the case with homelessness. The narrative of claimsmaking activities around homelessness began with a central activist group in the nation's capital, the Community for Creative Non-Violence (CCNV). The CCNV's creative and often confrontational claimsmaking activities stimulated various audiences to react to the group and their claims, the media to report on their actions, and both the media and select audience members to engage in claimsmaking activities of their own. It is through this interactive process that some collection of "socially circumscribed activities and processes" or condition-categories (Ibarra and Kitsuse 1993:26) becomes a social problem. In this chapter I compare two separate CCNV claimsmaking campaigns in the city where homelessness initially was constructed as a social problem, with a focus on the activist sector and its role in the emergence of a social problem.

THE COMMUNITY FOR CREATIVE NON-VIOLENCE
TAKES ON THE ISSUE

At the center of activities that would ultimately construct homelessness as a "new" social problem in Washington was a local radical activist group, the Community for Creative Non-Violence (CCNV). By 1977, this group of about two dozen self-described "Christian anarchists" devoted to the promotion of peace and social justice through "prayer, service and protest" (Sabath 1976:30) had begun to focus on what founder and former Paulist priest Ed Guinan called "the violence of wasted lives" in their local community (Rader 1986:57). Specifically, the group began a feeding program in 1972 and shortly afterward decided to open their communal home to serve as a winter shelter for their homeless neighbors (Sabath 1976). By 1977 the CCNV had also opened a free food store, started an urban land trust, found a multifamily abandoned building on Fairmont Street, and were engaged in negotiations with the city to purchase it for renovation (*Washington Afro-American* August 13, 1976). In addition, the group had opened a shelter for indigent men awaiting trial, a free medical clinic, a print shop that provided job training, and a referral service for evicted families (CCNV brochure 1977). All activities were funded through private donations.

In this early period of problem emergence, the CCNV pursued a dual strategy of pressing the city government and the local religious community for both emergency and longer-term housing solutions for the city's impoverished residents. The group engaged in activities intended to generate publicity and in relatively nonpublic claimsmaking (Gubrium 1993). One early relatively nonpublic activity conducted in the autumns of 1976 and 1977 included writing letters and calling eleven hundred area churches, synagogues, and mosques to urge them to provide shelter for the homeless poor (CCNV letter, September 29, 1977). By the winter of 1977, two churches had responded affirmatively and began to offer temporary night shelter to homeless people.

Another central nonpublic activity that symbolically and materially demonstrated the CCNV's commitment to treating homeless people with dignity was what the group, in Catholic Worker tradition, called "night hospitality" (Murray 1990). This involved CCNV members making the rounds of known street sleeping sites in a van and attempting to convince street dwellers they encountered to accept transport to the CCNV hospitality house or one of two shelters operated by religious organizations. In CCNV publications and publicity of this period, sheltering homeless people was referred to consistently as offering "night hospitality" (e.g., CCNV letter, March 14, 1978; *WP,* December 21, 1977). Homelessness was not yet defined as a "public problem" (Gusfield 1981) by the dominant press during this period. The *Post's* coverage of derelicts, vagrants, drifters, and street people, as they were variously termed, or those who helped them was sparse during 1977, including only five stories, three during the holiday season.

The emergence of homelessness as a social problem in the *Post* began with "Night Hospitality," an article by columnist Colman McCarthy, who spent an evening traveling in the CCNV's van and profiled the group and its leader, Mitch Snyder (*WP*, December 21, 1977). In this initial public forum in the *Post*, the CCNV's Snyder is portrayed as focused on the immediate needs of homeless street people—a bus to transport street dwellers to shelters so that more homeless people could avoid a freezing death. The group's larger vision was also mentioned. McCarthy explained that the CCNV was trying to raise money to renovate an abandoned apartment building (the Fairmont Street site) that city officials had recently turned over to what the group's fund-raising letters refer to as "the first urban land trust in the country" (CCNV letter, August 25, 1978). Though at first the CCNV envisioned using the building as a shelter, the group eventually hoped to renovate it to provide long-term housing for the poor (Rader 1986).

Claims about the immediate need for increased night hospitality dominated press reports of this period and were also the focal point of CCNV's own publications. Night hospitality, as the CCNV envisioned it, required offering more than merely shelter to what were often referred to as "street people." In a subsequent *Post* article about church-sponsored shelters, Mitch Snyder was quoted as saying the terms of the shelters "infuriate" him. He continued, "You must treat these people with dignity. You can't force religion down someone's throat and expect a miracle. These people need to be given friendship, respect" (*WP*, December 23, 1977). This marked the beginning of press coverage of CCNV's remarkably consistent message about treating the homeless poor with respect and dignity and providing night hospitality on terms that street dwellers would find acceptable.

Though the CCNV continued to press the religious community for assistance with providing shelter and for funds to continue its efforts, by the end of 1977, the CCNV had also begun calling for city government to take responsibility for homelessness. Their initial efforts met with several successes. In early 1978, the group met with the sympathetic director of the Department of Human Resources (DHR), Albert Russo, to plead for the opening of city-funded emergency shelter (*WP*, January 29, 1978). Their claims were bolstered by testimony of the religious community's shelter operators that their shelters were continually "filled beyond capacity" (CCNV letter to Russo, February 6, 1978) and by that winter's bitterly cold weather, which by January had caused three new freezing deaths. The city did open its first publicly financed emergency shelter in January 1978 and staffed it with DHR employees. By February, the CCNV publicized a planned "death watch" in front of the District Building to press the city for an expanded number of beds. This effort was also successful both in generating publicity for the issue and in that within forty-eight hours of the threatened protest the city opened a new shelter that more than doubled capacity to two hundred beds for homeless men (*WP*, February 10, 1978; CCNV press release, February 8, 1978). In a later news article, deputy director of DHR William Whitehurst admitted, "To be perfectly candid, the opening last winter of [the shelter] was directly attributable to our meetings with CCNV" (*District Star*, December 8, 1978).

These successes resulted in a bit more publicity for the CCNV and their issues in the coming months. The urban land trust was discussed in the *Washington Star* (February 12, 1978). Mitch Snyder was again profiled in the *Post* in relation to the CCNV's pressure campaign to get Holy Trinity Church, a wealthy Georgetown Catholic congregation, to reallocate a portion of their $350,000 building renovation fund to use in service of the homeless poor (*WP*, June 2, 1978). The group focused on this ultimately unsuccessful campaign of protests and fasts through the summer of 1978. They also, however, reminded DHR head Russo that he had made a public commitment to open additional emergency shelters by winter, and that they were holding him to this promise (CCNV letter to Russo, June 22, 1978). Claimsmaking activities in the second half of 1978 and the responses of intended publics to those activities would prove to be pivotal in shaping typification of homelessness as a social problem in Washington, D.C. The CCNV worked on two distinct campaigns during this period. Each aimed at evoking a response from a particular "public."

THE HOLY TRINITY CAMPAIGN

The idea for the Holy Trinity campaign appears to have originated in a conversation with *Post* columnist Colman McCarthy (Rader 1986). In early 1978, when funds for renovating the Fairmont Street building were drying up, Snyder took McCarthy on a tour of the building, hoping to get some publicity for the project. At this meeting McCarthy, who had "shared more than a few meals and evenings with members of CCNV" over the years (*WP*, August 20, 1978) told Snyder of another group's renovation project. In spring of 1978, Father James English of Georgetown's Holy Trinity Church (where McCarthy attended services) had asked his parishioners for $350,000 to preserve and bring up to safety code the church, a building widely recognized as one of Washington's architectural gems (Rader 1986). McCarthy told the CCNV that some socially conscious parishioners were unhappy about the renovation plans. After checking out the situation for themselves, the CCNV wrote a strongly worded letter to the pastor, questioning whether church renovation was the most Christian use of congregation money when "others not far away die for lack of shelter" (CCNV letter, May 1978). The CCNV suggested that some of these funds be diverted to the Fairmont Street project. The two groups were already known to each other. CCNV members had previously spoken and had been warmly received at the church, and Holy Trinity parishioners had donated food, money, and clothing to various CCNV activities concerning homelessness. A few parishioners were regular volunteers at the CCNV soup kitchen (Rader 1986).

CCNV members were told to bring their request for funding to the church's Social Concerns Committee, which distributed about $5,000 a year to worthy causes. The CCNV needed about $80,000 to complete renovations to the Fairmont Street building and also was convinced that the two renovation projects should be directly compared as to their value as Christian acts. So they shifted tactics from the relatively nonpublic claimsmaking activities of letter writing and committee meeting attendance to a more public campaign of leafleting Holy Trinity's wealthy parishioners before Mass on Sundays. The leaflets apprised parishioners of the needs of Washington's homeless people and urged them to divert a portion of the church renovation fund to renovating the Fairmont Street building. "When people in a position of moral leadership, people such as yourself, place buildings before human beings, something is wrong," the leaflet read in part (*WP*, June 2, 1978).

Instead of reconsidering the purpose to which building renovation funds were to be put, Holy Trinity Pastor English added another $50,000 to the building renovation fund so that the church's pipe organ could be refurbished (Rader 1986). Snyder met with Father English to ask him to reconsider, to no avail. So from mid-June through July the CCNV decided to "represent the poor with their own bodies" (Rader 1986:95) at weekend services. Several members stood silently through each Mass in protest of Holy Trinity's financial priorities. Meanwhile, the $400,000 was raised in seven months from the wealthy parishioners, renovation was scheduled to begin soon, and Pastor English refused to have an open meeting on the issue, although there was some support for reallocation from a minority of parishioners (*WP*, August 20, 1978; Rader 1986).

On July 29, the CCNV decided to begin a liquid fast in protest, a tactic that they would use again and again over the years. Eight members of CCNV, four Carmelite nuns associated with the parish, and two Holy Trinity folk Mass musicians fasted. Weekend Masses grew tense as standing became an obvious ordeal for the fasting protesters and discomfort among parishioners grew. One CCNV member recalled that a male parishioner started shrieking "I hope you die! You're poison, you're evil!" at her while she stood in the church (as quoted in Rader 1986:96). The fast continued, press coverage of the conflict increased, but the parish did not change its policy. On August 28, four CCNV fasters moved onto the church grounds and vowed to fast and to remain there until funds were reallocated to serve the poor. After forty days of fasting, a meeting by church council members was held and they agreed to reevaluate the building plans. Buoyed by this ray of hope, the protesters ended their fast. Just a few days later, on September 13, 1978 (Rader 1986), the city demolished the Fairmont Street building, citing the lack of renovation progress and the dangerous condition of the existing structure. The demolition of the Fairmont Street site would effectively end the CCNV's struggle to provide substantial long-term housing for the poor. In the short run, however, the group decided to continue to press Holy Trinity for funding reallocation to be used to provide emergency shelter and other services for Washington's homeless residents.

In the end, the church's renovation committee voted unanimously to accept the original budget and no funds were reallocated (*WP*, December 24, 1978). As Colman McCarthy stated, "CCNV felt badly betrayed" (Rader 1986:99) by this outcome. In response, CCNV's leader Mitch Snyder decided to begin a total fast on Christmas Eve, 1978, vowing to make the church "change its ways or I'm going to be dead" (*WP*, December 28, 1978). "Human beings are dying from starvation and homelessness," he stated, "while [Holy Trinity] has resources available to stop it but instead is using those resources for its own needs. By my fasting, we are creating a window onto that reality" (*WP*, December 24, 1978). Snyder received much local and Catholic press publicity for this action, including articles and columns headlined, "If Activist Dies, Who Is to Blame?" (*District Star*, December 29, 1978), "Exploring the Purpose Behind a Dying Man" (*WP*, December 31, 1978), "Anguish Pervades a Georgetown Church" (*WP*, January 1, 1979), and "Snyder's Fast Shows Who Values Life Most" (*WP*, January 5, 1979).

By January 4, 1979, the twelfth day of his total fast, Mitch Snyder's condition was described as "very perilous" by a physician attending him, who added that he could die within hours (*WP*, January 4, 1979). That same evening, Holy Trinity's parish council decided to reject the CCNV's request for funding for the poor. As it became clear that the CCNV would lose this battle and possibly their leader as well, the group and Snyder decided to put an end to the fast (*WP*, January 5, 1979). By this time, Catholic officials from the archdiocese of Washington had stepped in to attempt to mediate the dispute (*WP*, January 3, 1979) and Holy Trinity parishioners were reported as vehemently opposed to Snyder's action. "Let him die! . . . The world would be well off without him," was how one woman put it. "We feel very put upon" and "It's a kind of extortion," said another. "Let them do what they want with their money. We'll do what we want with ours," stated a male parishioner (*WP*, January 1,

1979). The press, too, generally expressed exasperation with Snyder, the *Washington Post* calling him "a kidnapper holding himself (and human feeling) hostage" (*WP,* January 5, 1979). The editorial concluded that the main issue was Snyder himself and that the paper found itself "commending his impulse to aid the poor, yet recognizing his pretense of martyrdom as the act of egotism it was" (*WP,* January 5, 1979). Washington's other major daily paper, the *Washington Star,* said, "Father English and his congregation deserve sympathy for maintaining a calm good sense under the publicized pressure, and sticking by their considered moral judgement" (January 6, 1979). Snyder was compared to suicide cult leader Jim Jones in Guyana. The *Star* editorial and a press summary published in the *Catholic Standard,* the Washington area archdiocese's weekly newspaper, noted that a fast that might result in suicide contradicts Catholic teachings and was an "act of violence" that Catholics should condemn (*Catholic Standard,* January 11, 1979). Michael Novak, a *Washington Star* columnist summarized by the *Catholic Standard,* agreed that the fast was a Snyder ego trip, even calling it an act of terrorism. McCarthy, not surprisingly, was most sympathetic, noting that the CCNV brought to the fore a contradiction between Catholic teachings and Catholic action (*WP,* January 8, 1979). Another *Post* columnist, William Raspberry, commended Snyder for his sincerity and for bringing issues of wealth and poverty to the fore (January 10, 1979). Several other news stories noted that the CCNV succeeded in getting the issue of local poverty and homelessness on the public agenda (*Washington Star,* January 5, 1979; *WP,* January 6, 1979). The *Star* continued coverage of the issue and even gave Snyder himself a column in which to express his views (January 10, 12, 15, 21, 1979). CCNV's claimsmaking activities around the use of church funds by a wealthy congregation did heighten the visibility of local homelessness and poverty. Because of this, in an interview in 1983, Snyder declared that the Holy Trinity confrontation "was our most successful campaign" (Rader 1986:109). Claimsmaking activities by the CCNV, however, were markedly unsuccessful in convincing a supposedly like-minded audience (other Catholics) of CCNV's moral position on the centrality of local homelessness and poverty as a social problem and on its solution (divert funds from wealthy Catholics) to dealing with the problem.

THE NATIONAL VISITOR CENTER CAMPAIGN

The Holy Trinity campaign was pursued vigorously during the summer of 1978 and picked up again at Christmas. In between, however, the

CCNV launched another claimsmaking campaign, this one aimed at the public sector. As the winter of 1978–1979 approached, the CCNV took the position that many individuals the advocacy group described as "hard-core street people" would not submit to either regulations imposed by the city shelters or the religious proselytizing at church-run shelters. Yet these homeless people remained in danger of freezing to death during the winter if they would not avail themselves of these shelters (*WP,* December 5, 1978). These claims were given credence and publicity when a local priest posed as a homeless man one night and reported on his adventures with an oppressive city shelter bureaucracy in a column in the *Post* in late fall (October 28, 1978). Snyder was quoted in a subsequent *Post* article as saying, "Many of them can't take the hassle, the controls. They don't want to have to give a name or a Social Security number at the [government] shelters, and they can't take the religious trip at the missions" (*WP,* November 30, 1978).

To dramatize the need for shelter reform, on November 30, 1978, scores of homeless people and advocates occupied an unused portion of the National Visitor Center, a part of Union Station, Washington's central commuter rail and Amtrak station. The group intended to set up and operate a makeshift, community-regulated shelter in the unused portion of the highly visible federal building for the duration of the winter or until demands to the city for a more adequate and less regulated shelter for street people were met. Prior to the occupation, they made their intentions known in a letter sent to the Secretary of the Interior, under whose jurisdiction the building fell. This letter was also released to the press. In it and other letters of the period, the right to shelter was defined by the CCNV as "people have the right to get in out of the cold, on any night of the year" (letter to Cecil Andrus, Secretary of the Interior, October 9, 1978) and "Our commitment is this: there must be adequate, accessible space for everyone who needs and wants it, offered in an atmosphere of reasonable dignity" (CCNV fund-raising letter, October 14, 1978). The *Post*'s coverage of the CCNV's call for dignified treatment of the poor typically focused on the antibureaucratic aspects of the group's demands, stressing their insistence on "hassle-free" emergency shelter for homeless people (e.g., *WP,* December 5, 7, 9, 1978).

Though the group only occupied the Visitor Center for nine days before being locked out by government officials and police officers, this direct action, with its arrests, sit-ins, and confrontations with police, received much publicity (*WP,* December 5, 7, 9–12, 14, 16, 1978). Six local TV and press outlets covered the takeover as did four Catholic publications and the *New York Times,* for a total of at least forty-six separate news stories, dramatic photos and footage of arrests, editorials, features, and letters to the editor. In an unsigned editorial, the *Post* characterized the takeover as a "dramatic gimmick" and urged the CCNV to cooperate with the DHR or offer to run a shelter for the city (December 9, 1978). This position was echoed in an editorial broadcast on a local news program (WHLA, Channel 7, December 10, 1978).

A few days later CCNV members did meet with DHR director Russo. They presented him with a list of eight formal demands growing out of the Visitor Center takeover and included documentation showing that shelter populations had declined recently (CCNV letter to Russo, December 13, 1978). Declining shelter use, the CCNV claimed, was a result of excessive regulation and demeaning and invasive treatment at the shelters, which made many homeless people refuse to come in from the cold. Although the city could have used these statistics to claim that shelter use was declining because homelessness was abating, the DHR instead tacitly accepted the CCNV's reasoning for shelter use decline and agreed to meet the group's demands on an experimental basis. The *Post* reported that "a key demand is 'elimination of all restrictions on the admittance of guests to city-run emergency shelters including identification and income verification" (December 14, 1978). Though Snyder commented that "we got DHR to say housing is a basic human right" (*WP*, December 16, 1978), all demands were focused on immediate steps the city could take to provide street people with emergency, not permanent, shelter that was less restrictive than was the case previously (CCNV letter to Russo, December 13, and response, December 15, 1978). Eventually, the DHR gave CCNV a shelter to run as a result of the Visitor Center occupation and, consequently, the group engaged in less direct action concerning homelessness and received little publicity from the *Post* for nearly two years (but see *WP*, January 19, 20, 1979; January 8, 1981). Moreover, the occupation did not succeed in involving the federal government in any substantial way in the problem of homelessness. This accomplishment was still a couple of years in the future.

The CCNV had been successful in garnering publicity for homelessness in the late 1970s; theirs was the dominant voice in typification of the issue at the local level. As translated by the *Post*, however, the group's notion of the "right to shelter" came across as a demand that emergency shelter should be provided to the city's truly homeless. The conception of dignity that textured CCNV members' lives and work with the homeless poor was reduced to a notion that the shelter should be "hassle-free." By the beginning of 1979, then, this early and prominent group of claimsmakers had had much success in the night hospitality arm of their campaign for the homeless poor and had witnessed terrible setbacks in their quest for more low-income housing. The group's early focus on building an urban land trust had met with stiff opposition from both religious and secular sectors and its plans to expand housing for the poor seemed further off than ever. On the other hand, the CCNV's call for emergency shelter for homeless people had received a positive reception from the local government. These early failures and successes would have a profound effect on the CCNV's next round of claimsmaking about homelessness and the group's longer-range goals for the issue.

CLAIMSMAKERS IN CONTEXT

The reconstruction of claimsmaking activities describes, in a "history of building" style, *how* claimsmakers acted as they attempted to construct a social problem and how audiences reacted to these activities. To understand *why* these claimsmaking activities took the forms and met with the response they did, however, it is necessary to examine the interplay of activities with the varying contexts in which they were embedded. The goal here is to identify how elements of context were used as resources or presented obstacles to claimsmakers and their audiences as they engaged in elaborating their social world. The focus remains on social interaction. The elements of context themselves must be understood as claimsmakers' and audience's *interpretations* of the symbolic, material, and relational contexts they inhabit. Though some interpretations have proven quite historically durable (e.g., the Catholic church); all are still dependent on current social actors and their activities for their meanings. In an analysis that construes context in a strictly interpretive sense as I do here, a better grasp on the *why* questions can be obtained by comparing two instances of contextualized social interaction.

Though both of the audiences for these disparate campaigns nominally shared the same physical location, Washington, D.C., and had some overlap, particularly in that the media were part of the intended audience for each campaign, the contexts differed markedly. Here I sketch some main elements of context as it was invoked and confronted by claimsmakers to illustrate how discerning and exploring generic elements of context can illuminate potential causal linkages.

I distinguish between two basic features of context. The *environmental context* is the material or physical aspects of the human-made and human-interpreted natural environment (such as a city or the weather). It also includes sedimented current power and bureaucratic relationships, including what social movements scholars have termed political opportunities, and accountability and mobilizing "structures" (McAdam, McCarthy, and Zald 1996). The *interpretive context* is the range of symbolic materials available to both claimsmakers and their audiences in interpreting "what to make" of a putative social problem (Benford and Snow

2000). The interpretive context is what "frames" are made from—the culturally specific and historically embedded elements of claimsmaking activities that are combined by claimsmakers in an attempt to make their version of a social problem persuasive to others (Goffman 1974; Tarrow 1994; Zald 1996). It is also the basis upon which publics evaluate claims-making effectiveness—the resonance of a particular framing of a social problem (Snow and Benford 1988).

In both interpretive and environmental aspects of context, claimsmak-ers actively use contextual elements as resources and find themselves confronted by obdurate typifications (made salient by other current so-cial actors) that present obstacles to their goals. The social world, of course, is a seamless web of environmental and interpretive elements. But discussing each separately and employing these two aspects of con-text as heuristic devices aids in discerning salient and generic features of context, thereby enabling some purchase on the question of why social life was elaborated as it was rather than in some other way. It is for this purpose that I employ them here.

THE INTERPRETIVE CONTEXT

One challenge for claimsmakers emerges when members struggle with one another to achieve an account of what is objectionable and what to do about it (Miller 1993). Although interpretive consistency or within-group cohesion is not necessary, a common interpretation of and re-sponse to the problem must evolve, both to sustain group solidarity and to facilitate consistent claimsmaking. At times, this *private*, within-group social problems work (Gubrium 1993; Holstein and Miller 1993) differs from how the interpretive context is *publicly* and *strategically* marshaled when claimsmakers attempt to frame the problem for targeted audiences.

Within-Group Interpretive Resources

In attempting to typify the problem to themselves and each other, CCNV members gleaned their interpretive and ideological resources from the theological and historical sources that made moral and emo-tional sense to them. These locally salient and available aspects of the interpretive context derived from members' biographies and social and historical locations (Mills 1959). CCNV members hailed from different religious, cultural, ethnic, and class locations, and these differences ensured a variety of interpretive resources. Indeed, the diversity of interpretive resources members brought to the group may have helped to ensure a wealth of creative claimsmaking ideas. Catholic sources of inspiration featured the Catholic Worker philosophy of Dorothy Day, with its attention to divestment from materialism, to serving the poor, and to living in poverty among those served. This philosophy itself was often linked by CCNV members to biblical accounts of the lives of service by very early Christians (such as Paul) as well as more contemporaneous ideas coming from the "liberation theology" branch of leftist Catholicism as it was developing in Latin America (Sabath 1976).

The civil rights and anti–Vietnam War movements also influenced CCNV members. CCNV founder Ed Guinan had been a young seminary student during "Freedom Summer," and had been impressed by nonviolent approaches to civil rights. He began to meet other civil rights activists such as the priests Philip and Daniel Berrigan and labor organizer Cesar Chavez and as anti-Vietnam activism grew, came to know the work of Vietnamese poet and scholar Thich Nhat Hanh, who advocated love and sacrifice, such as fasting, to achieve peace and justice. Guinan spent the summer of 1968 in Berkeley, where he met Mario Savio and learned firsthand of the ideology and tactics that had grown from Freedom Summer into the Free Speech movement. Also that year, he had contacted Martin Luther King and offered to help with the Poor People's Campaign. The influence of these central members of the civil rights and peace movements was reemphasized by Guinan's choice of seminary thesis topic—Thomas Merton's theology of nonviolence. Merton himself had been influenced by Aldous Huxley, Erasmus, Gandhi, and James Joyce, and the ideas of these men also became part of the ideational resources of the CCNV. Later, Mitch Snyder converted to Catholicism after meeting Daniel Berrigan while both were incarcerated in a Connecticut prison. The Berrigan brothers' nonviolent but outspoken approach to Christian activism was thus reemphasized during the years Snyder was a leader of the group (Rader 1986).

The interpretive resources that members brought to the group eventually cohered into three basic principles. First was a within-group Christian consciousness about the primacy of the "violence of wasted lives" and a need to live lives that directly addressed poverty. Second was that this should be done through both service and political action. Third, and reflected in the group's name, was a loose consensus that dramatic nonviolent direct action was to be a central component of their political efforts. How to forge these central commitments into a specific social problem agenda was discussed and fine-tuned during the group's many, often contentious meetings (Rader 1986). In addition to guiding a direct action agenda, members' moral framework provided a foundation for the emotional commitment to the social problem necessary to sustain claimsmaking activities, especially oppositional projects such as those profiled here. Emotional commitment is a central, but often overlooked, piece of the social problems claimsmaking explanatory terrain (Benford 1997; and see Loseke 1999).

The Strategic Use of the Interpretive Context

The CCNV, especially during Mitch Snyder's involvement, was highly attuned to public and media responses to its efforts. Thus the selection of persuasive symbolic materials was based on a combined and evolving assessment of what problem typification was *privately* consistent with core moral beliefs and what framing of the problem and its solution made *strategic* sense. This is generally typical of claimsmakers. Here, the CCNV's private social problems work resulted in the adoption of a non-violent stance toward its public claimsmaking activities. More specifically, the CCNV adopted the approaches of Gandhi and Thich Nhat Hanh and the American civil rights and antiwar movement tactics of peaceful protest demonstrations, sit-ins, and other symbolic uses of their bodies—particularly fasting—to highlight the problem. These basic commitments, however, were strategically employed to target specific audiences such as government, media, or religious organizations.

For example, the CCNV's commitment to service-Christianity led the group to frame homelessness as a problem of "neighbors in need" when attempting to get Holy Trinity parishioners to reallocate their building fund. In their letters and leaflets to church leaders and members, the Christian spirit of giving and Catholic tradition of taking responsibility for the poor were invoked (e.g., CCNV letter to Pastor English, spring 1978). In hopes of resonating with their specifically Christian audience leaflets were passed out that depicted Christ with the saying, "How can you worship a homeless man on Sunday and ignore him on Monday?" In press coverage of the campaign, the Fairmont Street project was described by CCNV members as the group's response to the question, "How do you carry Christian and non-violent values over into those things you want to see changed?" (*Washington Star*, February 12, 1978). When Snyder was given a forum in the *Star* to explain the Holy Trinity actions, he started his commentary with a biblical quote about the wealthy's relationship to those in desperate need (January 21, 1979).

Erving Goffman (1974) suggests that interpretive "frames" such as those employed by the CCNV provide organizing principles for interpreting social actions, events, and situations (also see Benford and Snow 2000; Snow and Benford 1988). To understand how claimsmakers construct a social problem, we need to examine their methods of framing subjective understandings of relevant circumstances and events. By viewing context in terms of its possible framings, we gain access to the interpretive practices by which everyday "facts" are built up and sustained as aspects of social problems. The CCNV, for example, consistently framed homelessness using a specific Catholic Worker–inspired message: the poor deserved night hospitality because they were "the least of my brethren" (Murray 1990). This message explicitly tied Christian principles to social activism, framing homelessness as a challenge to all Christians.

Though it stemmed in part from radical-Catholic sources, the CCNV's commitment to peace and civil rights also enabled the more secular framing of homelessness as a "rights and justice" problem, a typification they invoked consistently in their dealings with city government and the broader public. In addition, they invoked the rational-legal language of bureaucracy and the law when engaging in claimsmaking activities aimed at this broader secular audience. In their letters to DHR director Russo, they employed legal language and statistics on shelter use and freezing deaths to mount their appeal for increased shelter (e.g., CCNV letter to Russo, February 6, 1978). In a subsequent press release they indicated in a legalistic fashion that a previous agreement with city officials was not being honored. The threatened "death watch" in front of the District Building was framed as an action to point out that the city had a responsibility to provide each of its citizens with shelter (CCNV press release, February 8, 1978).

In November, when the group began its occupation of the National Visitor Center, the same "rights and justice" frame was invoked. In a much quoted press release, Mitch Snyder stated in secularized terms that the CCNV has "felt a growing commitment to the creation of adequate, accessible space, offered in an atmosphere of reasonable dignity, for every human being in the District of Columbia who needs and wants to get in out of the cold" (CCNV press release November 1978, and *Rock Creek Monitor,* November 30, 1978). The occupation of a highly visible public space was also calculated to heighten awareness of the government's failure to meet its responsibilities towards poor citizens. Although there were shades of "neighbors in need" and "rights and justice" frames in both political action campaigns, they were differently emphasized in hopes of resonating with two somewhat disparate audiences.

The media, of course, constitute a distinct social problems audience. Here the CCNV was straightforward and quite strategic in the way it framed homelessness. The group tried to maximize the dramatic elements of all its claimsmaking activities so that the media would find the CCNV's efforts newsworthy. Snyder's claims that he was willing to die for his cause and his increasingly emaciated body provided the media with drama during the Holy Trinity campaign, evoking an image of Christ-like suffering timed to take place during the holiday season. The National Visitor Center takeover, streets blocked by sitting protesters, and their passive arrests likewise were reminiscent of earlier powerful images—those of civil rights protesters. These practices highlight CCNV members as social actors creatively combining and framing contextual elements to construct the social problem of homelessness.

Frame Resonance

Like all social actors, social problems claimsmakers use symbolic materials as resources with which to make moral-emotional sense of social conditions and to execute rhetorical strategies in pursuit of their goals. Likewise, recipients or audiences also mobilize symbolic resources as they interpret and react to the claimsmaking activities of others. Receptiveness to particular rhetorical "pitches" in part depends upon how well claimsmaking messages resonate with recipients' interpretive frames for the situations at issue (Snow and Benford 1988).

Here, the secularized "rights and justice" frame proved to be more persuasive to an audience of elected officials, city bureaucrats, and "average citizens." Claimsmaking activities thus configured resulted in the eventual opening of a new homeless shelter and the relaxation of shelter regulations in all of the city-operated shelters. In contrast, the overtly Christian "neighbors in need" frame clearly failed to persuade its audience at the Holy Trinity Church, where parishioners declined to reallocate church renovation funds to be used to shelter homeless people, even during Mitch Snyder's near-fatal fast.

A partial explanation for these disparate outcomes can be found by examining the differences in frame resonance. The "rights and justice" framing of social problems has become well-known and well-ensconced in the public's interpretive lexicon in the decades following the Black civil rights movement. In Washington, D.C., particularly, many Black-government officials (including Mayor Barry) had themselves been actively involved in civil rights activities and were direct beneficiaries of civil rights expansion. Thus this framing of the problem and the tactics the CCNV used to promote it were not only familiar but were also viewed as legitimate.

The more radical Catholic message of service to the poor, in contrast, is a longstanding one, dating to the beginnings of Catholicism. However, it is a central tenet of Christianity only to a tiny minority of American Catholics. In addition, it clashed with other compelling American frames for personal responsibility, including individualism, self-interest, and self-reliance—frames that resonated strongly with Holy Trinity parishioners. The CCNV's framing of homelessness may simply have been too antimaterialistic to resonate well with the much more affluent Catholics who constituted the CCNV's social problem audience. By identifying these central elements of the interpretive context *as claimsmakers' audience members used them,* we can offer cautious explanations for *why* the construction of homelessness as a social problem took the forms it did. An even richer portrait of these disparate outcomes becomes available if we also consider the environmental context of social problems claimsmaking.

THE ENVIRONMENTAL CONTEXT

Incorporating the environmental context into constructionist analyses points our attention to relevant aspects of the material world (for instance, the weather) and to sedimented and systematized relationships (such as the Democratic Party), asking how these present obstacles to, and provide resources for, claimsmakers and their audiences. Again, it is how claimsmakers and their audiences experience and interpret these aspects of the material world that is the focus of analysis, with the intent of identifying why claimsmaking activities proceeded as they did proceed and produced the observed outcomes. Often it is local manifestations and embodiments of these relationships that are most salient as resources or obstacles because these are the social actors (i.e., the mayor, the pastor) that claimsmakers directly confront. But the wider sets of systematized relationships that these actors embody (democratic government, the Catholic church) also shape local actors' interpretations and actions. Among the most salient are the *political-authority, economic,* and *physical* aspects of the environmental context.

The organization of power and authority, for instance, was quite distinct in the CCNV's two audiences. The National Visitor Center campaign and related activities was primarily aimed at local elected officials (and local community members in their role as citizens of the District). The city government is a democratic institution. In this case, it was also a Democratic Party institution. Public service is the central mission of city officials, who ultimately gain their power from the electorate. In the democratic context, civic leaders are always vulnerable to highly visible public campaigns aimed at embarrassing them into taking action. In the case of Washington, D.C., in addition, liberal Democratic control of the government made for an activist bureaucracy, at least insofar as always stringent budgetary constraints allowed. These institutional arrangements predisposed a positive response to CCNV's request for additional shelter. This was especially the case when a rights and justice framing of the problem—a frame particularly resonant with Washington's Black majority—was coupled with actions geared toward negative publicity for the city such as the "death watch" or Visitor Center occupation.

From an economic standpoint, the CCNV's request to the city was construed as a reasonable one. The city owned abandoned buildings, particularly schools, that it could easily convert to temporary winter shelters, staffing needs could in part be met by volunteers such as the CCNV, and the group's demand for less regulated shelters also did not impose an additional economic burden. In fact, acceding to the CCNV's demands was an economical way to make the city government look like it was acting swiftly to "solve" what was perceived as a growing public problem. Claimsmaking activities by the CCNV were thus framed in a fashion that gave city officials the ability to act in a manner consistent with their Democratic Party values, in part because demands the CCNV made required a minimum commitment of funds for a minimum duration of time (the winter months).

In contrast, the Catholic church is not a democratic institution, though Vatican II reforms had sought to democratize church leadership through the creation of "parish councils" to aid in congregation decision-making. Still, the parish priest is seen as the shepherd to his flock and parishioners seek his guidance. In this case, the CCNV challenged the charismatic Father English and his decision to renovate his church building. That Mitch Snyder, with his equally strong and charismatic personality, was the leader of the group making the challenge did not help bring about a change of heart (Rader 1986). The CCNV threatened the authority of English and questioned his discretion. Because this congregation and its building were nationally important, these actions were easily viewed as a radical threat to Catholic priorities in general. CCNV's criticism's implied that this congregation might "talk the talk" of Catholic responsiveness to the poor, but it did not, in the more radical Catholics' opinions, "walk the walk." This was an untenable position for those in authority and quite likely the reason that in the end, it was the "immorality" of Snyder's suicide threat that became the focus of the Catholic hierarchy response to this campaign, instead of serious reflection on church funds and their use. In this sense, the ongoing interaction between the CCNV, Snyder in particular, and the Catholic church confirms an analytical stance that emphasizes the reflexive and recursive nature of context and claimsmaking.

The socioeconomic status of Holy Trinity's parishioners was also a relevant factor. This was the church of the Kennedys, of then HEW secretary Joe Califano, of senators Hollings and DiConcini, representatives

Bonior and Obey, and of CBS journalist Roger Mudd (Rader 1986). These and other members of the elite (their government roles notwithstanding) did not often have their private economic priorities directly questioned.

When the CCNV attacked Catholics' right to spend their money as they please, Colman McCarthy noted in a postcampaign column, their reactions "were examples of the complete secular mind: Call this nut's bluff, don't let him push us around, we have our rights. That thinking," McCarthy continued, "was the logical outcome of a mindset dominated by worldly values. It had nothing to do with Christianity: Turn the other cheek, go the extra mile, love your enemy, if you are asked for your cloak, hand over your tunic." In a pinch, McCarthy accused, his fellow Catholics "rely on secular values, not Christian values" (*WP*, January 11, 1979).

Finally, the physical contexts of these two claimsmaking narratives differed. The occupation of the Visitor Center, while problematic for local law enforcement and various levels of government, was undeniably the occupation of a public space; such is the nature of federally owned buildings in a democracy. Likewise the "death watch" site, on a sidewalk in front of a public building, was an action on public property. A certain amount of tolerance for such actions is typically the norm in the post-civil-rights era American democratic context. Another aspect of the physical context that unfortunately aided the CCNV's claims was the bitter winter weather and the freezing deaths of several homeless people. While the CCNV sought to avoid this very outcome, ironically, these deaths could be marshaled as resources to add urgency and poignant underline to the CCNV's demand for more and more accessible shelter.

In contrast, the CCNV Holy Trinity campaign began in the summer when the consequences of hunger and homelessness were less evident. Thus the group did not have the dramatic evidence of need ready to present to reluctant parishioners and church officials. By the time the campaign was reinvigorated by Snyder's fast during the holiday season, the CCNV was facing an audience whose attitudes had already hardened. Moreover, the fasting of the youthful, mostly white, mostly educated CCNV members were seen by some as a matter of personal choice and thus egotistical, in stark contrast to a street person's freezing death. The Holy Trinity campaign intimately involved, and even threatened, the church, a space that is understood to belong to the Catholic church and its parishioners, regardless of any "all are welcome" policies that existed. It was easier to view the CCNV as unwelcome trespassers with no "right" to protest. These were perhaps not the most important elements of context in this case but combined with political-authority and economic aspects of the material context, these physical elements did help to shape claimsmaking and its outcomes.

In sum, claimsmaking activities by the CCNV were framed in a fashion that enabled Washington's local government to act in a manner consistent with its liberal Democratic Party values, in part because demands made on it required a minimum commitment of funds for a minimum duration of time (the winter months). In contrast, what the CCNV asked of Holy Trinity was a quite radical departure from "business as usual" and a significant commitment of funds in comparison to the cash donations typically given by the congregation for this type of specific request (less than $5,000 in the previous year).[1] Moreover, though what the CCNV asked was consistent with Catholic *values* toward the poor, it was not consistent with mainstream Catholic *practices*. Thus this framing of the issue necessitated much more of a "stretch" than what the CCNV asked of from the city government.

These two campaigns were the opening acts of claimsmaking around the social problem of homelessness in a time when few members of the public considered homelessness to be a social problem. If social problems however, in constructionist style, are considered to be *the activities of claimsmakers* as they seek to persuade other social actors of their view of conditions (Spector and Kitsuse 1977), then it is crucial to include these earliest actions. As early activities, they influence the subsequent choices of claimsmakers and the ongoing audience reactions to claimsmaking activities. They may also result in the emergence of additional claimsmakers and in other ways elaborate the context in which future claimsmaking activities occur. Here, the failure of the Holy Trinity campaign coupled with the destruction of the Fairmont Street building resulted in CCNV members channeling their energies in the direction of short-term night hospitality instead of emphasizing the need for low-cost permanent housing. Their success with a secularized government-directed campaign and their failure to influence the priorities of the Catholic church also influenced how they framed the issue in future campaigns. Claimsmakers' private social problems work and their strategic presentation of a social problem to others evolve as their activities interact with the social context as it is embodied by other social actors such as the press, politicians, and other audience members. It is in this way that the career of a social problem such as homelessness proceeds.

NOTE

1. The *Washington Post* reported that Holy Trinity's activities in 1978 included $500 a month to Father Horace McKenna's work with the poor at St. Aloysius Church; $100 a month to the House of Ruth, a homeless shelter for women; $500

to the Higher Achievement Program, a tutoring and counseling program at a local high school; and $200–$250 a month to the So Others May Eat (SOME) soup kitchen. In addition, one group of parishioners prepared and served the meal once a month at SOME and another performed the same service at the House of Ruth (January 4, 1979).

2

Government Officials as Claimsmakers

INTRODUCTION

In this chapter, I examine what role the second member of the iron quadrangle—government officials—played in the emergence of homelessness as a social problem. Often, as was the case at first in New York City, government officials and social problem activists have an adversarial relationship. But claimsmaking activities are not always structured so that advocates stake out one side of the claimsmaking terrain, government officials, the other. In Washington, some government officials were sympathetic to activist claims while others were neutral. The features of context that were confronted by government officials in each context largely explain these differences in approach to social problems claimsmaking by government officials.

THE EMERGENCE OF CLAIMSMAKERS AND THEIR ACTIVITIES IN NEW YORK CITY

In New York City, homelessness emerged as a public issue somewhat later than in Washington. Importantly, no advocacy group as adept at garnering public attention as the CCNV emerged during this crucial period to shape the kind of issue homelessness was to become. Instead, early on, homelessness became an issue of importance to powerful political insiders who struggled to make their characterization of the problem dominant. Unlike Washington, where government officials mostly played a reactive role to claims made by the central advocacy group, in

New York City, government officials on several levels were themselves the predominant claimsmakers.

In 1977 *New York Times* coverage of the issue was restricted to crimes committed by "vagrants" with one exception—a human-interest story about the lives of steam-tunnel dwellers beneath the city. In 1978 as well, most news stories concerned a rash of murders of "skid row bums" (seventeen separate articles in 1978 reported on this theme). In November of that year, homelessness was presented as a social problem in the *Times*. Times Square was reported to have a problem with "sleepy winos" and "aggressive street-corner drinkers." This was because, the paper reported, these street dwellers had judged the Times Square area to be safer than the Bowery, where a rash of "muggers, drug addicts, the conversion of flophouses to loft apartments, and the influx of released mental patients" had made the area unlivable (*NYT,* November 14, 1978).

Early homeless advocates in New York, meanwhile, pursued a non-public political strategy. In late 1979, attorney Robert Hayes filed a class action lawsuit as part of his *pro bono* efforts on behalf of homeless people (*Callahan v. Carey*) to force the city to provide public shelter for derelicts during the winter (Blau 1992:98–100; *NYT,* October 27, 1979). This suit proved successful: On December 9, a state Supreme Court judge in Manhattan ordered the city to provide 750 beds for the "helpless and hopeless men of the Bowery" (*NYT,* December 9, 1979). Two more years passed before negotiations between advocates and the city resulted in a court-entered consent decree that endorsed a de facto right to shelter and set minimal conditions for its provision (Blau 1992). In exchange for a city agreement to provide sufficient emergency shelter in large institutional settings, however, advocates were forced to give up their demand for increased community-based shelter and low-income housing. The *Callahan* suit received little press coverage in the *Times* during the negotiation period. Behind the scenes, however, mayoral policy response to city homelessness was shaped by this advocate-initiated legal victory.[1]

The first act of grassroots advocacy for the "new homeless" in New York City to be given publicity by the *Times* took place in August 1980. The Community Service Society, the Catholic Workers, other activists, and homeless people had staged nightly vigils in the churchyard of nearby St. Francis of Assisi Church. Activists were protesting the removal of street people from the area surrounding Madison Square Garden, where the 1980 Democratic National Convention was held (August 14, 1980). In the aftermath of these events, these and other activists formed what would later become the city's central advocacy group: The Coalition for the Homeless (Blau 1992:96). These events sparked a September article by the *Times* on Madison Square Garden "vagrants" (who had returned to the area after the convention). In the September article, the paper discussed the city's inability to deal effectively with what is described as a growing population and "problem" (*NYT*, September 26, 1980).

In December of 1980 the *Times* reported that the New York State Department of Social Services had been pressuring Mayor Koch to set up additional shelters for the homeless in all five boroughs of the city. Koch was reluctant to do this, because, as mayoral aide Robert Trobe said, large shelters have a damaging effect on neighborhood preservation and economic development (*NYT*, December 30, 1980). Trobe went on to state, "Although we don't have hard data on it we think that one-third to one-half [of single homeless men] have some history of psychiatric hospitalization, probably in state facilities."

The *Times* reported in the same article, "[New York State] Governor Carey has reacted with anger to the way city officials link the increasing number of homeless people with the release of patients from state psychiatric institutions." It continued, "Last week the Governor's office issued a memorandum suggesting that the *city* (my italics) had actually displaced thousands of people by giving tax breaks to owners of single-room-occupancy hotels who upgrade their buildings."[2] The next day, the governor denied that he believed the city was to blame, but the *Times* noted that the memo claiming gentrification was to blame for homelessness also attempted to document that deinstitutionalization of patients from state psychiatric facilities had *not* led to increases in homeless people. The memo, edited by an assistant secretary to the governor, also said that "city housing policies were 'the single greatest cause' of the problem," according to the *Times* (December 31, 1980). The reporting continued with this sentence: "These statements infuriated city officials who said it was 'obvious' that many former mental patients were wandering about the city."

The *Times* prefigured its own allegiance to deinstitutionalization as a causal model for homelessness when it reported the following in the December 30, 1980 article:

> The debate over which level of government is responsible for the mentally ill and homeless dates as far back as the early 1970's when the state embarked on a policy of "deinstitutionalization" releasing thousands of mental patients to a network of community shelters some of which never materialized.
>
> That transfer also represented a transfer of financial cost because the former patients became eligible for Medicaid reimbursement, which is shared by the state, city and Federal governments. Patients in state psychiatric centers between the ages of 21 and 65 are not eligible for Medicaid, forcing the state to pay the entire cost of their care.

At this point in 1980, the state, bound by a social services statute, had declared itself willing to pick up half of the cost of sheltering homeless New York City residents. This action itself can be interpreted as a tacit acceptance of deinstitutionalization as at least a partial explanation for the apparent growth in the numbers of homeless New Yorkers (*NYT*, December 30, 1980).

By the end of 1980 then, city officials and the editorial staff of the *Times* were poised to characterize the city's homeless as primarily consisting of deinstitutionalized mental patients. Even the state, which received bad publicity from this characterization and so publicly argued in favor of gentrification as the main culprit behind homelessness, was ready to accept some financial responsibility for the homeless because it was both politically and fiscally expedient. It simply was more cost-effective for the state to accept partial responsibility for the city's homeless and to pay for half of their care in a city-run shelter than to foot the entire bill at the state level were these people to become wards of the state.

CONSTRUCTING HOMELESS PEOPLE IN NEW YORK CITY

The next year, the characterization of the homeless as unwilling victims of deinstitutionalization was codified by the release of a study conducted by an established Protestant charity organization, the Community Service Society (*NYT*, March 8, 1981, reporting on the Baxter and Hopper study). The study received a substantial amount of television and newspaper coverage (*NYT*, March 8, 11, 21, 1981; NBC featured its authors on two shows in December 1981). Several pieces of data about homeless people analyzed in the study also received press coverage by the *Times* (Baxter and Hopper, 1981:10; *NYT*, March 11, 1981). One was an estimate made by the State Office of Mental Health, which claimed that "45% to 50% of the homeless are mentally ill" (from a State Office of Mental Health internal memo cited in Baxter and Hopper 1981:10). The second was the results of psychiatric screenings that took place at Wards Island men's shelter in 1980 that found that 70 percent of residents suffered from psychiatric problems. Though the Baxter and Hopper study presented a complex portrait of those living on the street and how they got there, the *Times* coverage of the study highlighted deinstitutionalization as a main cause of homelessness (March 8, 11, 1981).

Indeed, nearly every 1981 *Times* report on homeless people included terms such as "former mental patients" (March 11); "bizarre characters," who are "too confused to seek [government help] properly" (March 21); "tragic people, strange and unclean rather than violent, they inspire more hysteria than pity" (August 31); and "these aimless, troubled and sometimes violent discards of our society"(August 25): all emphasizing the mental derangement of the homeless.[3] In an editorial on the problem of homelessness written on the day the Baxter and Hopper study made page one, the *Times* stated, "Government agencies have failed to face the problem and have made it even worse by discharging many patients from state mental institutions" (March 8). In a later editorial, the *Times* again claimed, "State mental institutions continue to dump them on the streets" (August 25).

In addition, the use of Sarah Connell, the regional director of the state's Office of Mental Health, as a consulted expert on homelessness in the *Times* helped to promote the view of her office that homelessness was a public problem of insufficient mental health care. In mid-1981 she was reported as saying, "If someone said to me what is the single greatest problem in New York City today I would say there is no question, the homeless" (*NYT,* June 28, 1981). Her position as a state-level mental health official added weight to a psychiatric-patient view of homeless people. This accumulation of coverage characterizing homeless people as improperly deinstitutionalized mental patients came to a climax in late 1981, when Mayor Koch openly accused the state of dumping its client load on the city in order to save money (*NYT,* November 20, 1981).

In New York City, homeless people were portrayed as "dangerous victims"—people who were ill equipped to survive on the streets and people who might pose a danger to themselves and possibly to others. Prominent claimsmakers, who included Mayor Koch, Mayoral Aide Robert Trobe, Sarah Connell and most editorial and news story writers of the *Times,* called for a highly regulated shelter system to house these troubled individuals, preferably far from residential neighborhoods. Shelters, according to this consensus, would at least in part be funded by the state of New York because it had caused the problem. The cause of this malady, its subjects, and the solution to homelessness are thus constructed in a comparatively consistent and clear-cut fashion in New York City. Early advocates such as Hayes, Baxter, and Hopper clearly had called for expanded low-income and supportive housing as part of the solution to homelessness in New York. The nature of the publicity advocates received during this period, however, made it appear as though claimsmakers of all kinds, including politicians, advocates, and the nation's "paper of record," the *New York Times,* were all united in their construction of the problem.

CONSTRUCTING HOMELESS PEOPLE IN WASHINGTON

By the time politicians, the press, and advocates had started making claims about homelessness in New York City, public problem construction in Washington, D.C., largely driven by the CCNV, was well under way. The problem had received regular publicity from the city's newspapers and television channels, the city government had acknowledged it, and advocates had even scored a victory in that the city had taken some financial responsibility for providing emergency shelter. During the next several years, CCNV continued to set the agenda for what kind of problem homelessness was and what should be done about it. In the years before 1982, when homelessness was at best emergent as a *local* social problem, Washington city government officials were not claimsmakers of note around homelessness. Instead, they were merely reactive to the main claimsmaking group, the CCNV.

Indeed, the CCNV had little local competition for "ownership" of this social problem. Almost all other parties with a relationship to the problem at this time were involved as groups reacting to the demands or actions of the CCNV or were quietly providing services without seeking to influence the public perception of the problem. Thus during this period the CCNV was free to portray homeless people in a fashion that derived directly from their roots in radical Catholicism and from depression-era images of "unaccommodated men" (Hopper 1991:108). The subjects of this social problem were portrayed in a "least of my brethren" fashion, dramatized as somewhat unsavory characters who nonetheless deserved community care. Indeed, the CCNV often portrayed homeless people as an overwhelmingly service-resistant population. Though descriptions that characterized hard-core street people as "alcoholics" or "mentally or emotionally impaired" (*WP*, November 30, 1978) were frequently given by the advocacy group, the CCNV nevertheless consistently portrayed homeless people as rational human beings capable of making choices that were in their own best interests. "Street people" troubled by alcoholism and mental health problems who were unwilling or unable to cooperate with shelter rules and regulations quickly became the dominant image in numerous subsequent reports about homeless people in the *Post*. At the same time, however, this population was often portrayed in various human-interest stories in the paper as persons making choices, if unconventional ones, about sleeping sites and lifestyle. Portraying the homeless as mostly competent, if at times troubled, adults appeared in article after article during this period. The CCNV also emphasized this portrayal of homeless people, one drawn from years of service to this population. This image of homeless people proved to be a resonant and enduring one in Washington's local press and among other prime local social problems claimsmakers, such as politicians and social service providers.

For example, Henry Mitchell, who wrote occasionally about homelessness in the *Post*, related a story of a man who lived for a time in the shed behind Mitchell's house (*WP*, February 8, 1980). Mitchell portrayed the man as someone interested in preserving independence and the right to live as he would, a harmless individual, who, though he might drink a bit and occasionally engage in eccentric behavior, had the right to be left alone. In the following month, the *Post* published another story of a "happy hobo," a harmless and charming alcoholic who had been befriended by a group of firefighters who gave him changes of clothes and an occasional shower (March 19, 1980). A twelve-part series written by a young reporter, Neil Henry, who went undercover as a homeless man himself for two months, additionally strengthened the idea that most derelicts and bums, as he referred to them, were down on their luck, had a tendency to drink, wanted to maintain both their dignity and independence, and were highly resourceful in finding innovative ways to meet their daily needs. (The series ran from April 27 to May 8, 1980.) Thus *Post* human-interest stories about the character of local homeless people portrayed them in a fashion that suggested that these social deviants either did not want or would not accept an offer of assistance. Indeed, in the period from 1977 to 1981, homeless people of Washington often appear to have in some sense *chosen* their lifestyle or at least were stubborn and fussy about accepting help. In a column (*WP*, January 10, 1981), Colman McCarthy related a tour of heat grates taken by Mayor Marion Barry, who is cited as "telling the media that he offered aid but that most of the men on top of the grates don't want to come in from the cold."

In Washington, the causal model driving homelessness was left largely unarticulated by claimsmakers in 1980 and 1981. Instead, the focus was on the character of homeless people and short-term solutions to ensure their survival during the cold winter months. As 1981 closed, Colman McCarthy presaged the coalescence of a causal model for homelessness in Washington in a holiday season column. "A myth persists that the dispossessed and rootless prefer life on the street, that vagrancy has its advantages and that this ragged population of 'bums' and 'shopping bag ladies' is too proud to ask for help. . . . Only lately . . . has the uncomfortable truth emerged. America has a permanent refugee class, people driven into the streets . . . from pressures created only recently" (*WP*, December 27). In this column, McCarthy correctly anticipated and contributed to a sea change in problem construction in Washington, still mainly accomplished by the CCNV, that took place beginning in 1982. At that

time, Washington advocates began to overtly and forcefully typify homelessness as having its base in economic inequality. By this time however,
the typification of homelessness and homeless people by claimsmakers
in New York City, who constructed this problem in terms of personal
deficiency, had already taken hold. It was this typification that would
come to dominate national views of this social problem.

CLAIMSMAKERS IN CONTEXT

In New York City, official claimsmakers quickly developed a coherent
view of the cause of homelessness, its subjects, and its "solution" in policy.[4] In Washington, by contrast, five years of social problems work resulted in an amorphously defined problem, a complicated depiction of
its subjects as both rational and troubled, and a focus on noninvasive
emergency shelter as the prominent "solution." It is tempting to account
for these differences by merely noting the different claimsmakers prominent in each location. In New York, Mayor Koch obviously benefited
from the legitimacy of his elected position and resultant access to the
media. The CCNV in Washington, in contrast, was an underfunded advocacy group working outside the enfranchised local political system.
The CCNV was comprised of politically savvy veteran activists, however,
with the result that in Washington the issue received much more press
coverage, most of it sympathetic, than it received in New York (Hilgartner and Bosk 1988). Furthermore, this group had little competition for
ownership of this social problem from political officials such as Mayor
Barry. Key city bureaucrats, such as DHR head Russo, were sympathetic
to many of the CCNV's positions and so did not use their status as city
officials to supply the media with a contrasting portrayal of the issue.
With these advantages, the CCNV would seem to have had the opportunity to construct a coherent typification of homelessness. That this did
not happen during these crucial years is inadequately explained by the
CCNV's lack of status and legitimacy. A richer account of why these two
instances of social problem construction took the varying forms they did
emerges from an examination of the interplay between claimsmaking
activities and the contexts in which they were embedded.

THE ENVIRONMENTAL CONTEXT

New York and Washington are similar cities in that they both are centers of national opinion formation. The print press in each consists of

dominant papers, the *New York Times,* and the *Washington Post,* that have long been influential voices in setting the tenor of local and national political debate. Other features of the environmental context, however, in particular, political, economic and housing conditions, differ markedly. First, Washington's status as a stateless "district" stands in marked contrast to New York City's position as the dominant city in one of the nation's largest and most powerful states. This arrangement of the *political-authority environment* ensures that the New York City political apparatus is a perennial powerhouse in its dealings with New York State. In stark contrast, Washington's city government has little influence with its next-level overseer and fiscal manager, the federal government.

Second, Washington, as the seat of the federal government and its huge bureaucracy, has a stable *economic environment,* albeit one that does not provide sufficient jobs for its less-educated citizens. It is a medium-sized city, a "one-horse town," with few resources and no pressing need to remodel itself as a center of some other economic sector. New York City, in contrast is a behemoth with a continual need for economic sector development in order to support its infrastructure and keep its labor force employed. During the early 1980s, manufacturing in the city was in flux due to the forces of globalization and a nationwide recession, and the city was experiencing a fiscal crisis. The Koch administration sought to stabilize the local economy by revitalizing the city's status as a world center of finance and banking.

This in turn affected the *physical environment* of New York City, in particular its housing stock, which, officials determined, was in need of "gentrification" if the white-collar finance sector was to be lured to the city. In contrast, Washington during this period had plenty of abandoned housing with few private parties interested in developing it and few public resources to devote to upgrading the housing stock. These varying "conditions of action" (Schwalbe et al. 2000:444) helped to shape who would become prominent claimsmakers in each local context, which types of claims would be promoted most forcefully by claimsmakers, and which would be emphasized in the dominant press.

The Environmental Context in New York City

New York City's fiscal crisis was one central feature of the local environmental context that indirectly led to the mayor becoming a central claimsmaker around the social problem of homelessness. After taking office in 1978 in the midst of a severe recession in the city, the mayor set out to reaffirm the city's place as a world financial center by enticing banks and other multinationals to locate their corporate headquarters in

New York City. In addition to granting tax abatements to big business to relocate to Manhattan, the mayor's office expanded real estate tax abatements for the purpose of substantially expanding middle-class professional housing in Manhattan. Oftentimes, this resulted in gentrification, or the conversion of housing the poor could afford to housing that was priced for the professional classes. Indeed, substantial numbers of SRO hotels were being converted to upscale apartments in segments of the city and no replacement housing for individuals with marginal incomes was forthcoming (Blau 1992). Advocates, the state, and the media had already pointed to the connection between gentrification and a rising number of homeless people. The city's growing commitment to gentrification during this period lay at the heart of the mayor's interest in cornering the construction of homelessness as a social problem. He was further spurred to become a central claimsmaker around the issue by the press, which had begun to characterize homelessness as one of the city's unsolved social problems, an implicit criticism of city government (e.g., *NYT*, November 14, 1978; September 26, 1980).

In late 1980, after a threatening exchange in which the governor's office pointed to New York City tax policy encouraging gentrification as the cause behind homelessness, the mayor's office saw opportunities to protect itself from political vulnerabilities by instead configuring homeless people as victims of state psychiatric facility deinstitutionalization (*NYT*, December 31, 1980). First, this causal view of homelessness held the promise of deflecting responsibility for this ever more visible problem away from the mayor's office. Second, citing deinstitutionalization as the culprit deflected possible criticism of landlord reinvestment policies that the mayor hoped would improve New York neighborhoods and housing stock and also increase Mayor Koch's popularity with voters and business interests. Third, it was a more appealing typification than either of two possible alternatives, that of portraying homeless people as victims of poverty and unemployment or as criminals. Criminalizing the mostly male homeless population would have indicated a need for better city policing (requiring funds the city did not have) and would have been a disincentive for enticing corporations and their professional-class workers to move to the city. Admitting the extent of poverty in the city would likewise have been poor advertising and might have led to increased calls by liberal factions for more investments in antipoverty programs, a substantial portion of the city's budget even under the best of economic conditions. By making the state directly culpable, the mayor's office stood to gain state financial assistance to deal with homelessness. Blaming the state enabled a typification of homeless people and their needs that diffused the issue into a more manageable social problem for the city.

In the end, the state was vulnerable to this criticism because it was demonstrable that state psychiatric facility commitment rates *had* shrunk. The state was also somewhat willing to accept this construction of the problem because New York State's fiscal health is much affected by economic conditions in New York City. If gentrification could help revitalize the city's economy, the state would gain by improved tax revenues and a lessening of the need to provide services for the city's unemployed. Beyond this, the Koch administration tacitly acquiesced to admitting that homelessness in New York City would be handled as a *local* problem, thus alleviating the state's need to revisit the deinstitutionalization issue again.

In addition, by claiming that the state had caused homelessness through excessive deinstitutionalization, New York City officials could avoid acknowledging, at least for a time, that the city had a severe shortage of affordable housing. Behind the scenes, the affordable housing crisis was growing in saliency for the mayor's office due in part to the legal efforts of Robert Hayes and similarly minded advocates who sought to make housing a right for all city residents. As a solution to growing levels of homelessness in the city, these advocates had demanded that the city provide scattered-site community housing for the poor. The 1979 court ruling in favor of a general right to housing for the poor, if enacted in any substantial way, could curtail the city government's gentrification efforts. Thus nonpublic social problems work by legal advocates affected typification by forcing the mayor's office to push its view of homeless people more forcefully.

Advocacy groups such as the Coalition for the Homeless, which might have provided an alternative typification of homelessness in New York, were in the initial stages of organizing during this early period and were not yet much involved in publicized claimsmaking.[5] The charity group most prominently involved in the issue during this period was the Community Service Society. This group's early study of the street and shelter population was somewhat misrepresented in the press, which sensationalized its figures on deinstitutionalization and the population of homeless people (see Chapter 5) rather than focusing on the study's overall message. This resulted in an interpretation that backed the mayor's typification of homeless people as primarily deinstitutionalized mental patients. The legal advocacy efforts of Robert Hayes during 1979–1981 did not receive much press attention until after this crucial emergent period. Together these factors worked to make the mayor, other government officials, and the *New York Times* the dominant claimsmakers during the first two years of the 1980s.

The *New York Times,* in its role as local paper and defender of the city's interests when they collided with the state's interests, also found this causal model easy to support. In several editorials during this period, the *Times* defines the homeless population as largely comprised of people with psychiatric problems, many of them former wards of the state (*NYT*, March 21, August 25, 31; December 15, 1981). The paper also lays the blame for their homelessness squarely on the state. This editorial position is understandable as a classic "hometown paper" advocate's stance. The *Times* both provided access to those proposing a deinstitutionalized mental patient typification of homeless people and allied itself with this portrayal of the problem in its own editorializing.

In New York City, then, three crucial conditions of context influenced who became interested in homelessness as a social problem and how they attempted to typify it. The first was a local fiscal crisis. The second was a redevelopment policy in response to that crisis promoting a shift in the allocation of housing toward the professional classes. The third was the state, which could be held culpable for state-level mental health policy and therefore seemed a reasonable entity to blame for causing the problem. Moreover, for reasons stated above, the state went along with this typification. For many interested and powerful claimsmakers, representing homeless people as deinstitutionalized mental patients during this period was a workable typification.

The Environmental Context in Washington

The CCNV in Washington, in contrast, posed homelessness as a more complex moral problem, the responsibility for which lay with an amorphous "public." Although the CCNV blamed the city (and church groups) for not doing enough to aid homeless people, it did not point to the District as the cause of the problem. Unlike in New York City, a causal model with a specific public entity named as the party responsible for the problem was never clearly articulated during these early years of problem construction. Thus a political element of context (blaming the state) that aided in a rapid coalescence of typification efforts in New York was absent prior to 1982 in Washington.

The CCNV was able to pursue a line of claimsmaking in which the subjects of the problem were unconventional citizens requiring assistance on their terms and the party responsible for their plight remained underspecified because no other competing claimsmakers came forth to challenge the CCNV's portrayal. This, in turn, occurred largely because Washington as a local context had few economic resources to devote to this problem, nor any political interests to protect. Thus there was little to lure others into becoming claimsmakers.

In Washington, homelessness was not posed as a problem of deinstitutionalized state mental patients. Since Washington, D.C., is a self-contained district with no state of its own to which it might appeal for aid or on which it might place blame, the CCNV or any other possible claimsmakers had little impetus to suggest this construction of homeless people. Washington, at that point a chronically impoverished city, had no major redevelopment plans at stake, which might have influenced claimsmakers such as Mayor Barry to come forward during this period. Typifying homeless people in any particular fashion had no discernible larger political purpose, as was the case in New York City. Thus, homeless people interested relatively few claimsmakers and certainly none as powerful as state-level department heads or big-city mayors. Though homeless people were a problem for Mayor Barry of Washington just as they were a problem for Mayor Koch of New York, Barry lacked access to any state resources and any ability to entice a new economic sector to his city. There was therefore no impetus for him to take a proactive stance regarding homelessness.

Although the CCNV often received sympathetic gestures from city officials, including Mayor Barry, and from church organizations, the group could not entice these sectors to coalesce around its claims about homeless people or their needs. Presenting homeless people as a service-resistant population simply went against what these organizations saw as their mandate—to rehabilitate the destitute. Thus, in Washington in the emergent years of this problem, homeless people were constructed in a way that made other possible interested parties hesitant to commit resources or to enter into an alliance with the CCNV.

In addition, because there were no clear material advantages to posing an alternative representation of homeless people, neither party attempted to pose them as something other than service-resisting recalcitrants. Instead, both church groups and the city government, while continuing to offer emergency services to the homeless, did not much participate in constructing the public view of this social problem. Thus the CCNV could represent both homelessness and homeless people according to their ideological preferences, which were then left largely unchallenged.

The *Washington Post*, another possible participant in claimsmaking activities or alliances, took a mixed position on homeless people. At times the paper portrayed them as self-sufficient if somewhat problematic independents; at times it lamented the freezing death of a homeless victim. At times it commended the CCNV for its efforts; at times it portrayed the group as unhelpful to the cause of aiding homeless people (for example, *WP*, December 9, 1978; January 12, 1981). Unsigned and therefore "official" editorials published during this period called for a very limited response to homelessness. DHR director Russo is commended in one editorial for working with the CCNV to provide a city-sponsored emergency shelter (*WP*, January 29, 1978). Another editorial admonished the CCNV to work with the city and perhaps contract with it to "show by example, how best to help the homeless" (*WP*, December 9, 1978). Again, since the city had little to gain from any particular typification of homelessness, its major newspaper had little impetus to either challenge or ally itself with the CCNV's construction of this social problem.

The *Post*'s view of itself is also implicated in the paper's editorial stance toward what was then viewed as a local social problem. Though the *New York Times* has long considered itself the nation's paper of record, it is also overtly committed to being New York City's major local daily and to being the city's advocate. In contrast, the *Post*, during the years that followed the Watergate scandal, a story the *Post* famously broke, was striving to define itself as the nation's political news daily. It concentrated much effort on covering national political news and was less devoted to being the daily paper of the average citizen of the District. Though the *Post* showed interest in homelessness, the paper did not spend much editorial space on the issue until it began to be perceived as a national social problem. Thus prior to 1982, the *Post* was not itself much of a claimsmaker around homelessness.

Because of its commitment to insuring the privacy and dignity of homeless people, the CCNV constructed the problem in a fashion that allowed others to minimize the need to do much service provision (homeless people as the CCNV had portrayed them could easily be said to really not want services). Other possible claimsmakers with limited resources themselves found it convenient to go along with the CCNV's typification. The resulting construction of the subjects of this social problem as service-resistant men enabled Mayor Barry to rescind early promises of aid he had made as the city slipped into recession in the early 1980s with little political danger to himself (*WP*, January 1, October 23, 1981). The CCNV's combination of a complex typification of homeless subjects and bureaucratically difficult demands for amelioration of their problem resulted in only sporadic acts of intervention for homeless people by the city government. Even these inadequate efforts remained very vulnerable to the wavering of public attention or economic downturns in the city.

Later, after the Reagan administration had implemented tax cuts and the recession grew worse, the CCNV did receive publicity for its causal model—one that posited the economy, unemployment, and general unequal distribution of wealth exacerbated by Reagan administration policies as the culprits behind homelessness. In this sense, the Reagan administration acted as an important political resource—like the state in New York, the responsibility for the problem could be laid at its door. In these earliest years of claimsmaking, however, the CCNV did not have a conservative federal government as a convenient entity to blame. By the time it did, the New York City version of homelessness, with a generalized focus on individual deficits as causing homelessness and emergency shelter as the solution had gained the upper hand in the national construction of the problem.

THE INTERPRETIVE CONTEXTS OF NEW HOMELESSNESS

Although dissimilarities in the environmental context help explain variations in problem construction, interpretive context differences are equally important. Two layers of interpretive context influence typification success. The first is the historical and cultural material that resonates with claimsmakers and from which they construct an image of a social problem (Snow and Benford 1988). The second is how these efforts at framing a social problem are interpreted by audiences exposed to the typification efforts of claimsmakers, leading some to align themselves with a particular interpretation (Bockman 1991; Snow and Benford 1992). Though in the constructionist view all meanings are "socially constructed, deconstructed and reconstructed" (Benford 1997:410) important members of the iron quadrangle are more likely to view some meanings as reasonable and as resonating with everyday experience (Benford and Snow 2000; Kubal 1998). These are the claims that most often come to typify a social problem because they foster the formation of a coalition of claimsmakers who strengthen a certain view of a problem.

In this case, only one major type of claimsmaker was prominent in each city during the emergent period. The radical-Catholic commitment to peace and civil rights that motivated the CCNV in Washington, D.C., made the framing of homelessness as a "rights and justice" problem resonate, especially with certain members of the city government such as Albert Russo. The group's commitment to service-Christianity led it to additionally frame homelessness as a problem of "neighbors in need," especially in its appeals to other Catholics. This Christian-focused frame failed to resonate with its intended audience, at least at the level required for a financial commitment to be made. Instead, Holy Trinity parishioners had felt put upon, even blackmailed. Their values and giving habits had been exposed and scrutinized even in the media. They had been accused of not being generous enough, often a sore spot for the wealthy. The rights and justice frame, however, found more strategic success.

The city agreed that it should provide shelter for its homeless men and opened several city-funded shelters during this period. Even the CCNV's more radical claims regarding the immorality of having to relinquish the right to freedom from search and seizure and the right to privacy merely to access shelter found success when the city relaxed its shelter regulations in early 1979. According to this civil-rights-influenced frame, despite homeless people's differences from "normative citizens," they still deserved "equal treatment under the law." Operating under this conception of the social problem, the CCNV did not need to make homeless people seem more normative or deny that some had mental health, substance abuse, or other problems, as basic rights should not be denied on account of difference. The success of this frame made it increasingly the dominant theme in the CCNV's efforts,[6] with ironic results as environmental constraints encouraged translating this framing of the problem at the local level as the need to do less for homeless people since they were characterized as "service resistant."

The elected officials and bureaucrats in New York, by contrast, were either embedded in the public service industry (i.e., Connell) or found it politically convenient to ally themselves with it (i.e., Koch). In the past few decades this industry had seen its fortunes rise with the successful medicalization of deviance (Conrad and Schneider 1980) and the accompanying rise of the therapeutic state (Polsky 1991). The dominant trajectory of medicalization was an expansion in the populations deemed appropriate for therapeutic diagnosis coupled with shifts in service delivery policies. One strand of these policy shifts can be located in the deinstitutionalization movement of the previous decades (Trattner [1974] 1989). With the advent of effective psychiatric medications and the availability of federal funding outside state hospitals many people previously thought to need the constant supervision of mental health professionals in a psychiatric facility could now be rehoused in the community (Hopper and Hamburg 1984).[7] In part, as Loseke notes, the trend to deinstitutionalize psychiatric patients reflects general attention to the civil rights of all kinds of people during this era (1995:265). A contravening trend in the social service community, however, worked against what could have been a complementary characterization of homeless people to that promoted by the CCNV. This trend stressed the continuing professionalization of the social services by adopting the medical model (Trattner [1974] 1989; Polsky 1991). This required increasing attention to creating diagnostic protocols, defining new populations in need of services, assessing "patients" for newly defined therapeutic needs, and constructing organizations to deliver services. The medical model allowed homeless people to be easily categorized as one more population in need of specialized social services (Snow, Anderson, and Koegel 1994).[8]

This characterization additionally seemed a reasonable one to the public. Many of the homeless people most apparent to casual observers were obviously troubled individuals who at times displayed behaviors typically associated with mental illness. The prominent New York City typification of homeless people thus fit well with how a reasonable middle-class public also saw these individuals. The support of New York's large base of human services workers for this view of homeless people and its fit with casual observation made this typification persuasive.

A rights and justice perspective required more commitment from the public to maintain for it implied more radical social change, a tolerance of the street presence of homeless people, and possibly, redistribution of wealth (hardly a popular idea among most Americans). Despite gains made by civil rights movements, CCNV members were making a much more difficult and contentious argument. Beyond political or other advantages, claimsmakers in New York had a clearly defined interpretation of the issue that meshed well with casual observation. It additionally implied that homeless people would be removed from the sight of the middle class, thus reducing discomfort levels while simultaneously mitigating public guilt for homelessness by promising humane treatment for these troubled individuals (Loseke 1995). The official status that was enjoyed by Koch, Connell, and other government officials engaged in claimsmaking in New York also added to the legitimacy of their framing of this social problem.

Public officials gained the upper hand in New York City's typification of homelessness, not because of their status and power per se but because features of the surrounding context motivated them to be active claimsmakers and use their positions and status to their advantage on this issue. In addition, New York's official claimsmakers were able to frame the problem in a fashion that was quite resonant with many other New Yorkers. Though New York's advocates won an incredible legal victory for homeless people during this period (the right to shelter), this victory went largely unnoticed in the press. Meanwhile, the public typification of the problem went largely unaddressed by local advocates during this period, leaving public officials to "own" the problem's portrayal.

In Washington, activists had brought the problem into the public sphere and got homelessness to be recognized as a public problem. But they had not yet managed to typify homelessness and homeless people coherently nor had they successfully pinpointed a cause for the problem. A causal argument is often central to making "solutions" to the problem resonate with important elements of the public. Given the obvious power differences between advocates and official power holders, government claimsmakers almost always have the upper hand in a battle to typify a social problem. This is why the third member of the iron quadrangle, the media, is so crucial. I next take up the media's role in the claims-making process. In particular, I examine how a relatively powerless group like the CCNV can, with the help of the media, take on the federal government and prevail in typifying a social problem.

NOTES

1. I thank Harry Murray, Kim Hopper, and Joel Blau for their comments on this point (private communication). For instance, the city opened the Keener Building as a men's shelter in response to the original injunction and upgraded its staffing and funding after being threatened with more legal action in 1980 (Blau 1992: 141).

2. As Blau points out, the replacement of cheap single-room-occupancy hotels (SROs) with condominiums and high-rent apartments for professional employees of the service industries was part of an overall reinvestment strategy to aid New York in overcoming its 1975 fiscal crisis (Blau 1992:134–36; Hopper and Hamburg 1984:38–40).

3. Liberal columnist Sidney Schanberg later was an exception to this trend but during this period seemed to support it (e.g., columns August 25 and December 15, 1981).

4. The idea that the "solution" to homelessness could consist primarily of highly regulated congregate emergency shelters proved to be short-lived as family homelessness reached crisis proportions in the city in the mid-1980's (Kim Hopper, private communication to the author, 1999). During this period (prior to 1982), however, it was unclear to most involved in the issue that single men were merely the "tip of the iceberg" of New York City's housing shortage.

5. As Hopper and Baumohl point out, even in later years advocates often employed "a (strategically) misplaced simplicity" in their demands for a solution to homelessness. This was because calling for emergency shelter provision seemed at the time the most efficient way of garnering resources in an era increasingly more hostile towards the poor (1994:524).

6. Later, the extent to which this civil rights frame resonated with *local* voters was made evident in the passage of Initiative 17. This city referendum, which the CCNV fought hard for, established the right to shelter in the District. It passed by a wide margin (72 percent approval) in 1984 (*WP*, November 7, 1984), no doubt due to the Black majority's strong commitment to civil rights.

7. Unfortunately, much of the community-based housing that was supposed to be converted to house former psychiatric ward inmates never materialized.

8. Eventually homeless shelter programs would encompass the results of this trend by offering a vast array of services including parenting classes, substance abuse counseling, and "life skills" training (Gerstel, Bogard, McConnell, and Schwartz 1996).

3

The Role of the Media in Constructing Homelessness

INTRODUCTION

National social problems are media products. Without publicity, it is unlikely a social problem will be recognized as such by the public or by social actors, such as politicians, with the power to ameliorate it. This chapter spotlights the media as the third member of the iron quadrangle of social problem construction. Unlike other claimsmakers in the iron quadrangle, the media are not merely claimsmakers in their own right. They also act as a conduit for the claims of others. In this chapter I explore how the media began to offer themselves as a regular context in which other claimsmakers could press their case for homelessness as a social problem of import. And I argue that it is during this time period, late 1981 and 1982, that the *Post* and the *Times* become claimsmakers about homelessness in their own right.

So far in this volume, the print media in particular have been used to reconstruct the "gist" (Ibarra 2002) of how homelessness was constructed as a social problem. In this chapter that use of the media is continued. In addition, however, I examine how claimsmakers interacted with the media in order to press their positions. I also consider how the "communicative conventions" (ibid.) or genres of reporting and editorial writing shaped what aspects of the story were highlighted and to what effect.

The relationship between the media and other claimsmakers is of course an interactive one. In this case, the CCNV learned early on how to forge relationships with the press and how to stage a "media event" successfully. It was also effective in pursuing elements of a social problem campaign that were sure to draw in the media by linking these events to important social actors such as politicians, celebrities, and the courts. Appearance in Washington's key media outlets, particularly the *Post*, in turn suggested to other media outlets, policymakers, and the reading public that the CCNV was a serious player on the issue of homelessness (Gamson and Meyer 1996). New York claimsmakers did not pursue the media in the same fashion.

EARLY MEDIA IMAGES OF HOMELESSNESS IN WASHINGTON AND NEW YORK

Washington

Reaganville—Population Growing Daily

As part of its actions on behalf of Washington's homeless and hungry, the CCNV had hosted a public Thanksgiving dinner every year since 1978 (*Philadelphia Inquirer,* November 29, 1985). All who had nowhere to go for Thanksgiving were welcome to the traditional turkey and trimmings served by CCNV members and other volunteers on Thanksgiving Day. By 1981, the CCNV was pointedly serving this traditional meal in front of the White House in Lafayette Park. Thanksgiving has traditionally been a day of light news coverage so this themed event was widely photographed and distributed. Many of the nation's papers carried photographs of the poor eating a CCNV-prepared meal on Thanksgiving Day with the opulence of the White House in the background. Although the CCNV's motives surely were focused on feeding the poor, the group was also cognizant of the powerful impact made by a line of poor, mostly African-American men standing in a "soup line" in front of the presidential mansion. On Thanksgiving Day the president and his family are usually also featured in the press enjoying a traditional and finely prepared and presented version of the same meal. The images made a poignant contrast.

In addition, that Thanksgiving Day, the group erected "Reaganville" in Lafayette Park, a village of ten tents with a sign proclaiming "Welcome to Reaganville—Population Growing Daily—Reaganomics at Work" (*NYT*, November 27, 1981). Meant to evoke the depression-era "Hooverville" encampments and dramatize the plight of current homeless people, Reaganville, along with Thanksgiving for the poor, attracted some media attention on the slow news day following Thanksgiving (for example, *Boston Globe, San Francisco Chronicle, NYT,* November 27, 1981). That might have been the end of the story, if not for the fact that the federal park police refused to grant the group a permit for the encampment. The following days' stories around the country featured photos and copy of protesters being carried away and arrested by United States Park Service officers for refusing to leave the encampment (for example, *Seattle Post-Intelligencer, San Diego Union, Philadelphia Inquirer, Baltimore Sun*, November 28, 1981). The American Civil Liberties Union took up the case and by November 30, the CCNV had secured a one-week permit to "symbolically camp" in Lafayette Park (U.S. Dept. of the Interior Public Gathering Permit No. 81–966; *NYT*, December 1, 1981). The tents could remain, the activists could not. Federal officials warned that arrests would be made if activists slept in the tents.

Along with the tents, forty-five crosses and a painted plywood tombstone were erected to symbolize the freezing deaths of Washington area homeless people since 1976 (*WP*, December 2, 1981; *National Catholic Reporter*, December 11, 1981). By Christmas Eve, U.S. District Judge Charles R. Richey had reversed himself and allowed sleeping in the tents as part of free speech rights protected by the First Amendment, although Richey stayed the ruling until the U.S. Court of Appeals ruled on the case (*WP*, December 24, 1981). Meanwhile, the CCNV had collected names of people from many states who had died due to homelessness, and the Reaganville cemetery had grown to more than five hundred white crosses. This made an effective visual display, which was photographed by the Associated Press and widely circulated in the nation's newspapers (*Evening Sun, Bremerton Sun, Springfield Daily News*, December 29, 1981).

The U.S. Court of Appeals heard the case on January 15, 1982. The CCNV meanwhile vowed to keep Reaganville alive as a symbol at least, until the last day of winter, whether or not the group had a permit. If live bodies were not permitted to testify to the plight of the poor, the group asserted, "the dead would have to issue the cry for justice" (CCNV letter, January 1982). The U.S. Court of Appeals found in favor of the CCNV and stated that National Park Service regulations "plainly allow [the group] to sleep in the tents as an intrinsic part of their protest" (as quoted from the ruling in *WP*, January 23, 1982). The ruling led to a new round of publicity for Reaganville and its aims, including more photographs (*Guardian*, February 3, 1982), and a column by Colman McCarthy, a longtime supporter of the CCNV (*WP*, February 21, 1982). Reaganville again received coverage in March when the encampment was taken down by the CCNV (*New York Rocker*, March; *NYT*, March 21; *Philadelphia Inquirer*, March 24, 1982).

The Apple Pie Bite Back Event

In July 1982, the Republican Party staged a national media event that the CCNV found irresistible. As the *Washington Times* reported, "The

Senate Republican Conference announced yesterday it has ordered 'the world's largest apple pie' for a celebration tomorrow of the nation's 10 percent tax cut" (June 30, 1982). Flyers were distributed inviting guests to "get your slice of the tax pie" and celebrate the tax cut with a free piece of the pie and "a free Pepsi to wash it down" to the first "2000 people" to show up (Republican Party flyer, July 1982). CCNV created its own counterflyer for the event, a statement about class difference entitled "Whose Pie?" It starts "Pardon us, dear friends, for the fracture of good order. We have—with purpose and forethought—come here to-day to disrupt these activities" (CCNV flyer, July 1, 1983). And disrupt them they did. Five CCNV members dressed in pillow-stuffed suits as named "fat cat" Republican contributors and supporters (including brewery corporate chief Joseph Coors and conservative media mogul Walter Annenberg) pushed through the media-infused crowd and leaped into the pie, "squishing the apples and shouting, 'It's all mine, it's all mine!' " (NYT, July 2, 1982). As the Times further reports, "Momentarily stunned, staff members of the Senate Republican Conference, who had worked hard to arrange the event, sprang to the defense of their pie, leaping into the apples and attempting to drag out the offenders. By the time the Park Police showed up, almost everyone involved was covered with goo" (July 2, 1982).

The photographs from this protest were dramatic and, as they lent themselves to clever headlines, were widely distributed around the nation on July 2, 1982. Some examples include, "Pie-Party Protest" (WP), "Pie-In" (News American-United Press International), "Apple Pie Slip-Up" (Dayton Daily News), "Slice of Life" (Los Angeles Times), "Applesauce" (Philadelphia Daily News), "Some Folks Have a Lot of Crust" (Seattle Times), and the politically revealing "Giveaway Spoiled" (Houston Chronicle). Many accompanying stories and photo captions mentioned the CCNV by name or mentioned that the protesters were claiming that the poor were shortchanged by the tax cuts. The five protesters were arrested and charged with disorderly conduct and destruction of property. They were immediately dubbed the "Apple Pie Five" by the press and their story and photos reappeared in widespread coverage in November when the jury charged with deciding their case declared itself "hopelessly deadlocked" (WP, November 2, 1982). Eventually, the Apple Pie Five pleaded no contest, and the matter was dropped. But they had certainly parlayed a Republican celebration into press coverage for the cause of America's poor. As it happened, this event dovetailed nicely with the CCNV's main summer activity—a campaign against food waste.

The "Beggar's Banquet"

On June 11, the CCNV wrote a letter to area food wholesalers and retailers announcing a new campaign (CCNV letter, 1982). For the past eleven years, the group said, they had been feeding the poor on surplus, donated, and scavenged food. Much of their food came from shipping terminals and wholesale markets, where the group intervened before excess produce was sold to pig farmers or discarded. They also regularly scavenged in dumpsters at these locations and at supermarkets to claim and reuse food discarded by others. Because garbage is considered private property, the group had often been harassed for this practice, threatened with arrest, and even ordered out of dumpsters at gunpoint. Store managers had at times poured bleach or other toxic chemicals in their dumpsters to prevent scavenging. The letter called on these businesspeople to instead work with the CCNV to enable the distribution of usable food. This letter was followed a few days later by one to the CCNV's supporters who were called on to support the new initiative (June 22, 1982). Thus began the CCNV's campaign to extend feeding the poor beyond a daily activity and into the arenas of public problem construction and policymaking. As the news reported record jobless rates (*NYT*, June 20, 1982) and increases in housing shortages for the poor (*WP*, June 27, 1982), the CCNV approached several like-minded representatives, including Tony Hall and Mary Oakar (both Ohio Democrats), to cosponsor a banquet for Congress made from the city's cast-off food. And to advertise the event they recruited Representative Pete Stark (D-Calif.) to join them in dumpster diving—as the cameras rolled (*WP*, July 24, 1982). Media representatives were also recruited to accompany CCNV members on their daily "food runs"—visits to dumpsters and wholesalers to collect the food the group needed to feed between three hundred and five hundred impoverished people seven days a week.

The banquet was held in the federal Rayburn Building's Gold Room and was attended by Senator Ted Kennedy (D-Mass.), and about thirty other members of Congress and dozens of reporters. The menu—made exclusively from scavenged food—included crab quiche, potatoes au gratin, green bean casserole, and a shortcake topped by boysenberries. Photographers' shutters whirred as the senator from Massachusetts tasted "dumpster quiche." Attendance by political stars ensured amused national coverage of the event (*WP*, July 29; *Philadelphia Inquirer*, July 29; *Cleveland Plain Dealer*, July 25; *Los Angeles Times*, July 25, 1982). Congress members used the luncheon to launch a House resolution urging the enactment of a national "Good Samaritan" law. The proposed law would exempt from liability lawsuits food distributors and retailers who donated instead of discarding their waste food. The CCNV, which had suggested this legislation, also gained a national platform from which to argue against wasted food. The event even made the national news weeklies, *Time*, and *Newsweek* (August 9, 1982), and *Newsweek* did a follow-up story on dumpster scavenging, its use by the CCNV, and its growing respectability due to the nation's recession (August 23, 1982). Columnist Colman McCarthy wrote a follow-up article about food salvaging in which he featured the nation's new foodbank programs, such as Second Harvest, which, by late 1982, had forty member groups in cities spanning the nation (*WP*, October 2, 1982).

America's Dispossessed

Media coverage of homelessness and hunger in Washington closed 1982 with a reprise of the previous year's concerns. The CCNV held its annual Thanksgiving Day meal in front of the White House, featured in a large photo on page one of the *Washington Post* (November 26, 1982). The *Times* carried a photo from the Lafayette Park meal and a story stating that "tens of thousands" of Americans around the nation had had to seek their Thanksgiving Day meal from charitable organizations (*NYT*, November 26, 1982). A Thanksgiving Day editorial in the *Post* focused on destitution, homelessness, and the need for a redistribution of surplus food (*WP*, November 25, 1982). The paper had begun to cover homelessness and hunger in earnest by this point, both as a city problem, "Large Poor Families Face Critical Shortage of Public Housing" (October 6, 1982), and as a national one, "Cities Stagger Under Needs of 'Newly Poor' " (October 14, 1982).

Most importantly, the *Post* decided to run a series of editorials on "America's Dispossessed" for the holiday season. A three-day assessment of the problem was offered, beginning with "Christmas on the Grates" (offering a description of long-term homeless people). This was followed by "The New Migrants" (about the revival of homeless people crisscrossing the country in search of work), and "Searching for Jobs" (about the consequences of the newly globalized economy) (December 25–27, 1982). The *Post* finished the year with a four-part editorial on what sorts of policy changes needed to come about to alleviate these national ills entitled, "America's Dispossessed: What Needs to Be Done" (December 28–31, 1982). The paper encouraged federal policy to "focus on helping people hurt by economic change" and stated, "for God's sake, stop cutting . . . important social programs that are the last line of defense for the 'old' and 'new' poor alike" (December 29, 1982). The *Post* urged emergency aid for the homeless (December 29, 1982), extending unemployment benefits, retraining and relocating displaced workers, and

toughening educational standards so that students would be better prepared to take on the new economy's challenges (December 30, 1982). In
the final editorial, the paper urged cuts in defense spending and fiscal
policy aimed at lowering the then staggering interest rates (December
31, 1982). While these issues were being discussed in the editorial segment of the paper, columnists Henry Mitchell also wrote about housing
the homeless (*WP*, December 17, 1982) while Colman McCarthy described "the first congressional hearing on homelessness since the Depression in 1932" (*WP*, December 26, 1982). News stories covered
America's overloaded soup kitchens and shelters (*WP*, November 23,
1982) and the doings of the CCNV. Mitch Snyder was reported urging
the use of federal buildings for shelters (*WP*, December 16, 1982) and the
tent city issue again became salient. The CCNV had gone back to court
to win permission to camp in Lafayette Park (tents had been allowed
but sleeping in them had not) (*WP*, December 4, 1982). The CCNV decided not to erect the tents again as people sleeping in them had been
the point of the symbolic act. Instead, the group brought cardboard boxes
and camped in front of the District Building, the seat of the city government. This action received much photographic attention from the
local television news, though not from the *Post* (*Washington Times, Baltimore Sun*, December 29, 1982). By year's end, the local papers in Washington had begun to cover hunger and homelessness frequently and with
seriousness.

New York

The coverage of homelessness in New York in late 1981 was scant.
The *Times* covered a mayoral hearing concerned with the disappearance
of SRO hotels (*NYT*, November 20, 1981) and *Times* columnist Sidney
Schanberg wrote a scathing column on the state's deinstitutionalization
policy and the city's gentrification policy, saying each had contributed
to the growing numbers of "expendable people" (December 15, 1981).
"Channel 4 News" covered homelessness and the lack of adequate city
policy in a series called "The Homeless: Shame of a City" (December 7–
14, 1981). And the city paper devoted to presenting an African-American
perspective—the *Amsterdam News*—reported that "homelessness among
Blacks [is] now epidemic" (December 26, 1981). This story was followed
shortly by another one about neighborhood resistance to the opening of
a large shelter in a poor and minority Brooklyn neighborhood. Although
residents were sympathetic to homeless people, some felt as though they
were being relocated from the Bowery so that area could be gentrified.
One resident said, "When the city put them here they weren't helping

them, they were dumping them on a community that can't help them" (*Amsterdam News*, January 2, 1982).

Much more coverage of local homelessness occurred as the new year began. The *Times* reported that "Housing Aid Cuts Affect Poor" (January 3, 1982), and on sheltering efforts ("Judge Approves New York's Plan to Shelter Men," January 6, 1982) and complaints ("Lawyer Terms Shelters for Women Inadequate," January 8, 1982). The *Christian Science Monitor* reported that "[New York] has been unwilling to admit that the conversion of single-room occupancy hotels (SROs) into expensive housing has contributed to the problem of homelessness" (January 12, 1982). At the same time, the *Times* reported, "3,000 Families in City to Lose Welfare Funds" (January 9, 1982) and "Many Families in East Harlem Seek Food Aid" (January 28, 1982). Other stories featured personal tales such as the story of homeless man Bobby Cruz (*NYT*, January 16, 1982). A column by Anna Quindlen about homeless men was entitled, "The Priorities of Life by a Fire in the Cold" (January 13, 1982). The *Times*'s longtime program of donation to the poor, "The Neediest Fund," featured homelessness that month as well (*NYT*, January 28, 1982). The *Daily News* also wrote about homeless men in the Bowery in its feature, "Into the Heart of Darkness" (January 26, 1982). At the end of January, 1982, Rebecca Smith, a woman who had lived for eight months in a cardboard box on Tenth Avenue froze to death in her makeshift home (*NYT*, January 31, 1982).

The Death of Rebecca Smith

Rebecca Smith, the *Times* reported, had been a college-educated woman, the valedictorian of her class, gifted in music, a pianist. She had spent ten years in a psychiatric facility as a child. She had married, had had a child, and later left her husband and daughter because she had not wanted her mental illness to be a burden to them. She was originally from Virginia and had moved to New York to live with her sister. She had spent some time in a local psychiatric hospital and about ten years prior to her death she had struck out on her own to become independent. She had managed to achieve this goal with the help of public assistance and Thorazine, a psychiatric medication she took somewhat irregularly. She had lived in an SRO hotel on the upper West Side until her public assistance check had been cut off because she had failed to show up for a recertification meeting. Though social welfare workers had subsequently tried to arrange the meeting, Rebecca Smith had disappeared. Eventually she had resurfaced on the corner of Tenth Avenue and Seventeenth Street. Other social welfare workers had visited her for ten days prior to her death to try to convince her to come out of the cold, but she had refused help. According to the workers, their attempts to get a court order forcing her to be sheltered had come too late for the sixty-one-year-old (*NYT*, January 31, 1982).

Rebecca Smith's story seemed to encapsulate homelessness for many. The *Post* featured a column on her story (Richard Cohen, February 4, 1982) and many letters to the editor were written about her plight, not all of them sympathetic (*WP*, February 13, 1982). The *Post* also wrote an editorial about her case, supporting a subsequent New York law that would enable the city to go to court and within seventy-two hours declare a person mentally ill. This law also allowed the city to shelter homeless people against their will (February 16, 1982). Radical psychiatrist Thomas Szasz wrote a guest column in the *Times* and argued that taking away her personal liberty by incarcerating her in a psychiatric facility early in her life had made Rebecca Smith refuse help later in life (February 16, 1982). A *Times* editorial wondered why Rebecca Smith was allowed to refuse help if she was mentally ill (January 29, 1982). Later, the *Times* endorsed the "forced shelter" law, noting that it had sufficient safeguards for the protection of rights, even according to the ACLU (February 19, 1982). The *Daily News* ran a feature entitled, "Should We Seize Homeless People against Their Will?" (February 14, 1982).

After the Rebecca Smith story ran its course, coverage of homelessness in New York again became muted. Still, sporadic stories continued to appear in the media. The *Times* ran an article claiming that "young and able" New Yorkers who could have found other housing were deciding to stay in homeless shelters because of improved conditions in the shelters (April 26, 1982). The same court-ordered agreement the city had signed that had improved conditions so much that people had flocked to shelters, according to the *Times*, had resulted in little change, "Shelter Program Still a Bummer," according to the *Daily News* (May 4, 1982). Robert Hayes, longtime homeless activist and attorney, filed a class action suit against the city on behalf of mentally ill people without housing (*NYT*, May 21, 1982). The *Times* noted that nationally homelessness continued to increase, taxing various cities' ability to cope (May 3, 1982). New York was "Trying To Add Shelters for Its Homeless," and the city was looking for private groups to provide additional space for the 40 percent rise in need over the previous year (*NYT*, July 26, 1982). The Community Service Society released a follow-up study that, while recognizing that shelters had been expanded and improved, also noted that "distressing deficiencies remain" (*NYT*, July 28, 1982). A *Times* editorial stated that New York City and New York State officials were "finally doing a good job of housing the homeless." The editorial also noted that the population had changed, from white male Bowery drunks, to mental patients, to a population that was increasingly "young, Black, Hispanic, and female" (July 30, 1982). Later in the summer however, both the *Times* (August 16, 1982) and the *Daily News* (August 16, 1982) noted that more beds were needed for the upcoming cooler months. The *Times* reminded their readers in an editorial that "the homeless won't go away" and admonished city officials to "show some political courage" to add more supervised housing for the mentally ill homeless (August 23, 1982).

In October, Hayes's class action suit was dismissed (*NYT*, October 5, 1982). In an editorial, the *Times* chided both state and city officials for their failure to develop a comprehensive plan to deal with homelessness (October 15, 1982) and complained again about bureaucratic and legal stalemate in a subsequent editorial (November 15, 1982). A third editorial called for the state to transfer mental health funds to urban areas where, according to the paper, most homeless mentally ill people lived (December 1, 1982). State Mental Health Director Sarah Connell wrote a letter to the *Times* stating that the state was not "dumping patients" and that indeed, it was aiding many with psychiatric problems (October 27, 1982). During the holiday season, the *Times* twice ran news stories about the "new homeless," unemployed people crisscrossing the country in their cars in search of a job (December 15, 24, 1982). The *Times* covered the first congressional hearing on homelessness, wherein homeless people spoke about their plight and advocates urged Congress to provide additional aid (December 16, 1982). The paper also ran a column by Anna Quindlen about people donating time and goods to the needy (December 22, 1982). On Christmas Day, the paper published a news story that stated that New York clergy were blaming the government for failures to house the homeless. Another feature on the holiday noted that "For Homeless, the Cheer Is Gone from Christmas" (*NYT*, December 25, 1982). In this early stage of homelessness developing as a social problem, city residents mostly heard about their government not doing enough for an increasing population.

THE MEDIA AND CONTEXT

Thanksgiving 1981 until the close of 1982 marked a crucial stage in the development of the role of the Washington media as a resource in which to press claims and as a claimsmaker in its own right. The CCNV during this period continued to cultivate close relationships with the local press and began to forge relationships with media with more national venues. Moreover, the group began to envision how to use the media as a resource for pressing its view of the entwined problems of hunger and homelessness. In contrast, the New York media mostly stuck to their role as reporters of news of local interest and made only modest forays into pressing hunger or homelessness as local problems to be solved. Although the *Times* is widely read by the nation's intellectual and political elite, the paper did not engage much in attempts to construct homelessness or hunger as national social problems. Local advocates made little headway in getting their perspective on homelessness heard, either as a local or national matter of interest. To examine further why the social context was elaborated in the way that it was, I first examine the environmental and interpretive contexts available during this time period. I then examine the media as context in addition to their claimsmaking role.

The Environmental Context in Washington

In this phase of problem construction, Washington, as the seat of national government, proved a crucial element of context in several senses. First, as the seat of government, Washington is the location where the nation's political agenda is set. Thus, operating in Washington gives activist groups or others seeking to be claimsmakers an added advantage—there is an increased potential that an issue raised here will be noticed by important federal power brokers and thus become nationalized. Second, Washington has a high concentration of political and media personnel. Thus, there is increased potential that connections with important national figures can be made. Third, a high concentration of media workers makes it much more likely that claimsmakers can find someone willing to publicize their issue, particularly if it is presented in a media-friendly, dramatic fashion. The CCNV used all three of these elements of the environmental context to press its claims during this phase of problem construction.

Even as early as 1981, the CCNV was well-known to politicians and reporters in Washington. The past occupation of Union Station brought the group to the attention of many in Washington. Though most politicians were probably in their home districts for the Thanksgiving holiday and did not witness the Thanksgiving soup line, the symbolic cemetery and Reaganville tents became noticeable features of the capital-area landscape during the winter of 1981–1982. Politicians and reporters passed these symbols on the way to their jobs. Given that being informed is a central feature of both political and media work, most Washington politicians and media workers were probably somewhat familiar with the CCNV and Reaganville and its message. On a less public level, some politicians had no doubt followed the CCNV's First Amendment case.

Many politicians and reporters are avid, even obsessive news absorbers. If a claimsmaking group can get noticed by some element of the media, other media workers proide a willing "first" audience—and one crucial to expanding media coverage of claimsmaking activities (McCarthy, Smith, and Zald 1996). The coverage of the Apple Pie event and Ted Kennedy eating salvaged food were no doubt noticed with amusement by media workers and politicians. Even if these groups were not yet much interested in the issues these events tried to raise, the CCNV and its antics were an increasingly noticed local phenomenon. As purveyors of drama themselves, it is reasonable to suspect that many in Washington's political and news businesses had a grudging respect for the CCNV's increasing ability to get itself public attention. The CCNV's success in generating publicity for Reaganville, the Apple Pie Bite Back, and the Beggar's Banquet thus put the CCNV and its issues on the map in Washington (Ryan 1991). Once noticed, the CCNV was in a better position to forge relationships and ally itself with other more powerful claimsmakers.

In this phase of problem construction, the group began to move toward cultivating relationships with sympathetic national politicians as a way to further its cause. Though Reaganville and the Apple Pie event must be seen as classic examples of oppositional politics, celebrity food salvaging and the Beggar's Banquet required alliances with national-level politicians. Approaching Representative Stark and convincing him to engage in some well-publicized dumpster diving served both to publicize the issue of wasted food and gave Stark a way to stand out from his fellow House members. Likewise, the Beggar's Banquet allowed politicians to suggest that hunger was a problem the Reagan administration had neglected or exacerbated. It also allowed House members from the agricultural states of California and Ohio to suggest legislation (the "Good Samaritan" resolution) that might help combat hunger while reducing risk to those who produced and distributed the nation's food. Cultivating relationships with politicians helped garner the CCNV and its issues increased access to the media and increased publicity. Forging relationships with national political figures also put the CCNV in a position to potentially influence the types of changes to social policy that the group increasingly felt were necessary to alleviate the problem. Thus pursuing the increased media coverage that accompanies linkages with national-level politicians also enabled the CCNV to forge ties with the very people who could help them forge ahead on the legislative front (Kingdon 1984; Kielbowicz and Scherer 1986).

The press is an important resource for any claimsmakers. Reporters deal in the currency of drama and celebrity. Early on, the CCNV had demonstrated an ability to dramatize its activities effectively—the National Visitor Center campaign and Reaganville were two examples of dramatic and photogenic protest activities. When political celebrities were added to the mix, either inadvertently as they were in the Apple Pie event, or purposively, as they were at the Beggar's Banquet, the press naturally became more interested in the CCNV and its activities. Beyond these enticements, the CCNV actively worked to forge relationships with members of the press, thus helping to ensure the media would remain "open" to covering the issue (Gamson and Meyer 1996). The most consistent of these over the years was Colman McCarthy of the *Washington Post*. The breadth of coverage the group received, however, indicates that other reporters for other news organizations were also cultivated. It also suggests that the CCNV learned quickly how to make the most out of Washington's overabundance of media workers.

The Interpretive Context in Washington

Washington, as the nation's capital, is imbued with a wealth of symbols, settings, and people that can aid claimsmakers in dramatizing issues such as homelessness. One such interpretive resource is the physical space of the nation's capital. Because the Capitol Building, White House, and other of the city's landmarks are widely recognized as shorthand for the nation's power and its democratic values (freedom, equality, justice), using Washington as a stage from which to dramatize claims takes on special significance. The CCNV managed several times early on to use these widely shared symbolic resources to good effect (Zald 1996). Though using the National Visitor Center as the setting for making a statement about increasing shelter was effective on a local level, few Americans outside the Beltway recognized Union Station or understood the significance of using this would-be tourist destination as a homeless shelter.

Washington was much better used as a stage in the Thanksgiving Day meal and in siting the Reaganville encampment and cemetery. Almost all literate Americans recognize the White House as the home of the president. What otherwise would have been a local gesture of good will by a charitable organization—the feeding of the needy at Thanksgiving—became a poignant symbol of inequality when the line of destitute, mostly African-American men filed past the White House to get their free holiday meal.

Likewise, staging Reaganville in Lafayette Park evoked, at least among the historically savvy, images of veterans who had similarly built a squatter's village to demand their pensions during the nation's last time of mass unemployment in the 1930s. Most Americans were aware of the "Hoovervilles" built by the desperate homeless poor that had sprung up with the Depression and some even remembered these squatters' camps. "Reaganville—Population Growing Daily" worked well as theater because it linked the Reagan administration and its policies directly to the nation's worst economic collapse in a way familiar to most. The cemetery of those who had died for not having shelter likewise used the opulent backdrop of the White House to eloquent symbolic effect. There was simply no better stage upon which to nationalize a social problem, especially one in which government intervention would seem to be required.

The CCNV's other main events of the year, the Apple Pie Bite Back and the Beggar's Banquet, used settings similarly symbolically. In addition, politicians constituted a second interpretive resource. In the Apple Pie event, Republican House members set the stage, using the backdrop of the Capitol Building as a symbol of their power and ability to cut citizens' tax rates. The pie too, was oversized to represent the people's returned wealth, with apple giving it quintessentially American flavor. By disrupting this event the CCNV was able to turn this setting on its head, making the Capitol into the place where powerful insiders (the "fat cats") made their deals. The pie in the disrupters' lexicon was the people's money being cut up and distributed to wealthy Republican campaign contributors. Though Republican House of Representative members attended the event to demonstrate their commitment to low taxes and their power to enact such a policy, for the CCNV, they became props that signaled Washington's collusion with moneyed interests. Here again, Washington and its politician inhabitants became the perfect stage for raising the issue of inequality.

At the Beggar's Banquet, the same physical symbols and personnel were used for opposite effect. The Rayburn Building Gold Room was used to demonstrate that not only edible food but a gourmet meal fit for Washington's elite could be prepared from discarded food. Politicians who agreed that food was wasted when many were in need of it were used as political celebrities, notables whose presence would help make sure the issue was noticed by the media and publicized. Moreover, the presence of these Democrats and Washington insiders symbolized that powerful men and women cared about the issue of hunger. Their attendance lent credence to the importance of solving this social problem.

Finally, the Beggar's Banquet and the food scavenging events, which had included inviting news reporters to follow CCNV members as they scavenged and filming Representative Stark as he dumpster dived, were staged with an audience and its reaction in mind. The audience the CCNV had most in mind for these events was the press itself. The banquet and food scavenging events signaled that the issue was worthy of press coverage because it could be dramatically presented and starred national politicians, who were by definition worth media attention. In this early phase of problem construction then, the CCNV gradually learned that important audiences (politicians, the media) must be enticed and honed to turn members of these sectors into social problems claims-makers. The press and some politicians were increasingly looked to as allies in generating interest in the issue so that a more general national audience could be reached and so something might be done about the issue. Politicians who were inimical to viewing homelessness and hunger as serious social problems were used as props and foils and in that capacity they also helped generate media and popular interest in the social problems of concern.

The Environmental and Interpretive Contexts in New York

Several characteristics of New York City's environment colluded to prevent homelessness from being treated as other than a very local issue during this time period. Although New York was a national center of intellectual and media activity, it did not have the relevant concentration of national political power brokers that comprised Washington's elite. New York may be a city of celebrities but, unlike the case in Washington, none were obvious candidates to approach and interest in promoting homelessness as a social problem. New York's homeless advocates and its local politicians already had a working relationship with one another, one best characterized as that of negotiating partners. Mayor Koch for example, was unavailable as a public foil nor was he much of an ally with advocates on the issue. He had already publicly conceded that homelessness was a social problem. And he had been through years of negotiations with advocates as to how the city would meet its court-ordered responsibilities to the destitute. Thus in some way, homelessness in New York was already a "solved" social problem, however inadequately.

In any event, New York City has never been the best place to typify a national social problem, in the sense that New York is not viewed as representative of the nation. For most of its existence, the city has been viewed by its residents and by others as an exception—with problems as well as glitter unlike anywhere else in the country. New York's concerns have not often been viewed as America's. A social problem publicized in the "Big Apple" was instead likely to be viewed as a "big city" or even "New York" problem in a way that problems identified elsewhere were not. Moreover, its readily available symbols were those of a great city, not of a nation. If nationalizing a social problem was the issue, Washington was a much more amenable setting for the task. Though the individual-deficit model of homelessness was originally produced in

New York, New York was not the venue best suited to convincing salient members of the public that homelessness was a national social problem.

Moreover, it is certainly not clear during this period that advocates in New York were much interested in nationalizing the issue in the same sense that the CCNV was. New York was a huge city with a large homeless problem, one that by all accounts continued to grow worse as the months proceeded. It made sense for advocates to focus on the local situation, particularly since they had had some success in forcing the city to recognize housing as a civil right. The strategy that had so far produced success for the advocates was a mostly unpublic one—that of filing lawsuits. Though there had been demonstrations in New York and advocates there were in close contact with their peers in Washington, what had worked in New York were the behind-the-scenes methods of lawsuits, court proceedings, and legal negotiations with the city. Advocates saw little reason not to continue to pursue what had worked locally. Besides, the CCNV was better positioned both by location and style to make the case nationally.

The issue of Rebecca Smith's death was probably the single chance to nationalize homelessness from the vantage point of New York during this time period. Here again, however, New York's reputation as a huge and, to some, callous city made the issue seem like one that only occurred in New York. It was also a hard story for advocates to promote symbolically since Smith's death represented all that was difficult about solving the problem of homelessness. Here was a woman whom the social welfare bureaucracy had made homeless but had also tried repeatedly to help. Smith was not a quiet victim desiring aid and not being offered it, but a resistant and difficult person of uncertain mental health. Should she have been locked up against her will? It was a thorny story, not one easily galvanized into a symbolic representation of homelessness and what should be done about it.

The media reflected these conditions in their representation of homelessness during this period. Although a few national stories were featured in the *Times* and elsewhere, most coverage of the issue revolved around two topics, the first, that the problem continued to grow, and the second, that local and state efforts to ameliorate it were inadequate. In most media representations of the issue in New York, the solution to homelessness was clear—providing more shelter space for the "new" homeless and providing a more permanent solution—either rehospitalization or supervised housing—for the mentally ill. This narrow vision of the problem and solution combined with a legalistic approach to it perhaps prevented the more broad definition of the problem favored by the CCNV from emerging.

THE EMERGENCE OF MEDIA AS CONTEXT

The media offer other claimsmakers a context in which to promote their construction of a social problem such as homelessness. But this is not a blanket offer as Gitlin (2001) and many others have observed. Instead, the media must be seduced by drama, celebrity, or the unassailable importance of an issue or event to decide to devote space or time to it (McCarthy, Smith, and Zald 1996). There is always competition for space in the public arena (Hilgartner and Bosk 1988). Once the decision to report a story is made, the media in some ways become the primary claimsmakers. It is reporters who decide which person to interview, which angle to pursue. It is photographers who decide how much footage to take and how to dramatize the event visually. Then editors and producers determine the placement of copy in the paper or segments in the program, how much time or space to devote to it, which quotes to use and which to leave on the cutting room floor. Often, the result of this process bears scant resemblance to the intentions of the advocate or other claimsmaker who was interested in wooing the media in the first place (Klandermans and Goslinga 1996; Gitlin 2001). Yet for claimsmakers desiring to use public persuasion as a means to get others to take notice and act to ameliorate a social problem, dealing with the media is critical, for it is the industry in charge of the distribution of information. Therefore it is the conduit through which claimsmakers generate public concern for an issue (McCombs and Shaw 1972; Neuman 1990; Page and Shapiro 1992).

The media as context is a terrain steeped in fog—claimsmakers can never be sure of stepping on solid ground. Although outcomes can never be certain, there are discernable methods by which to gain the media's attention and these were well used by the CCNV. Because of media's bias in favor of drama and celebrity, low-status claimsmakers wishing to have an impact on this member of the iron quadrangle must supply the media with recognizable fodder. As discussed above, this the CCNV did, through its dramatic—even outrageous—visual representations of its issues and through its celebrity-studded events (Margolis and Mauser 1989). Although the CCNV had little control over what would be reported in the news about it, at this stage, perhaps the content and cast of the issue took a back seat to generating publicity itself. In these early years, the CCNV tried to raise homeless and hunger as "valence issues," which Nelson describes as issues that are rather unspecified but that "attempt to *reaffirm the ideals of civic life*" (Nelson 1984:28). There may also be an advantage of sorts when advocates are introducing "new victims" of a social problem to the media (Best 1999:131). In the honeymoon phase of media coverage of an emergent social problem, the media rarely pursue a policy of balanced coverage. The advocates for a time had an ability to press their case unopposed by counterclaimsmakers.

To help ensure that media content reflected the group's intentions, the CCNV developed ongoing relationships with journalists. At the *Post* it was Paul Valentine who almost exclusively covered the National Visitor Center takeover. Colman McCarthy gave the group its first public recognition in his "Night Hospitality" column (*WP*, December 21, 1977). And it was he who most reflected the CCNV's views on the issues of hunger and homelessness. Henry Mitchell, another sympathetic *Post* columnist, also often reflected views that were cognizant with those of the CCNV. Additionally, the group had cultivated its relationship with the *Washington Times* and this paper also covered the issues of homelessness and hunger regularly. As many who have wrangled with the press will concede, it is relationships, however, rather than "events speaking for themselves" that ensure that claims made by a public group, especially a controversial one such as the CCNV, will get a fair hearing. The CCNV and perhaps especially Mitch Snyder became adept at giving the media something they could use. This was a firm foundation upon which to build the personal relationships that produced frequent and often sympathetic coverage of homelessness, hunger, and the Community for Creative Non-Violence. Because of the structure of advocate claimsmaking in New York, no equivalent relationships emerged. Instead, the mayor and his administration continued as the main generator of news about homelessness. Mayor Koch had nearly unlimited ability to use the media as a context in which to press his claims, because as the mayor, he was by definition a dramatic, newsworthy celebrity deserving of media attention.

THE EMERGENCE OF MEDIA AS CLAIMSMAKER

In print journalism, there are several categories of claimsmaking. First, there is "all the news that's fit to print" as the *New York Times* so tellingly puts it—the news and photographs that editors have decided are worthy of coverage. Because the media are susceptible to drama, some symbolic representations of social problems compete successfully with other events or issues, and even attain page one coverage, but then are dropped as the media's attention is diverted (Hilgartner and Bosk 1988; Dyan and Katz 1992; Best 1999). The National Visitor Center takeover and Apple Pie Bite Back event could be categorized as such dramatized moments in the press. If a social issue merely attains momentary notice and quickly fades from view, the media remain at best a temporary context for other claimsmakers and do not act as much of a claimsmaker in their own right. Coverage validates the issue as worthy of note, but it is unclear that this is because the issue is an ongoing social problem (rather than a momentary diversion or dramatic moment). The signal that a daily newspaper has become a claimsmaker in its own right around a social problem lies in a pattern of sustained news coverage that is also evident in elements of the newspaper that are reflective in nature. These include its regular columns, its letters to the editor, its guest editorials and news analysis segments, and particularly, its corporate editorials.

Although columnists often have much leeway in deciding which issues to pursue, they are certainly amenable to the editor's suggestion or coercion. Guest editorials indicate that a topic is important enough to require "experts" to weigh in on it. Letters to the editor may come from active claimsmakers or just concerned readers: the selection of which letters to print, however, reflects editorial decision-making. News analysis pieces are typically reserved for topics the paper thinks are extremely important or pressing. Corporate editorials, more than any other single category of print journalism, signal that the paper's editors have decided that the issue is worthy of direct claimsmaking. These unsigned editorials typically *presume* the problem and recommend a certain approach to it be taken or congratulate those taking an approach with which the paper's editors agree. Frequent corporate editorials about a certain social problem such as homelessness are a good indication that the paper has decided to engage in claimsmaking about the issue.

It seems clear that 1982 marked the time when the *Washington Post*'s editorial board joined the effort to construct homelessness as a social problem in earnest. The paper ran twelve editorials that it indexed as pertaining to homelessness, seven during the holiday season. Columnist Colman McCarthy wrote on homelessness four times in 1982. Another columnist, Richard Cohen, wrote on Rebecca Smith's death in New York and five letters to the editor responded to this article. A corporate editorial on the same topic followed. The clearest indication that the *Post* was becoming a claimsmaker on homelessness-related topics, however, was the seven-part editorial series run during the holiday season. It is unusual for a newspaper to write such a lengthy editorial series. This end-of-the-year series made it evident that the paper viewed homelessness as a national problem and its solution a responsibility of the Reagan administration.

The *New York Times* also became a claimsmaker on homelessness during this period, albeit of quite a different sort. The paper ran five editorials on the topic and in each case, it was New York's problem with homeless and mentally ill people that was at issue, not the nation's.

Likewise, the letters to the editor, all from advocates or government officials, were responses to some local issue pertaining to homelessness covered in the paper. The paper also ran three columns during 1982, again all local construals of homelessness. There is no doubt that the *Times* during this period began to see homelessness as a local social problem requiring editorial comment. But there was also little indication that the *Times* felt it was its responsibility to participate as a claimsmaker in the national construction of homelessness as a social problem. Again, the preponderance of coverage had to do with housing homeless New Yorkers.

One telling difference between the two papers is its indexing of the issue. In 1982, the *Post* introduced the term "homelessness" into its annual index. The *Times* introduced the terms "homeless persons" and "homeless" (but not homelessness) into its index. Prior to this year, all material related to this topic was indexed under "vagrancy" in both papers (and in the *Times* the category "tramp" additionally appeared). This change in language itself speaks to the emergence of homelessness as a definable "new" social problem. In 1982, both papers used both "vagrancy" and the new variants on "homeless" in their indexes. In the *Post* almost all articles on the topic were indexed under "homelessness" (with the exception of the Rebecca Smith story). In the *Times*, almost all articles of this sort were listed under "vagrancy." Employing the word "homeless" to describe and categorize coverage of this issue is in itself a claim that this is indeed a definable and somehow "new" social problem—a problem with qualities discernable from those of "vagrancy."

In this chapter I have described how other claimsmakers in the iron quadrangle, particularly CCNV activists, began to effectively use the media as a *context* in which to press their claims. I also noted the emergence of media entities, particularly the nation's two most important newspapers, as *claimsmakers* in their own right. It is also important to identify the combinations of relationships, enticements, and pressures that makes newspapers decide to become claimsmakers for a particular social problem such as homelessness. None of these elements is probably sufficient on its own to entice a newspaper or other media entities to become claimsmakers. A combination of these elements, many of them present in their nascent stages during the period discussed above, were effective in convincing the media to take up claimsmaking around this social problem.

First, is the enticement of a "big" or ongoing story. If the story line around a social issue promises to have ongoing dramatic moments, such as those suggested by the Reaganville First Amendment case and the general confrontational politics of the CCNV, media attention is likely. Second, if celebrities (by definition newsworthy individuals) take up the issue, the media will follow (Best 1999). By 1982, Mitch Snyder himself was fast becoming at least a local celebrity and one prone to dramatic acts. Moreover, interactions and alliances with Congress members and other powerful Washington insiders made the *Post* notice the issue in a fashion that would not have happened without these political stars.

Third, regular beat reporters and columnists must be enlisted in the cause. If a columnist regularly comments on a social issue it becomes important somewhat exclusive of its immediate newsworthiness. The *Post*'s Colman McCarthy served this function particularly well for the issues of homelessness and hunger, as did Henry Mitchell and feature writer Neil Henry (who went undercover as a homeless man for an early serial feature about being "down and out"; *WP*, April 27–May 8, 1980). In the *Times*, Sydney Schanenberg played this role, though more sporadically than did McCarthy.

Fourth, continuous pressure by other sorts of claimsmakers helps convince the media that this is truly an issue in which they should become involved. In Washington, the CCNV consistently brought up the issue on multiple (and often dramatic) fronts, including feeding the poor in front of the White House, publicly fasting, occupying a central train station, sitting in cardboard boxes in front of the District Building, and erecting tent cities and symbolic cemeteries. In New York, legal action and Mayor Koch's response provided continued evidence that this was a story worth editorializing about. The bylines of letter writers to both papers offer additional evidence that advocate claimsmakers used this venue to gain attention for their issue. Public response to features or other articles also pricks the media's attention—these serve as an informal polling mechanism suggesting what issues resonate with readers. Here too, there was evidence of the beginning of a public audience for homelessness as a social problem.

Finally, there is the political reputation of the paper or other media venue. The *Wall Street Journal* may not have given much attention to the issue, especially at this emergent stage. But papers of a more liberal or Democratic bent feel compelled to become involved in social problems, especially those pertaining to social inequality. Surely this constituted a part of the impulse felt by editors at both of these national papers.

These enticements and pressures are constituted from a combination of interests and interactions. The media, advocates, government officials, and policymakers and experts have separate and evolving agendas around the social problem at issue. In addition, each group has more general interests, such as gaining or retaining power and influence. How a social problem is elaborated depends on what relationships are formed between these separate groups, each replete with somewhat separate visions of what is important. In this case, the *Post*'s interests in drama, celebrity, and social responsibility were cemented by the relationships forged between the paper's writers and the local issue advocates. These advocates (at this point the CCNV and some national politicians) pulled the issue in the direction of becoming a national one, an additional enticement to the *Post*, which viewed itself as the nation's paper of politics. In New York, little effort was made by local advocates or local politicians to nationalize the issue, but significant effort was made by both groups to make homelessness into a local problem of growing importance. The *Times* responded to these efforts by taking positions on the resolution of several homelessness-related issues of local concern. This period then marks the entrance of the media, here represented by the nation's papers of record, into an active role in the construction of homelessness as a social problem. This role was to become much enhanced as the eighties progressed.

4

The Interactions of Claimsmakers and Issues

INTRODUCTION

During 1983 the problem of food for the homeless and destitute became a prominent national poverty-related issue. For the CCNV, highlighting the problem of hunger was perhaps even more central to the group's mission than was the very closely related problem of homelessness. After all, the group had been feeding Washington's hungry for over a decade and was in a good position to notice that the numbers of those who were in need of a free meal grew quickly during the early Reagan years. The CCNV was again influential in raising the issue and making it appealing to a segment of Democratic members of Congress. As the year unfolded, the CCNV kept up a program of dramatizing this issue and ended up nationalizing it with a series of events in Kansas City, home of a major storage facility for the nation's surplus dairy products. Various levels of Democratic and Republican politicians took up the issue as a matter of policy, calling for federal intervention to release more of the surplus to use to feed America's hungry poor. The national media, especially in Washington, responded to these stimuli by activists and government officials by covering hunger-related events and weighing in on the issue in columns and editorials. Thus, in a very short period of time, the problem of hunger and how surplus and discarded food could solve the problem were squarely on the nation's agenda.

Meanwhile, homelessness stabilized as an important social problem in New York and Washington. Increasingly, during this period, it was discussed as a national issue of importance. This chapter focuses on how interaction facilitates the construction of social problems in two senses. First, I demonstrate how the interactions between the relevant social problems sectors—at this point including activists, government officials, and the media—helped to create a stable framework in which to press claims about homelessness. Second, I delineate how, in this case, raising a related and complementary social problem, that of hunger, helped to solidify the place of homelessness as a social problem on the national agenda.

LEGISLATION, HEARINGS, AND LAWSUITS

The year opened with Congress actively engaging with poverty-related issues. Michigan senators Donald Riegle and Carl Levin asked the Department of Agriculture to release more surplus food to the poor (*Richmond-Times Dispatch*, January 1, 1983). Later in the month, the House Democrats unanimously called for a program of emergency economic assistance. In this early attempt at forging a national policy on the issue, the Democrats called for the creation of public service jobs, the provision of shelters and soup kitchens, and the cessation of foreclosures on homes and farms (*NYT*, February 2, 1983). Locally, the Senate Subcommittee on the District held hearings at which city officials stated that the number of shelter beds was adequate. Mitch Snyder and other shelter providers claimed that there were far too few beds (*WP*, January 25, 1983). At the hearing, chaired by Senator Arlen Spector (R-Pa.), Snyder also raised the possibility of using federal buildings as shelters, an idea the senator thought worth considering (*Washington Times*, January 25, 1983).

The hearing in part focused on the prevention of freezing deaths during the winter months, a subject emphasized by the recent death of Freddie, a longtime Georgetown street person who was known to many in both the advocate and political communities (*WP*, January 24, 1983). His had been the third homeless freezing death of the winter. A few days after the hearing, the *Post* reported that the White House was investigating the idea of employing unused federal facilities to house the homeless. The idea had been presented to the President's Task Force on Private Sector Initiative, reported the *Post*, by "some private charities," causing the White House to ask the Department of Defense (DOD) whether unused military base buildings could be used as shelters (*WP*, January 29, 1983). The CCNV was to return to this issue later in the year.

The continuing battle about whether camping in front of the White House was a protest activity protected by the First Amendment also kept homelessness in the news. During the first week of January, the full U.S. Court of Appeals decided to hear the case and the hearing began the following week (*WP*, January 15, 1983). Meanwhile, the National Park

Service granted the CCNV and 150 supporters permission to pitch tents and protest 24 hours a day in Lafayette Park as long as the group did not sleep in the tents (*WP,* January 6, 1983). A private memo from Interior Secretary James Watt stated that it was his "intention to prohibit such activities and require that they take place on the Ellipse" (Note to Moody Tidwell from James Watt, January 12, 1983). The Court, by a 6–5 majority did not agree with this sentiment and allowed "demonstrators who use their bodies to express the poignancy of their plight" to use sleep as a form of protest.

As many First Amendment cases do, this case received widespread media coverage (for example, *WP, Washington Times, Waterbury Republican (CT), Idaho Statesman,* March 10, 1983). A week later Supreme Court Chief Justice Warren Burger banned the sleeping protest in an emergency ruling (*WP,* March 18, 1983), a ruling with which conservative editorial writer George F. Will concurred (*WP,* March 20, 1983). The Burger ruling came at the request of Solicitor General Rex E. Lee. Watt's Interior Department was quoted as being "extremely pleased" with the ruling (*Washington Times,* March 18, 1983). Many of the nation's newspapers covered this story, some with photographs (for example, *Daily News, Baltimore Sun, Philadelphia Inquirer,* March 18, 1983). The CCNV decided not to defy this ruling and for the time being the tents were removed from the park.

The CCNV also held a "People's State of the Union" in January in conjunction with the president's annual speech (*Mother Jones,* May 1983). The event sought to highlight the plight of the poor and several hundred protesters marched with signs such as "Food, Shelter, Jobs" and "Words Won't Feed Our Kids" (*Philadelphia Inquirer,* January 26, 1983). The protesters held a prayer vigil in the Capitol Rotunda and 162 protesters, including longtime activist Rev. Phillip Berrigan, were arrested after refusing to leave when the police declared the building closed (*WP,* January 26, 1983). The *Daily News* stated that the protesters were using a different style but the same message as the Democrats, whose response to the State of the Union address charged that Reagan did not care that his economic policies had been devastating to millions (January 26, 1983). The *Times* was silent on the alternative state of the union event (except in a Schanberg column, see below). It did report, however, that the U.S. Conference of Mayors had called for an emergency economic package for the country's cities that included aid for the homeless and hungry (January 29, 1983).

In the cold month of February the *Post* ran an article detailing longtime street person Freddie's path to the street (February 9, 1983). In addition, the paper took up the issue of a large tent city in Houston that was under attack by local authorities and eventually closed down (February 5, 8, 1983). Columnist Colman McCarthy traveled to Chicago and experienced Midwestern-style homelessness for three days, an adventure that included trekking across town in the snow only to find filled shelters. He eventually had to resort to being "subjected to religious zealotry" at the mission shelter and spent a night in jail after requesting arrest so that he could obtain shelter (January 30, February 6, 1983).

On the local scene, the *Post* ran an article about suburban social service agencies "referring" their homeless clientele to District shelters (February 19, 1983) and followed it with an editorial stating that since suburban homelessness seemed here to stay a regional plan might be in order (February 27, 1983). An advisory commission to Mayor Barry recommended a policy for forcibly removing homeless people from the streets if the temperature fell below freezing (*WP*, April 5, 1983). Washington's local Coalition for the Homeless published its second newsletter in early 1983. The coalition opposed cuts for homeless services in the District's budget. It also noted that family homelessness was on the rise and that more services were needed to serve this group. Four more churches had been convinced to open shelters, the newsletter reported (February/March 1983). The coalition had been formed the prior year and on February 12, 1983, held its second annual organizational meeting.

Nationally, the shelter news was that the Reagan administration planned to house the homeless temporarily at military bases (*WP*, February 22, 1983). Meanwhile the *Post* chided the Reagan administration for its "Dumb, Mean Budget Cuts," an editorial in which the paper lamented the White House's new rounds of cuts to poverty programs (February 17, 1983). The paper also ran a series called "Losing It," about eviction and its aftermath. One day's installment included several articles. One was about middle-class evictions, another described how bad some landlords felt about eviction, a third detailed the skid from a $20,000 a year income to homelessness, and a fourth portrayed how for families who had been evicted home had become a motel (*WP*, February 23, 1983).

At the end of the month, the Reagan administration decided that local governments and charitable organizations would be permitted to set up emergency shelters in some vacant federal buildings (*WP*, February 26, 1983). Shortly thereafter Army Reserve facilities in counties surrounding the District were offered to private and public agencies to use for homeless shelters. A consortium of a dozen organizations unanimously rejected the offer, which consisted of making warehouse-like space available only between 5 P.M. and 7 A.M. The space was out of the way and would not "lend itself to the dignity and self-respect for innocent victims of the existing depression who, through no fault of their own, are now rendered helpless and homeless" according to the committee's chair (*WP*,

March 16, 1983). Washington was not alone in rejecting military space for homeless shelters. More than three hundred other cities also rejected the Reagan administration offer, saying that the facilities were unsuitable for overnight stays (*WP*, March 17, 1983). This offer of unused federal space, however, would later prove troublesome to the Reagan White House when Mitch Snyder decided to take Reagan up on the proposal. Shortly after military bases were resoundingly rejected as solutions to homelessness, the Federal Emergency Management Agency (FEMA, the agency that was handling homelessness at the time) announced that states and cities would be getting federal emergency money to feed and shelter homeless people during the summer months (*WP*, April 6, 1983). This marked the Reagan administration's first attempts to take federal action to ameliorate homelessness and was part of a Reagan White House policy project dubbed "Project Homeless."

FEED THE HUNGRY, NOT THE RICH

Also in February, the CCNV wrote Congress members to suggest courses of action to meet the needs of hungry and homeless people. Written in language that stressed accomplishable legislative goals, this letter suggested that at least $150 million be appropriated for emergency shelter through the Community Development Block Grant Program. The CCNV also suggested that the Department of Housing and Urban Development (HUD) and not FEMA be designated the "pass-through" agency for homeless shelter management. The group additionally reiterated its support for using federal buildings as emergency shelters. In the area of hunger, the CCNV supported Republican senator Dole's bill to release surplus commodities but thought that $2 billion of the $4 billion in storage should be released rather than the $1 billion in the Dole proposal. The CCNV's prior effort to suggest food waste legislation (House Congressional Resolution 381) had passed both houses shortly after it was introduced at the Beggar's Banquet in July 1982. The group now requested that the intent to distribute more food and discard less be coupled with legislation that would provide local funds to mayor's offices so that pick-up and distribution of waste food could proceed (CCNV letter to Congress members, February 22, 1983).

This letter turned out to be a warm-up activity for the CCNV's biggest campaign of the year—the Kansas City Campaign. The campaign kicked off quietly with an appeal to supporters in mid-March (CCNV letter, March 15, 1983). In the letter, the group stated its intention to set up an encampment and begin an open-ended fast on July 4, 1983, in

Kansas City/Independence, Missouri. This site was chosen because large limestone caves in the area contained nearly two hundred million pounds of surplus dairy products. The CCNV said the fast was intended to "encourage the release" of a portion of the surplus food stockpiled by the U.S. Department of Agriculture, a move the Reagan administration opposed. Reagan had recently gutted a bill sponsored by fellow Republican Bob Dole to release $1 billion of the surplus commodities, removing requirements for mandatory distribution (CCNV letter May 17, 1983).

Meanwhile, several local stories about homelessness were covered in the *Post*. In spring, the local Coalition for the Homeless asked Mayor Barry to keep shelters open during the summer months (April 2, 1983). The mayor responded by proposing a new policy for winter shelter for the homeless (April 5, 1983). The following day, however, the *Post* reported that federal emergency aid was on the way to help the District deal with sheltering homeless people during the summer months (April 6, 1983).

That spring, the Republicans gave the CCNV another opportunity to foil a rally. In this case, Republican Congress members tried to get press coverage for their opposition to a Democratic bill to raise taxes. Claiming that the average American family would not be able to buy thirty-seven weeks of groceries if the Democratic plan passed, the Republicans pushed thirty-seven grocery-filled shopping carts to the rally site on the Capitol Hill lawn. Just a few feet away, CCNV supporters staged a counterrally and heckled the Republicans with shouts of "Feed the hungry, not the rich." The group waved placards and piled 5,530 pounds of food—valued, the CCNV said at $2,075—behind the Republican display. This amount, said the CCNV, was what the average middle-income family had lost due to Reagan administration budget policies. This event received national press coverage, but not exactly of the type hoped for by the Republicans (*NYT*, April 15; *WP*, April 19, 1983).

A few days later, a one-day soup kitchen was set up in the Capitol building. After rain threatened a planned outdoor rally in support of more food support for the poor, House Speaker Tip O'Neill provided space for the demonstration in the House Ways and Means Committee Room (*WP*, April 23, 1983). Columnist Colman McCarthy called the event the only immediate, certain, and definable help the federal government was providing for the destitute and homeless and then proceeded to criticize the disorganized fashion in which federal policy was taking shape. Four agencies were at the time involved in the Reagan administration's new Project Homeless: HUD, DOD, the General Services Administration (GSA), and FEMA. With this many agencies involved, McCarthy warned, the Reagan administration's Project Homeless could easily become Project Aimless (*WP*, April 23, 1983).

GOIN' TO KANSAS CITY

Kickoff publicity for the Kansas City events first appeared in an article offered by Gannett News Service, a news distributor catering to medium-sized newspapers. In it, the planned fast and its purpose was described, with quotes from Snyder saying, "When large numbers of Americans are hungry, we don't see the point of sitting on $5 billion worth of food" (*Pacific Daily News*, May 3, 1983). The article went on to describe what types and amounts of surplus food the federal government owned. Views by various politicians were featured including some, like Representative Leon Panetta (D-Ca.) who, though sponsoring a food distribution bill, worried that food giveaways would be an excuse for the Reagan administration to make further cuts in programs already in place. Indeed, the Reagan administration had announced plans to cut cheese distribution in half, citing that commercial sales had been hurt by giveaways, though no verification of this was offered (*WP*, June 5, 1983). Meanwhile, the CCNV continued to plan and noted that over ninety organizations around the nation had decided to cosponsor or endorse the campaign (CCNV letter, May 7, 1983).

Several members of Congress who had been supporters of the previous summer's Beggar's Banquet helped this year's campaign by committing to tour the Kansas City food storage facility on June 27 (*WP*, June 5, 1983). Mary Rose Oakar (D-Ohio) led the delegation. Colman McCarthy publicized the effort in a column in which he mentioned that in a survey of emergency food programs, more than half reported increases of 50 percent or more in the prior year. "The food warehouses get bigger while the food lines get longer," McCarthy summarized (*WP*, June 5, 1983). Even the *Wall Street Journal* was prompted to cover the Kansas City surplus facility, stating that overproduction of dairy products was the problem and the solution was to cut milk price supports (June 14, 1983). The paper did, however, state that in a world where hunger was the most common problem, such surpluses were absurd and shameful. By mid-June, some CCNV members had traveled to Kansas City and the *Kansas City Times* began to publicize the event (June 16, 1983). The same day, the House of Representatives passed a bill authorizing the Department of Agriculture to dip into a wide variety of government surplus food for two years and distribute it to those in need (*WP*, June 17, 1983). The bill passed 389 to 18 after the representatives voted to defeat an amendment proposed by the cheese industry. The U.S. Conference of Mayors also took up the issue at their annual meeting, where mayors told of the rise of hungry people, soup lines, and food pantries in their cities (*NYT*, June 17, 1983). "Meanwhile," the *Times* editorialized, "the

Reagan administration wants to slice another billion out of food stamps, and cut $400 million more from the child nutrition budget in 1984" (June 17, 1983).

With the ACLU arguing for the CCNV, the Kansas City Parks Board was convinced that recent federal rulings in the Reaganville case made sleeping in a park as protest a free speech right protected by the First Amendment (*Kansas City Star*, June 22, 1983). There was obvious distress about the CCNV coming to Kansas City. The local press repeatedly mentioned that they were ex–Vietnam War protesters who relied on protest methods such as confrontation and civil disobedience (*Kansas City Star*, June 22, 1983). In one article, CCNV member Carol Fennelly was quoted as saying, "A lot of people see us as flaming commie pinkos" (*Kansas City Star*, June 26, 1983). The visits from Congress and the kickoff press conference were page-one news in Kansas City on June 27, even though television crews were denied permission to accompany the congressional delegation on its tour. [A letter to Secretary of Agriculture John R. Block from Mary Rose Oaker suggested that the Beatrice Foods conglomerate had something to do with the denial of access and asked the secretary to investigate this (private letter to Block from Oaker, June 30, 1983).] An article about the event noted the rise in hunger and pointed out that taxpayers were billed $239 million a year to store commodities in private warehouses around the country. Stockpiled commodities continued to increase despite giveaway programs (*Kansas City Star*, June 27, 1983).

FASTING FOR FOOD

The fast began as planned on July 4, 1983. The *Philadelphia Inquirer* publicized the event with a profile of the CCNV and its activities in Washington as well as Kansas City (July 4, 1983) while the *Hartford Courant* headlined, "Crisis Is Foreseen Unless Surplus Food for Needy Is Increased" (July 5, 1983). The Kansas City press carried the story with a large photo of the protesters foregrounded by a waving American flag (*Kansas City Times*, July 5, 1983) while *Time* magazine did a story about the food storage facility (July 4, 1983). *USA Today* reported that the "Fast Continues by Surplus Food Activists" (July 6, 1983). Though neither the *Times* nor the *Post* covered the fast as news, Colman McCarthy weighed in with a column entitled, "The Politics of Cheese," in which he noted that Congress members trying to see publicly owned cheese were not allowed to bring photographers with them. Reagan was, McCarthy opined, obsessed with the idea of "no free lunch." He continued, "His welfare queen who drove her Cadillac to the supermarket to cash in food stamps apparently is now stopping at the cheese lines to fill her trunk with a tub or two of USDA brie" (*WP*, July 10, 1983). The protest was receiving frequent local television coverage in Kansas City (Rader 1986) and regional newspapers paid some attention but the fast did not get much national press coverage.

The fast continued for two weeks, with about twenty activists participating (*Post-Dispatch*, July 24, 1983). After two weeks, the *National Catholic Reporter* published an article about surplus food and an editorial supporting the fasters' aims. The editorial stated that only politics could be getting in the way of distributing the surplus and featured the CCNV's Carol Fennelly stating, "When the administration is singing, 'Happy days are here again,' they don't want pictures of long food distribution lines" (July 15, 1983). On July 19, comedian and social activist Dick Gregory joined the hunger strike (*Chicago Tribune*, July 19, 1983). The *New York Times* finally covered the issue with a sympathetic story entitled, "U.S. Hunger on the Rise" (July 19, 1983), giving the CCNV the media break it needed. Charles Kurault ran a segment on the hunger issue on his CBS program, *Sunday Morning* (Rader 1986). After three weeks, Mitch Snyder had lost thirty pounds and the Department of Agriculture commented on the idea of releasing surplus foods. Robert Leard of the Department of Agriculture said that the fasters needed to think more about their request, that they probably had not thought through this request very well, and that the government must monitor giveaways to keep out the undeserving (*Post-Dispatch*, July 24, 1983). By the end of the month, the *Detroit Free Press* ran an editorial supporting the intentions of the fast, calling hunger in America "the paradox of bulging storehouses and empty bellies" (*Detroit Free Press*, July 27, 1983). On July 29, 1983 the *Kansas-City Kansan* reported, "In light of protesters at Kansas City, Mo. who are in their fourth week of a fast, House Speaker Thomas P. O'Neill Jr. Thursday asked Agriculture Secretary John Block to release government surplus food."

Meanwhile, an investigative report from Nashville also appeared to have an impact on the story line. Hundreds of thousands of pounds of surplus cheese had rotted in a Tennessee storage facility and had been taken to a landfill. This outraged local residents concerned about hunger (Rader 1986).

After twenty-eight days of fasting, one young protester, Eddie Bloomer, was close to death. Carol Fennelly, the CCNV's media coordinator for this event, began in desperation to call senators, such as Bob Dole (R-Kans.), who had been supportive of the issue in the past. Finally on August 3, 1983, Agriculture Secretary Block traveled to Nashville. In a speech delivered there, he reversed previous administration policy, promising that within a month the amount of surplus food distributed would increase significantly. Eddie Bloomer was immediately given juices to end his fast and others ceased fasting the following day when Ronald Reagan announced to the nation that he was "perplexed" about news stories and other accounts of growing food lines in America. He then directed a task force to look into both reports of increased hunger and problems with government surplus distribution. In a letter to supporters, the CCNV acknowledged that the taskforce meant little but that hunger was now on the nation's agenda as a pressing social problem (Rader 1986). As CCNV chronicler Rader put it, the CCNV had once again successfully engaged with "the politics of exposure" (1986). As proof, comedian Johnny Carson joked on his popular evening television show that the food surpluses were so huge that next year's tax refunds would be given out in cheese (*Star,* October 4, 1983). The hunger issue had also galvanized Senator Bob Dole to make another attempt at passing legislation. Just before members left for summer vacation, the senator shepherded a bill through the divided Congress that strengthened and expanded the food surplus giveaway program. The *Kansas City Times* reported on the new bill in a blow-by-blow description of the political wrangling that had resulted in the legislation's passage (August 6, 1983).

In August, the *National Catholic Reporter* did a major story on the fast, and also covered the government's policies on hunger, street homelessness, and unemployment (August 12, 1983). The next month it was reported that Agriculture Secretary John Block and his family would live a week on a food stamp budget, demonstrating the adequacy of current levels of aid (*New Republic,* September 5, 1983). The Reagan administration concluded a huge deal to sell grain to the Soviet Union, but, as the *New Republic* pointed out, seemed "stubbornly resistant to change" when it came to feeding hungry Americans (September 5, 1983). Colman McCarthy asserted that if Ronald Reagan needed to learn about hunger, there was no reason to form a task force. He could learn about it "right in his neighborhood," which McCarthy described as Washington's "hunger belt" (*WP,* August 13, 1983).

SOUP LINE EATERS

During the time the CCNV had turned its attention to the surplus food issue, Washington's press coverage of homelessness revolved around New York City's homeless situation (*WP,* July 16, August 16, September 7, 9, 1983). It was also noted that local shelter demand in the District was greater than supply (*WP,* October 14, 1983).

That autumn, two hundred homeless activists and advocates from around the country convened in Chicago to discuss political strategies. Coordinators of the event noted that the conference marked a new phase in national alliance building and political activism around the issue. Delegates discussed the need for a coordinated political strategy given that local efforts to provide emergency housing were only partially successful. They met impoverished people's immediate needs but failed to deal with the underlying causes of homelessness, nor were shelters and soup lines long-term solutions. These advocates suggested that the conception of what was pertinent to deal with under the rubric of homelessness should be broadened. One CCNV member attending the conference, Mary Ellen Hombs, identified the larger issues as being related to unemployment and lack of decent low-income housing. Paul Selden, coordinator of the National Coalition for the Homeless in New York, said, "We've got millions of people in shelters, but big deal. It doesn't take you anywhere. What happens to the homeless when they leave the shelter?" He then stated the need to press for low-income housing and other supports for the poor, noting that these were beyond the private sector's capacity to provide. At the end of the conference, the National Coalition for the Homeless was charged with drawing up a national agenda on homelessness. Groups represented at the conference would approve the plan (*Los Angeles Times,* October 27, 1983).

As Thanksgiving approached, the press covered needy families seeking food and shelter (*WP,* November 21, 24, 1983) and noted that there was a dramatic increase in the numbers of volunteers showing up to help distribute free Thanksgiving meals to the poor (*WP,* November 25, 1983). The CCNV held its annual Thanksgiving Day meal in front of the White House (*Dallas Morning News,* November 25, 1983). Behind the scenes, Secretary of Health and Human Services, Margaret Heckler was working on a plan to redistribute another type of surplus food. Nonmarketable food (such as dented cans and food without labels) owned by the Department of Defense would be transferred, under HHS direction, to a nationwide network of food banks, which by this time had over two hundred members (*Los Angeles Daily News,* November 25, 1983). More publicly, Representative David Bonior (D-Mich.) showed up at soup kitchens around Washington with a tape recorder, asking homeless people what they wanted Reagan's poverty policy to focus on. "Jobs" was the resounding answer, one he delivered in homeless people's voices when the Democrats responded to the president's weekly radio address (*WP,* December 4, 1983).

In an editorial, the *Washington Post* stated that homeless people's living conditions "alarms and concerns any thinking person." The editorial continued by bringing up deinstitutionalization and considering whether it had been an effective policy. It noted that Representative Stewart B.

McKinney (R-Conn.) suggested it might be time for new legislation revoking the Health Services Act provision, which mandated psychiatric patients be housed in the "least restrictive setting." Instead, he believed, it might be more appropriate that they be helped in an "optimum therapeutic setting" (*WP*, November 13, 1983). This marked the first time that McKinney was linked closely with homelessness policy. His words "optimum therapeutic setting" would eventually become central to the first federal homelessness legislation package, an Act that would bear his name.

As December arrived, columnist McCarthy suggested that area business people get used to their "new neighbors," fifteen homeless men housed in a business district shelter (*WP*, December 3, 1983). The *Times* reported that all over the nation, soup kitchens were overflowing. One clergy member involved with feeding the homeless called the idea that private charities could compensate for public budget cuts "a kind of lie" (December 4, 1983). Presidential Counselor Edwin Meese, in stark contrast, contended in an interview that "people go to soup kitchens because the food is free and that's easier than paying for it." He said the president had appointed a task force on hunger to find whether hunger was a problem and if so, why (*NYT*, December 10, 1983).

Predictably, these comments were not well received by Democrats or the advocacy community. Sister Catherine Rowe, who operated a soup kitchen in Paterson, New Jersey, invited Meese to "rub elbows with the poor and look them in the eye and tell them they're not hungry" (*Richmond Times-Dispatch*, December 10, 1983). The presidential advisor apparently did not take up the offer. At a press conference a few days later, Ronald Reagan said that some people who eat at soup kitchens may be undeserving, just as there are welfare cheats, but that most are "truly needy" (*Richmond News Leader*, December 15, 1983). A few weeks later the task force released its study, saying claims of hunger in America were "exaggerated" and though some malnourished children did exist hunger was "not a national problem" (*WP*, December 28, 1983).

A HOLIDAY "MIRACLE" OR TWO

On the housing front, the *Post* reported that half of the people with federal housing vouchers could not locate an apartment. At the same time, the Reagan administration continued to contend that there was no shortage of housing (December 18, 1983). Meanwhile, behind the scenes, the CCNV had written to the GSA asking it to donate a building it owned near the Capitol as a seasonal homeless shelter. By early December, the

CCNV had gotten the support of the Department of Health and Human Services (HHS), and in particular, Secretary Margaret Heckler, for the proposal. Initially, the group had approached Susan Baker, wife of White House Chief of Staff James Baker III, about the building. Susan Baker, described by CCNV member Carol Fennelly as a "very religious and compassionate woman who is genuinely concerned about the homeless" (Rader 1986:204), had been critical in getting the momentum going in favor of opening a shelter near the Capitol. Baker was involved in a federal task force on hunger and homelessness that had its home in HHS.

Eventually, Heckler, who was also personally committed to the issue, intervened with the GSA and committed the funds to get the GSA to consent to turning over the building to the CCNV. House Speaker Tip O'Neill had also actively supported the shelter (Rader 1986). The group was hoping it could obtain permission to open the shelter on the first day of winter (letter to GSA from James L. Oberstar, December 5, 1983). But city officials declared that the building at 425 Second Street NW— the former Federal City College Building—was not up to code (WP, December 23, 1983). District officials later reached an accord with the CCNV that enabled the building to open after some improvements to electrical and plumbing systems were made. While the CCNV scrounged funds and labor for the repairs, it also sought a temporary replacement shelter (WP, December 24, 1983).

Santa Claus appeared in the guise of Washington developer Oliver T. Carr, who had heard a televised message about the need for a temporary shelter. Carr owned a seventy-five-year-old hotel that he planned to demolish later that year and replace with an office building. Closed only a month earlier, the Presidential Hotel was mostly intact and had 137 rooms. CCNV members, Carr, his brother, and some of their employees quickly turned the building into a temporary homeless shelter. After Carr made a few phone calls, fuel was delivered and electricity and water were turned back on. The CCNV located cots by calling House Speaker Tip O'Neill, who called FEMA, who called the president, who had them shipped up from Georgia. Woodward and Lothrop department store donated two hundred satin-lined quilts and Dominique, a local restaurateur, donated ten cases of soup (Washington Times, January 2, 1984). By 10 P.M. on Christmas Eve, one hundred homeless people were sheltered at the hotel (WP, December 25, 1983). This story provided an irresistible holiday tale of goodwill, which received much local press attention (WP, December 26, 1983; Washington Times, December 27, 1983). The Richmond Times-Dispatch called it the "miracle on I Street" (December 26, 1983). By year's end, FEMA had delivered five hundred cots to the CCNV shelter and it was almost ready to begin operation (Washington Times, December 30, 1983). Record-breaking cold weather caused sixty exposure deaths around the nation in the last two weeks of the year (*USA Today,* December 27, 1983).

HOMELESSNESS AS ENTRENCHED SOCIAL PROBLEM
IN NEW YORK CITY

In New York City, homelessness remained mostly a local issue during this time. The *Times* started coverage of the year, however, with a report on a national survey that found that big city charities were increasingly unable to meet the needs of ever-growing numbers of poor people who appealed to them for help (January 1, 1983). Winter coverage of the issue in the *Times* mostly revolved around local shelters—a trailer being used as shelter in one case (January 9, 1983), the opening of three "properly equipped" shelters in another (January 22, 1983). Mayor Koch accused New York's Jewish community and other religious groups of not doing enough for the homeless; others suggested that it was Koch who was "trying to get out of municipal obligations" (*NYT*, January 20, 1983). The New York Board of Rabbis responded that they were providing some beds for the homeless (*NYT*, January 21, 1983). Rabbi Marc Tanenbaum accused the mayor of "scapegoating" synagogues and suggesting that "Jews are callous to human suffering," a comment that did not go unanswered by the mayor (*NYT*, February 5, 1983). Koch later mended fences with the Jewish religious community and visited a synagogue-run homeless shelter (*NYT*, February 9, 1983). Five new synagogue-run shelters opened later in the year (*NYT*, October 19, 1983).

A story labeled as news analysis documented Koch's court-prodded shift from opposition to sheltering homeless New Yorkers to vocal advocacy of providing a mix of private and public shelters (January 22, 1983). By the start of 1983, homelessness was "on the front burner" in the Mayor's office, according to the *Times*. Mayoral aides stated that an "evolution" had occurred in the mayor's opinions on the issue. Advocate and attorney Robert Hayes thought two things were responsible for the mayor's shift in attitude: the courts and "how the people of New York feel" about the issue. And Koch himself said that criticism of his early performance had caused him to "focus attention" on the homelessness issue (*NYT*, January 22, 1983). On the same day, in a joint news conference, the mayor and Governor Mario Cuomo issued a statement on the twenty-four-hour services offered at one of the city's newly opened emergency facilities (*NYT*, January 22, 1983). The mayor and governor were applauded in an editorial commending them for responding to the needs of homeless people (*NYT*, February 11, 1983). A few weeks later,

Mayor Koch noted in the *Times* that New York City is the only place in the nation that provides aid to any homeless person who asks for it. The guest editorial, written by the mayor, described the various services available to homeless New Yorkers (February 26, 1983).

Only the *Daily News* covered homelessness in conjunction with the State of the Union address directly (January 26, 1983), though the *Times* had several national follow-up stories. These included Representative Charles Rangel (D-N.Y.) telling the U.S. Conference of Mayors that he would introduce legislation to provide federal assistance to help cities build shelters and provide homeless services (January 28, 1983). A follow-up story told of the mayors' conference supporting an "emergency urban recovery program" (January 29, 1983). This story continued a few days later with coverage of the announcement that House Democratic leaders unanimously committed themselves to an emergency economic assistance program (*NYT*, February 2, 1983). The *Times* also covered Defense Secretary Caspar Weinberger's announcement that armed services base commanders were searching for unused military buildings that could be converted to homeless shelters (February 5, 1983).

Human-interest stories about homelessness in the *Times* tended to be concerned with homelessness outside New York. A cathedral in San Francisco that served homeless people was highlighted (January 18, 1983), a Chicago couple's path to homelessness was traced (February 3, 1983), and the homeless people who frequented a railroad station in New Jersey were profiled (February 6, 1983). Another article discussed Atlanta's resistance to public toilets as it was thought that more homeless people would be attracted to the downtown areas to use them (December 19, 1983). The paper also noted that homelessness was starting to occur in France (January 27, 1983). In the only local human-interest story of the year, the *Times* briefly interviewed grate-dweller Buddy Gore, who commented on life as a street person (October 21, 1983).

In February, advocate attorney Robert Hayes won a class action suit which mandated that the city upgrade its three women's shelters to conform to the standards of men's shelters (*NYT*, February 9, 1983). New York's Human Resources Administration (HRA) reported that the winter's frigid weather was likely the cause of record numbers of New Yorkers asking for shelter from the city—a record 4,931 were sheltered in the city's thirteen public facilities on the night of February 9. HRA officials assured the public that there was room for more homeless people at city-funded shelters (*NYT*, February 11, 1983). In a follow-up column, Sydney Schanberg bemoaned how the nation and the city was becoming accustomed to increasing numbers of homeless people and even increasing numbers of homeless people who died from exposure each winter. Schanberg commented that New York City is "not alone as a breeding ground for this 1980s lifestyle; it is only the most visible symbol, since the largest colony of America's poor resides here" (*NYT,* February 15, 1983). He also quoted local activist Kim Hopper, who had been in Washington for the Alternative State of the Union event. Homeless people crisscrossing the country in search of work, pilfering from garbage cans for food, said Hopper, are "not the tokens of a civilized society. . . . Such signs are rather the stigmata of a society grown weary of caring, one seemingly resigned to accepting such unrelieved suffering as a routine fact of life" (*NYT,* February 15, 1983).

Governor Cuomo echoed these sentiments the following day when he established an emergency task force on homelessness, stating, "Our response to the problems of the homeless is a true test of our commitment to justice and human dignity" (*Daily News,* February 16, 1983). A letter to the *Times* from a priest associated with Catholic charities a few days later noted that housing had been the responsibility of the federal government "ever since the dark days of the Depression" and that the Reagan administration had taken actions recently to renege on that responsibility. The letter mentioned Reagan's recent veto of a bill designed to bring down mortgage interest rates thereby making housing more affordable and the passage of a budget resolution that all but canceled Section 8 rent subsidy and public housing programs (*NYT,* February 19, 1982).

Charitable acts by New Yorkers were also the subject of ongoing coverage in the *New York Times.* One such article covered a wealthy executive who solicited gloves from his friends for distribution to the homeless poor (*NYT,* March 2, 1983). Another profiled a Manhattan congregation because, along with operating a shelter, parishioners were encouraged to put New York City subway tokens in the collection plate. These were distributed to homeless people in need of transportation (*NYT,* April 11, 1983). Such sentiments of concern for the predicaments of homeless people were interspersed in the *Times* with continuing coverage of issues related to the city's shelter systems.

Shelter openings, expansions, relocations, summer closings, and expansion of services dominated news coverage in the *Times* during most of 1983. There were reports about religious and other charitable groups opening or expanding shelters (April 10, 24, October 19, 1983). The Partnership for the Homeless, a coalition of charitable organizations, met to discuss how to meet the needs of growing numbers of homeless people. By winter's onset, the group hoped to have one hundred shelters operating throughout the city (October 16, 1983). An article noted that none of the state funds granted to community groups in spring 1982 had been delivered. The state responded that the new State Housing Commissioner had blocked the contracts until a review could be conducted (*NYT,*

May 15, 1983). The Coalition for the Homeless ran a public service advertising campaign to ask for donations to improve existing shelters and build new ones (July 28, 1983).

Public sector shelter news also appeared regularly in the *Times*. A spring audit of emergency services concluded that there was an urgent need to improve the quality and delivery of these services (April 1, 1983), while another article commented on increases in illegal "doubling up" among New York's poor (April 21, 1983). A state Supreme Court justice ordered that homeless families with children had to be given habitable living quarters in emergency housing or a hearing if the city evicted them (June 26, 1983). A soup line plan for the Lower East Side was scrapped after residents presented the mayor with a petition signed by two thousand people, saying the neighborhood was doing enough to serve the homeless (July 23, 1983).

In August, the mayor released a statement responding to state officials who had complained about conditions in the hotels where the city sheltered its increasing numbers of homeless families. In it the mayor blamed the state for the "displaced family" situation because it had kept the welfare housing grant at an unreasonably low level for city rental prices. He also explained that the families in the city's care would be enrolled in all services for which they were eligible such as Medicaid and the Women, Infant, Children (WIC) nutrition program. New York was on the verge of beginning to refurbish twelve hundred low-income apartments for these families, said Koch (Mayor's Office press release, August 22, 1983). The *Post* reported that homeless New York families were being housed in New Jersey (July 16, 1983). The paper followed up with a story stating that these "exported" families had been returned to New York (*WP*, August 16, 1983). Shelters with expanded capacity opened up in various city locations (*NYT*, August 17, 1983), at times with residents protesting against the shelters (August 20, 1983). New funding for permanent housing and a small public jobs project was allocated by the city (*NYT*, September 16, 1983). Mayor Koch announced a plan to make homeless people perform odd jobs for their shelter, in order to instill a "work ethic" in them (*NYT*, September 7, 1983).

As winter approached, Governor Cuomo and Mayor Koch teamed up to announce that two thousand more beds would be provided over the next two years for the city's homeless (*NYT*, November 24, 1983). Koch also stated that he would be taking action against fourteen privately run shelters that were not meeting health and safety standards (*NYT*, December 21, 1983).

The characteristics of homeless people also made the news in New York. In December, the *Times* noted that the number of people in homeless shelters had continued to rise as had the proportion of those seeking shelter who were under thirty years old (*NYT*, December 11, 1983). Some state officials, noting citizen concern about the growing legions of homeless people in New York City, suggested that the group consisted mostly of former mental patients, chronic alcoholics, and the jobless. State Mental Health Office official Sarah Connell instead suggested that the recession and SRO conversion were to blame for increasing numbers of homeless people (*NYT*, November 24, 1983).

Local coverage of the issue ended 1983 with a report that Carnegie Hall sponsored a musical performance for women staying at a homeless shelter—the first of several events scheduled around the city during the holiday season (*NYT*, December 20, 1983).

Very little national perspective was evident in the *Times* coverage in 1983. Two legal matters regarding the issue were reported on in small articles: the CCNV's First Amendment case (March 13, 19, October 4, 1983), and a case in Los Angeles County stating that it was not legal to deny shelter to homeless people because they had no identification documents (December 21, 1983). The U.S. Conference of Mayors was the subject of several articles (January 29, February 2, 1983). In a letter to the editor, the city's comptroller criticized the Veteran Administration for not taking sufficient care of needy veterans. The comptroller noted that about one-third of the men being sheltered in New York's public shelters were veterans (April 8, 1983). Other stories that were national in scope were limited to acknowledging the continuing plight of homeless persons across the nation as the weather warmed and the efforts of the National Coalition for the Homeless to find solutions to the problem (*NYT*, June 3, 1983). Later in the year the paper noted that the past few months' economic upturn had failed to benefit unemployed homeless people (*NYT*, November 29, 1983).

THE INTERACTIONS OF CONTEXT, CLAIMSMAKERS, AND ISSUES

Hunger and Homelessness as Interactive Issues

Judging from the disorganized and (in the case of the *Post*) limited press coverage the issue received in 1983, efforts to construct homelessness would seem to have stalled for a time during this period, or at least to have taken a back seat to efforts to construct hunger as a national problem. Hilgartner and Bosk (1988) have argued that only so many issues can be given space in the media at the same time and that social problems compete to have access to the media. This argument suggests that coverage of hunger as a national social problem might have muffled or shrunk coverage of homelessness. Hunger, however, at least as construed by the CCNV and public officials during this time was too closely intertwined with homelessness to really be considered a separate social problem. Instead, both were posed as issues related to the truly destitute and in that sense successful social problems work on one enhanced the public profile of the other. Even though the CCNV, politicians, and supportive members of the media did turn their attention toward hunger to some degree, homelessness continued to develop as a social problem during this time, in part because of efforts made on the hunger front.

Efforts to construct hunger as a social problem in 1983 helped move the construction of homelessness forward by reshaping both the environmental and interpretive contexts in which homelessness was considered. The environmental context that shaped homelessness and hunger early on in Washington moved beyond one defined by local geographical or political-authority features. Instead, the context for these intertwined problems started to solidify as a national one. This was true in two senses. First, some of the claimsmaking action by national government officials and activists moved outside the District. Second, the Reagan administration and its policies become firmly entrenched as the political-authority structure against which these problems were constructed.

The relevant interpretive context also shifted during this period. It was during this year that a "signature framework" (Gamson and Modigliani 1987) coalesced, in part because of the claimsmaking activities around hunger. By this I mean a unified symbolic framework around which to organize claims about both homelessness and hunger as social problems. The problem, more and more during this period, became one of Reagan administration neglect. The solution was legislative aid for the destitute. Symbolically, claimsmakers of all kinds increasingly relied on the contrast between America as a land of plenty and the blight of homelessness and hunger that affected some of the country's citizens.

The Environmental Context

The Local Context as National Resource

Though homelessness was becoming a nationalized social problem, the local contexts did not disappear as sites from which to make claims about homelessness. In both New York and Washington, local matters about shelter openings, controversies, and services continued to get regular press coverage. Thus, in both New York and Washington as a city (rather than as the capital) homelessness was maintained as an issue of which the public was aware. But this is not a period where homelessness took on new shapes or meanings as were the previous periods in this social problem's history. By this time, in both cities, homelessness was recognized as a social problem. Both cities were providing a mixture of public and privately funded shelter and feeding programs to local homeless people. Thus, in the sense that ameliorative actions had been identified and taken, the problems of homelessness and hunger had been both recognized and "solved" as local social problems, however inadequately. If national-level actors had not continued to construct homelessness and hunger as national social problems, it is likely that the Reagan administration's insistence that these were merely local problems most properly dealt with by local charities would have held sway as policy. But because claimsmakers continued to raise homelessness and, particularly in 1983, hunger as national issues in need of federal recognition and deserving of federal policy solutions, both issues continued to develop as national social problems.

In this period it was concerted efforts by activists and advocates, local and national-level elected officials, and media figures working in concert that enabled the problems to continue to develop. Thus the context that is salient to the issue's continued development as a social problem became a national context, reinforced by continuing "maintenance work" reemphasizing the local situation in both New York and Washington. In both cities numerous press stories covered the issue of providing shelter—where it was done, how it was done, and how much it was done.

In New York, advocates such as the Coalition for the Homeless, the city's mayor, and the press independently of these claimsmakers, continued to make claims about the local shelter situation. Mayor Koch mostly promoted the idea that the city was doing an adequate job and that it was commendable that New York was committed to caring for its homeless citizens. He also, however, upbraided the Jewish community for not doing enough and he continued to note that some aspects of the city's policies, such as health and safety standards and placements for families, were inadequate. The advocates continued to bring lawsuits against the city, reinforcing that more needed to be done. The press, during this period began to cover the shelter situation as a matter of routine, thus signifying its ongoing importance. The shelter situation was given similar regular coverage in Washington, though national-level portrayals of the issue often took precedence. Perhaps most importantly, in neither city was the situation described as under control or adequate. Instead, the press mostly emphasized the inadequacy of the local response, even though—especially in the New York case—those in charge were portrayed as trying to meet the ever-growing need for aid. Together these claims formed a backdrop that emphasized the seriousness of the problem locally, which national-level actors could use as a resource when they claimed that these were not *merely* local-level problems. Thus the maintenance work of local claimsmakers reinforced the claims of those operating in the national context.

The Reagan Administration as Resource

It is also during this period that the Reagan administration, and its failure to deal with homelessness and hunger, solidified as the focal point of much national-level claimsmaking activity. The administration's reluctance to acknowledge that homelessness was a national issue or hunger a serious problem provided a rhetorical resource against which activists, political opponents, state and local officials, and the press could make counterclaims. Even when the administration acknowledged that there might be a national role for homelessness amelioration, its awkward and, some would say, disingenuous proposal to use excess military buildings for shelters provided a further resource for others to use to claim federal policy was inadequate. Ronald Reagan's publicized beliefs that the cheese industry needed protection from profit loss more than hungry people needed surplus food and his comment that he was "perplexed" about the idea of hunger in America gave opponents a chance to portray the administration as both ignorant and callous. Presidential Counselor Edwin Meese's unfortunate comment about hunger and the characteristics of people who sought food from soup lines was an additional resource that advocates, politicians, and the press used to good advantage to press their views of these problems. These initial steps into claimsmaking around the issues of hunger and homelessness by the Reagan administration can be categorized as either denying the problems existed at all or denying their magnitude. Rather than changing the shape of social problems talk about homelessness and hunger, these early counterclaims at the federal level enabled other claimsmakers to further emphasize and solidify their viewpoints. Thus the Reagan administration at this juncture is best considered a resource akin to that of a frigid January day—it enabled those who thought that these were serious social problems about which something must be done to drive home their points and drive up public sympathy for the issues. Thus, the federal political-authority structure during this period was an aspect of the environmental context that shaped claimsmaking by providing a sense of unconcern for the problems against which sympathizers could make their case for the seriousness of the issues.

The Interpretive Context: The Land of Plenty and Want

In 1983 the symbolic representation of homelessness and hunger coalesced around one dominant image with several variations. The CCNV had started to use the contrast between the opulence of the White House and the poverty of street men lining up for food at their first Thanksgiving Day soup line several years earlier. Now this theme was repeated in a number of new and ongoing activities. Though hardly unique, there was still much claimsmaking value to be gained in posing the problem as one of want in a land of plenty. In January, the cold tents of Reaganville again stood in marked contrast to the warmth and comfort of the presidential mansion. The "People's State of the Union" emphasized what the people did not have and were not getting from a Republican administration bent on cutting taxes and services. This stance was compared to the "Morning in America" theme sounded by the president. The soup kitchen in the Capitol likewise provided contrast between the plush rooms of the Capitol building and their symbol of plenty and the empty pockets of those who had to resort to a soup line to eat. Even the Republicans were inspired to use plenty and want (as symbolized by full grocery carts) in their symbolic representation of what they contended the Democratic tax plan would foist on the nation's families if passed. The CCNV had this same contrast between plenty and want in mind, of course, as they fasted near the cornucopia of surplus food below ground in Kansas City. In the autumn, the Thanksgiving soup line was repeated. Inadvertently, the well-fed presidential counselor Edwin Meese and his callous comment about soup line users reemphasized the idea that those with plenty were ignoring the plight of those in want.

This proved to be an effective symbolic resource, which could be employed as a framework in which to unite homelessness and hunger as interrelated problems. It was also an effective way to draw political attention to the problem for it suggested a course for legislative action to take—some redistribution of the nation's "plenty." For Republican senator Bob Dole this could be accomplished without threat to Republican tax cuts by instead shepherding bipartisan legislation to mandate the release of already stored surplus foodstuffs. Likewise, HHS Secretary Margaret Heckler responded to this powerful symbolic frame with her plan to transfer castoff military food to the nation's hungry citizens. The Democrats, as the traditional representatives of the have-nots, were well able to use this symbolic framework to make policy suggestions—though these were not very likely to go anywhere given Republican control of the Senate. Nevertheless, House Speaker Tip O'Neill underlined Democratic commitment to the redistribution of wealth by inviting the soup kitchen into the Capitol building. He later demanded that surplus food be released. The House of Representative members who had visited the Kansas City storehouse likewise were able to reemphasize their commitment to alleviating hunger and to the unwarranted government policy of continuing to build stores of foodstuffs when significant numbers of people were in need. Even Secretary of Agriculture John Block tacitly acknowledged the excesses of undistributed plenty by choosing Nashville (where so much surplus cheese had gone bad and was wasted) as the scene for his announcement that increased amounts of surplus foods would soon be distributed. Although known as the "Great Communicator," Reagan himself was not able at this time to use this symbolic framework to his advantage. Instead, his administration sounded as if hunger was suspicious (the Meese comments), or could not be understood (Reagan's perplexity at hearing about hunger in his country), or that meeting the needs of the poor would unduly interfere with making profit (the administration's contention that cheese lines would detract from cheese sales).

Finally, the press also found this imagery to have ongoing appeal. Most compelling were photographs that continued to appear in newspapers around the nation in which the needs of the poor were posed against the comforts of the wealthy. The *Philadelphia Inquirer* ran a photo of Reaganville with a prominent White House in the background (March 18, 1983). The *Dallas Morning News* showed the Lafayette Park Thanksgiving soup line (November 25, 1983). In the *Chicago Tribune*, activist and celebrity faster Dick Gregory and Mitch Snyder were pictured in front of a sign reading, "There is hunger in the land of plenty" (July 19, 1983). Most subtly the *New York Times* invoked this framework of contrasts when it showed a corpulent Ed Meese making comments that questioned the idea that people sought out soup lines because they were truly needy (December 10, 1983). Some papers, such as the *National Catholic Reporter*, invoked this framing of the problem overtly in their reporting (August 12, 1983), in others, such as the *Post*, it showed up repeatedly in the words and themes of columnists (for example, McCarthy, July 10, 1983). For all three sectors of the iron quadrangle that were relevant at this point in the construction of homelessness and hunger, the contrast between want and plenty proved a very useful and therefore well-used interpretive resource in which to frame claimsmaking.

INTERACTING CLAIMSMAKERS

Publicly made claims become part of the ongoing flow of social life. With regards to the construction of social problems, claims become subject either to being ignored or to acceptance, to rejection or to some form of reinterpretation. Once interpreted by members of an audience—whether these are other claimsmakers or members of a general public—reactions and counterclaims commence. I do not mean that claimsmaking activities proceed in any sort of linear fashion; indeed, claimsmaking often seems a cacophony of simultaneous activities arranged around individual claimsmakers' aims rather than any sort of organized discussion of a social problem. Yet the claims of some are heard by others and these others may respond to them or use them to pursue their own purposes. By this time in the construction of homelessness, interactions among several claimsmaking sectors were in evidence.

During this period hunger and homelessness began to mature as social problems in large part because advocates, government officials, the media, and—to a small extent—experts, began to work in concert as claimsmakers. This is not to say that these groups agreed on the nature of these problems or what should be done about them. But each for its own reasons took up homelessness and hunger as social problems worth sticking with and talking about. This concerted effort at social problems work assured that the issues became known to a wider general audience and that the Reagan administration was continually pressured (at times even by Republican allies) to deal with these areas of concern.

Here I focus on the intersections between prominent groups of claimsmakers to delineate what Nichols refers to as the "dialogical" (2003) aspects of social problems. In his work the term is used broadly to refer to the "communicative interaction among speakers" including claimsmakers and their listeners (2003:93). In this case, I apply it to communication between sectors of the iron quadrangle as they together created a framework in which the social problems of homelessness and hunger were considered. As Nichols says, social problems are "joint productions of extremely complex dialogues" (ibid.). This does not necessarily mean that these claimsmakers purposively or directly communicated with one another though they often did in the case of homelessness construction. But claimsmaking sectors existed in somewhat overlapping contexts and so actors had the opportunity to mutually influence one another (Jenness 1993), to learn from each other's successes and failures (Lowney and Best 1995) and to adopt topics or language from one another (Nichols 2003). The interplay between claimsmakers and claimsmakers is as intrinsic to the social problems construction process as is the interplay between claimsmaking and context. I focus on it explicitly here, however, because at this juncture the dialogue between claimsmakers becomes one of the most noticeable features of the construction process.

An early example was the conversation between New York advocates such as attorney Robert Hayes and Mayor Koch. At first, the mayor reacted to claims made by advocates by minimizing the importance of homelessness as a social problem. Once the class action suit had been won, however, the mayor saw it was in his interest to co-opt the claims of advocates instead. By 1983, Koch was notable for his regular raising of the issue and for making claims about the seriousness of homelessness as a New York social problem. He could be found urging private charitable groups to provide shelter and food, much as advocates urged him in the formative days of the problem in New York. Though the mayor in many ways was the most critical shaper of the conversation about homelessness in the city by this time, his claims are best viewed as savvy incorporations of earlier claims made by advocates. In many ways, this turn of the public conversation about homelessness in New York made it likely that claimsmaking by most parties focused on the narrow issue of shelter provision rather than the broader problems of unavailable and unaffordable housing and joblessness, which according to many advocates generated homelessness and kept it growing.

In the Washington case, the CCNV must be credited with raising the issue as a social problem. At first the "dialogue" the group engaged in was with local groups—the parishioners of Holy Trinity Church and local government officials. For various reasons discussed earlier, both these groups were mostly reluctant to participate in any dialogue about homelessness. When they had to respond, as the city government had to, they minimized the problem and offered to ameliorate it in minor ways. Local officials in Washington did not, however, become major claimsmakers around homelessness. As the years proceeded, the CCNV looked to engage federal officials in the issue. Federal officials, for various reasons, did respond with their own claims. In some cases, the CCNV and government claimsmakers elaborated one another's narratives about homelessness and hunger. For example, representatives such as Oaker and Hall replicated the basic message of the CCNV about the need to do something to feed the poor. Likewise, the CCNV learned from its interactions with federal officials and pursued legislative goals along with continuing to raise the issues by way of public protest. While senators first brought the issue of surplus foods to the nation's attention, the CCNV elaborated the issue with the Kansas City campaign. This interactive process also worked in reverse. For example, House Speaker Tip O'Neill co-opted the soup kitchen protest to use for his own reasons and also called for surplus food distribution after the CCNV had dramatized the issue. The CCNV was quite willing to work in concert and press the same claims as government officials—even Republicans—when they judged that these would help create a solution to homelessness and hunger. Those concerned with homelessness as a national social problem forged important coalitions during this period, organized loosely around the signature framework of want within a nation of plenty. Thus homelessness and hunger were constructed as social problems through the interplay of claims made by both these sectors.

The press played several roles in this joint production of reality. First, it provided a venue for the dialogue between others to be heard. Second, it guided the way the public conversation about homelessness would go by its coverage or noncoverage of the issue and by the texture of the coverage that it did provide. During 1983, press coverage was notable for normalizing homelessness as a regularly covered social issue, thus giving the other sectors more media access. This normalization of coverage can in turn be thought of arising from the continuing drama provided around the issues and by the fact that public celebrities such as Mayor Koch kept bringing it up. Third, the press acted as a direct claimsmaker for the issue. One important example here was the investigative reports of cheese spoilage in Nashville. This in turn became a subject worth reporting because of the actions of the CCNV in Kansas City and the regional coverage of that campaign. The media also sometimes engaged publicly with other claimsmakers in a dialogue-like fashion, such as when the *Times* would criticize or condemn the mayor's handling of the homeless or when the *Post* would applaud the CCNV for raising the issue or condemn Mitch Snyder for being self-serving.

Finally, the Reagan administration began, during this time period, to be a partner in the joint production of these issues as social problems. Prior to this year, the Reagan administration had mostly ignored claimsmaking by others. Now it began to interact with the claims of others by suggesting policy solutions or by casting doubts on the validity of the claims. Though the administration was mostly a useful resource against which others could pose the problem, it is also the case that it began to be part of the dialogue, not just the context during this period. This could be seen in the administration's suggestion that federal space be used to house homeless people, a suggestion raised initially by the CCNV in its National Visitor Center campaign and again in the House Subcommittee on the District hearings about homelessness in January 1983. The president also formed "Project Homeless" during this year, a response to the continual raising of the issue by other sectors of claimsmakers. Agriculture Secretary John Block and his family lived on a food stamp budget for a week in response to accusations that aid to poor Americans was insufficient and the Reagan administration also conceded to increase the availability of surplus food. A federal task force on hunger was formed. By the end of the year, Mitch Snyder had asked the Reagan administration to use the Federal City College building for a homeless shelter. HHS Secretary Margaret Heckler was attempting to redistribute military surplus food to the poor and was instrumental in turning over the Federal City College building to the CCNV for use as a shelter. This is evidence that the highest levels of the federal government were beginning to engage in dialogue with other claimsmakers. Indeed, the dialogue between the Reagan administration and other claimsmaking sectors would characterize the next phase of social problem construction around homelessness.

Though claimsmakers pursued their own agendas in the burgeoning dialogue about homelessness and hunger, during this period there was an extensive "conversation" of sorts going on—even if the various participants were as likely to talk past one another as to talk to one another. Thus homelessness and hunger became the joint production of activists and advocates, the media, and various levels of government officials, including the president himself. Homelessness and its cousin social problem, hunger, thus truly became national public problems (Gusfield 1981). It now remained for the experts to weigh in.

5

How Many Homeless?
Experts, Advocates, and the Struggle over Numbers

INTRODUCTION

Typically, much claimsmaking about a "new" social problem has already gone on before social science "experts" enter the fray (Blumer 1971). Such was certainly the case by the time experts weighed in on homelessness at the national level. By "experts" I mean trained social scientists, policy researchers, and others legitimated by their credentials and employment positions who are involved in collecting and analyzing data that become the "facts" undergirding a social problem.[1] This idea of "experts" is borrowed from the natural sciences and a conception of science as "value free." Under this traditional conception, scientists search for and discover facts about a certain phenomenon and report them in an objective, depoliticized fashion. In contrast, in the constructionist view, facts, such as statistics are "tools, used for particular purposes" (Best 2001:7). If social statistics and the experts that produce them were ever the standard-bearers of truth and objectivity removed from the taint of partisan politics, they have lost this distinction in the post-Watergate political era. In this sense, Americans are all constructionists now as we attempt to parse the "facts" provided by one camp's set of experts with those provided by the other's. Yet how the "facts" of a social problem are resolved is what determines if that problem becomes real, important, or acted on.

Here I look at the construction of one crucial fact about homeless people—how many were there in America in the 1980s? In what follows I reconstruct, then analyze, claimsmaking about the extent of homelessness from 1980 to 1987. This episode in the construction of homelessness can be viewed as a struggle between federal government forces and their experts on one side and advocates and their experts on the other. Was homelessness a problem of such national significance that even the hands-off Reagan administration had to intervene or could it be construed as being of a magnitude requiring only volunteer and local effort? The stakes were indeed high in claimsmaking over "how many homeless."

THE NUMBERS GAME, ACT I

Unsurprisingly, it was the CCNV that first decided to collect some statistics documenting the extent of homelessness nationally. As CCNV member Mary Ellen Hombs recalled, "In 1980, we discussed with the Department of Health, Education and Welfare [soon to become HHS] and other federal agencies of the need for a statistical analysis of homelessness. There were no statistics, nor were studies underway or planned which would attempt to gather that information. No federal agency bore responsibility for the homeless" (as quoted in Rader 1986:144).

As Rader recounts, Mary Ellen Hombs spent early 1980 gathering information on the nation's growing numbers of homeless people. For estimates of those in need, she relied on advocates in twenty-five cities and states. Hombs compiled these estimates for a report submitted to the House Committee on the District of Columbia on September 1, 1980. The report was also sent to the CCNV's fund-raising list with the encouragement to use it "to educate, to sensitize, and to mobilize" (CCNV fund-raising letter, September 1980). "At that time, CCNV concluded that approximately one percent of the population or 2.2 million people lacked shelter" (Rader 1986:144). During this period, the press showed little interest in the report, either locally or nationally.

There was only slight evidence in 1980 that homelessness had become a problem prominent enough that the press was beginning to grow hungry for statistics about it. Using CCNV as its source, the *Post* reported that there were "5,000 homeless men" in the District in May (May 5, 1980). During the holiday season that year, two Washington area stories carried CCNV-generated estimates of local homelessness. The *Washington Star* reported that "the group has no precise figures, but estimates that between 5,000 and 10,000 homeless men and women will try to survive this winter on the bitter streets of Washington" (December 27, 1980). The only other time numbers of homeless people were mentioned was as competing claims. "CCNV estimates the number of homeless between

5,000 and 10,000. The city believes 1,000 to 3,000 is a more accurate figure" (*District Star,* December 31, 1980).

In New York, a figure of thirty thousand attributed to "the Community Services Society, the Catholic Worker, Covenant House and other groups that provide shelter" was mentioned in an article covering the removal of homeless people from the 1980 Democratic Convention site in midtown Manhattan (*NYT,* August 14, 1980). The number had originated in an internal memo of the New York State Office of Mental Health (dated October 12, 1979). It was an estimate of the number of homeless men in the city and was based on the belief that public shelters were only serving 30 percent of the actual number of homeless men. In the previous year, the Men's Shelter had served nine thousand. The thirty thousand figure, then, can be thought of as a year incidence estimate, made "official" because it was a state agency that had generated it. It appeared in the New York press, however, only once for the first sixteen months after it had been generated.

Instead, it was the human side of homelessness—its texture—that dominated early publicity about homelessness in 1980. As is the case with many social problems, it was on the basis of emotional appeal, not rational documentation, that the press, public, and politicians first became convinced of the salience of homelessness. The documentation of extent, as is often the case, *followed* the demonstration of the problem's emotional appeal.

In March 1981, a well-respected, longtime charity organization, the Community Services Society (CSS), released a study of homeless adults on the streets of New York City, entitled "Private Lives, Public Spaces." The preface began, "According to official estimates there are 36,000 homeless men and women in New York City—a shocking statistic reflective of unrelenting social crisis" (Baxter and Hopper 1981:iii). This report was widely reported on in the media and the number at the very beginning of it rapidly became New York's de facto enumeration of homeless adults. Of special importance was a page one *New York Times* article heralding the study's release and findings. "In all, there are about 36,000 homeless on the streets of New York City—'a shocking statistic' the report says, especially when there are only 3,200 beds available in public shelters" (*NYT,* March 8, 1981). Citing the soon-to-be released report, the *Christian Science Monitor* stated, "There is no place where the estimated 36,000 homeless people in the city can take refuge" (February 6, 1981).

That the city had an "estimated 30,000 homeless men and 6,000 homeless women" (*NYT,* March 11, 1981) was a claim derived from the first part of the CSS study. In it, the authors reported the New York State Office of Mental Health figure and added to it an estimate of New York's "periodically homeless" women, which was said to number between 6,000 and 6,500. The source of this figure was the Manhattan Bowery Corporation report "Shopping Bag Ladies: Homeless Women" released April 1, 1979. Similar to the figure for men, it was based on "extrapolations from the numbers of women applying to the Women's Shelter during the period 1974–1977" (Baxter and Hopper 1981:9).

Repetition in the national and local press hardened this combined estimate into established "fact." For example, "36,000 people now live in the city's streets" (*Guardian*, March 18, 1981). Or, "According to a year-long study released last week by the nonprofit Community Service Society, there are 36,000 people who 'sleep rough' " (*Newsweek*, March 23, 1981), and "Sarah is one of the 36,000 homeless people in New York City" (*Daily News*, March 27, 1981). The *Times* repeated the estimate in nearly every piece about homelessness during the months after the CSS report appeared. Headlines read: "New York Is Facing 'Crisis' on Vagrants: 36,000 Homeless in City" (*NYT*, June 28, 1981), "Who Will Take New York's 36,000 Outcasts?" (*NYT*, Letters headline August 22, 1981), and "Ping-Pong for 36,000" (columnist Sydney Schanberg, *NYT*, August 25, 1981). Thus the homeless population of New York City in 1981 became 36,000. This occurred even though both estimates had been made several years earlier and despite CSS authors Baxter and Hopper's protestations that "the accuracy of the above figures cannot be vouched for, nor can the probable error in them be estimated with any precision" (1981:10).

With the city receiving negative publicity for its paucity of shelter beds, the Koch administration tried to mitigate the influence of this figure. In a *Times* editorial, the city's estimate appeared: "There are 36,000 homeless people in New York City, according to a Community Service Society study. No, say city officials, that's an exaggeration; there are probably fewer than 12,000. Whatever the number, it is small in a city of seven million" (August 31, 1981). In large part throughout 1981, however, the local press, including the *Times*, continued to use the more dramatic CSS figure. For example, "An estimated 36,000 persons, about 6,000 of them women—now populate this New York netherworld" (*Newsday*, October 15, 1981). And, "There are an estimated 30,000 homeless men roaming the streets" (*Daily News*, October 21, 1981). During the holiday season, NBC's national anchor station Channel 4, NYC, aired the following assessment of the extent of homelessness in the city. "A Community Services Society report estimates thirty-six thousand in New York City. City officials dispute that. They think it's less. But when you press them, they can't give you a figure. People without addresses are hard to count" (Channel 4, NYC December 7, 1981). By year's end, "The Koch administration, exasperated by the wide use of a statistic it disputes—that

36,000 homeless people live on New York's streets—has decided to commission a professional count of the city's vagrants and settle the issue" (*NYT*, December 30, 1981).

In Washington in 1981, press coverage of homelessness was scanty and mostly concerned itself with ideas for providing additional local shelter and biographies of those who lacked it. [For example, "The Drifters' Endless Odyssey: The Homeless Roam in City Powerless to Help" (*WP*, October 23, 1981).] When figures were mentioned, they were mostly those being proffered by the CCNV, which had estimated twelve thousand to as many as fifteen thousand by year's end. In contrast, the less frequently reported mayoral office's figure remained at between one thousand and three thousand, though numbers were said to be growing (*WP*, October 23, 1981).

Nationally, the press had not yet taken up the CCNV's figures nor had it mentioned any others. At Thanksgiving time, the CCNV issued a press release in conjunction with the Thanksgiving feast for the poor in Lafayette Park, across from the White House (*Boston Globe*, November 27, 1981). The statement detailed some of the figures from the study that Mary Ellen Hombs had undertaken in early 1980. These "statistics" consisted mostly of estimates provided by shelter operators and local advocates, and, in a few cases, by city and national officials. Figures garnered in one location were not commensurate with estimates provided from other cities. Some advocates had counts of how many they had housed in 1979, others provided raw estimates of "street people" in downtown areas, still others estimated future housing displacement rates and numbers of runaway children. The CCNV concluded that "there are no accurate figures for homelessness nationally [but] we can safely say that the number of homeless people in the country is in the millions" (CCNV press release, November 26, 1981). The year closed with a Christmas night story on homelessness, in which the Public Broadcasting System's "McNeil-Lehrer News Hour" reported that national estimates of the homeless range from 250,000 to one million (December 25, 1981).[2]

Columbia Broadcasting System (CBS) ran a story on homelessness in early 1982 on its popular investigative reporting show, "60 Minutes" (January 10). The show reported that between "500,000 and two million are believed to be homeless" (Hayes, *CBC Quarterly*, Spring 1982). Otherwise, there was little mention of the national extent of the problem until the end of 1982. The CCNV was publicly concentrating on other issues such as the Reaganville campaign and the Apple Pie Bite Back event (see Chapter 3). The *Post* ran a story entitled "1982's Homeless: Americans Adrift in Tents, Autos" in which a national figure of "at least two million" was provided by Robert Hayes, the New York–based attorney for the National Coalition for the Homeless (August 14, 1982). The same article lists the local District estimate as "between 2,000 and 5,000."

In New York, meanwhile, local claimsmakers became increasingly skeptical of the thirty-six thousand figure. "The figure on the homeless most often used is 36,000—a figure the city strongly disputes. Last year, officials said, about 12,000 men and 2,000 women passed through the shelter system," reported the *Daily News* (February 14, 1982). "City authorities challenged the 36,000 figure as much too high, although they offered no independent estimate," reported the *Times* (July 28, 1982). In the same article, the paper reported that the Community Service Society had released a subsequent report (Hopper, Baxter and Cox. *One Year Later: The Homeless Poor in New York City,* released July 27, 1982) stating that "too much attention has focused on the . . . 36,000 figure." The report urged that "attention should be concentrated instead on caring for the homeless rather than counting them" (*NYT,* July 28, 1982). It also criticized the city's planned enumeration saying that enumeration was costly, labor intensive, and unnecessary as a policy planning tool. The authors suggested that the city drop plans to count the homeless. A *Times* editorial following the report's release stated that "no one is sure how many homeless there are; last year, the society estimated 36,000. The city's estimate of 10,000 to 12,000 is probably nearer the mark. Whatever the number, the economy continues to push marginal people into the streets, there are many of them, visible, victimized, troublesome" (July 30, 1982).

Though the figure of 36,000 would continue to be uncritically used, even by the *New York Times,* this period seemed to put an end to New York City's emphasis on counting the homeless for the next few years. In September 1982, the city announced that it had dropped its plan to conduct an enumeration. "The city felt that controversy had died down over the figure of 36,000 homeless people published a year and a half ago by the Community Service Society, a private social welfare agency" (*NYT,* September 6, 1982). Robert Trobe, the HRA official in charge of providing public shelter, noted that the figure "is not really being used by the press that much. It's no longer a credible or used number," he said. The *Times* concluded, "Therefore the need to embark on an expensive survey to get a number was abandoned" (*NYT,* September 6, 1982).[3]

Contention over the numbers of homeless in Washington also subsided in media reports during the mid-1980s. The national controversy about numbers, however, was just heating up.

THE NUMBERS GAME, ACT II

On Wednesday, December 15, 1982, Congress held its first hearings on homelessness. Witnesses from eleven cities, including advocates, service providers, government officials, and homeless people testified to the House Banking Subcommittee on Housing and Community Development, chaired by Representative Henry B. Gonzales (D-Tex.) on the nature and extent of the problem. In a press release advertising the upcoming hearings, the CCNV stated, "Homelessness is a national problem of massive and increasing proportions affecting at least 2 million people" (CCNV press release, December 12, 1982). Indeed, in press coverage following the hearing, Robert Hayes of the National Coalition for the Homeless stated that "1 percent" of the nation was homeless (*NYT*, December 16, 1982), while CCNV's Snyder made headlines claiming that between two million and three million were homeless (*Boston Herald American*, December 16, 1982). Friendly *Post* columnist Henry Mitchell wrote about "the two million homeless Americans who live on the streets" (*WP*, December 17, 1982). *USA Today* ended 1982 by reporting that in its opinion homelessness was third on a list of top "ten vital problems for the new year." The accompanying table stated that the homeless were "hard to count, but perhaps 2.1 million are now without lodging across the country" (*USA Today*, December 30, 1982). The CCNV released its 1980 study, *Homeless in America: A Forced March to Nowhere*, on the day the hearing was held. In the introduction, the authors noted that while the original study stated that perhaps 2.2 million Americans were homeless, they were now "convinced that the number of homeless people in the United States could reach three million or more during 1983" (Hombs and Snyder 1982:xvi).

Suddenly, it seemed homelessness had become a central national social problem affecting "millions." For example, "Estimates of the homeless across the country range from 500,000 up to 2.5 million," stated *NYT* columnist Sydney Schanberg (February 15, 1983), while a letter by Catholic Charities representative Donald Sakono repeated, "Up to two million Americans are at this moment homeless" (*NYT*, February 19, 1983). For its part, the CCNV emphasized its claims about the extent of the problem in a letter to Congress members, stating, "Between 2 and 3 million Americans are destitute—lacking even the most minimal shelter" (CCNV letter, February 22, 1983). An article about a national conference on homelessness reported, "Leaders of the conference estimated the nation's homeless population at almost 3 million, up by about 500,000 from a year ago" (*Los Angeles Times*, October 27, 1983). Even the Department of Health and Human Services under Reagan had cited the CCNV figure occasionally. "Late in 1983, for example, HHS asserted that as many as 2 million were homeless" (*Progressive,* March 1985).

By the end of 1983, *USA Today* reported, "Two years ago, the Census Bureau counted 50,794 homeless people. Now the National Coalition for the Homeless, an advocacy group, estimates there are 2.5 million" (December 21, 1983). In same issue, guest columnist Thomas J. Main, described as a program officer for an unnamed private foundation, portended the future by disputing the advocate-generated estimates. "The plight of the homeless is not to be minimized. But there is no sense in exaggerating it, either. Some advocacy groups put the number [in New York] at 36,000. But even during a blizzard last winter, city-run shelters, which accept everyone who applies, took in only 4,771 people. And the shelter census, instead of going up, actually went down slightly."

In early 1984, the Reagan administration finally started to respond to claims about the extent of homelessness. "A new study will attempt to define the problem of homelessness in America, Housing and Urban Development Secretary Samuel R. Pierce Jr. said yesterday, but he thinks recent estimates of the problem are probably overstated," reported the *Washington Times.* " 'My perception is that it's not as big as it's been made to be,' Mr. Pierce told senior editors at a luncheon yesterday at the *Washington Times*" (January 12, 1984). The study was described as soon-to-be released and "months long." This announcement was no doubt timed to precede a new congressional hearing, held January 25, 1984. (In fact, the study was not released until May.) Dramatically, the hearing was held in the basement of Washington's newest shelter—the Federal City College Building, which had been given to the CCNV to run. The hearing featured mayors from New Orleans, Chicago, and Washington, a number of advocates, the chair of the House Banking Committee, Henry Reuss, who was working at the shelter as a volunteer, and Mario Cuomo, then governor of New York.

The *Post* reported that the backdrop provided "tangible evidence of a problem that some Reagan administration officials have dismissed as anecdotal" (January 26, 1984). In the *Times,* Robert Hayes was cited as estimating that "there were two million homeless people in the United States" (January 26, 1984), while Mitch Snyder reported that the Department of Health and Human Services had estimated homelessness at up to two million nationwide (*Philadelphia Inquirer,* January 26, 1984). Many government officials also favored big numbers over small. Mayor Harold Washington of Chicago told the panel that in his city there were at least twelve thousand homeless and that the number might actually total twenty-five thousand. Governor Cuomo said that sixty thousand had used homeless-related services in New York City during the past year.

Mayor Ernest Morial of New Orleans repeated that there were five hundred thousand to two million homeless people nationwide (Associated Press, as reported in *Richmond Times-Dispatch,* January 26, 1984). The mayors were on hand to attend a meeting of the U.S. Conference of Mayors, which had released a survey. The survey stated, "Demand for emergency food or shelter increased last year in 95% of the cities surveyed by the Conference," despite an improvement in the rates of employment (*NYT,* January 26, 1984).

This statement of concern by the mayors' conference was followed shortly by the infamous interview of President Reagan on ABC's "Good Morning America," in which he opined that homeless people lived on the street by choice. This comment received quite a bit of media attention (see Chapter 6).

At the beginning of May, HUD released its study of homelessness.[4] The *Post* headline read, "Agency Disputes 2 Million Figure: HUD Says Number of U.S. Homeless Falls Well Below Private Estimates" (May 2, 1984). This was followed by a lead that stated, "The Department of Housing and Urban Development said yesterday that there are 250,000 to 350,000 homeless people in the United States, a fraction of the 2 million to 3 million previously estimated by some national organizations." It continued, "Even the highest local figures produced an "outside estimate" of 586,000." Snyder was quoted as calling the HUD figure "an absolute absurdity" (*WP,* May 2, 1984) and "utterly ridiculous" (*NYT,* May 2, 1984). A spokesperson for the U.S. Conference of Mayors termed the figures "a very conservative estimate" (*WP,* May 2, 1984) and said they "sound low" (*NYT,* May 2, 1984). The *Times* article summarized the methodology used in the HUD study. It was "based on over 500 interviews with knowledgeable local observers . . . in 60 metropolitan areas" and included a national survey of emergency shelter operators, ten site visits, discussions with advocates and a fifty-state survey of state activities, local studies, and reports.[5]

Post columnist McCarthy commented, "Whether or not HUD is playing politics, it is playing games. Until now, it has shown little interest in homelessness" (*WP,* May 12, 1984). The *Times* reported that "a new Government estimate that there are only 250,000 to 350,000 homeless people in the country has so angered [the CCNV] that it has demanded that the Department of Housing and Urban Development recall the two-week old report and concede that there are 'serious questions' about its 'veracity, fairness, objectivity and reliability.' " The group, the *Times* said, "is preparing to take the unusual step of seeking a Federal court injunction to prevent Secretary Samuel R. Pierce Jr. from distributing the Government document further." The paper also stated that the following week two

House housing subcommittees, from the Banking and Government Operations committee, would hold a joint hearing to assess the accuracy of
the HUD report (*NYT*, May 18, 1984).

At the subsequent hearing, expert testimony was heard from several
social scientists critical of the report, including Kim Hopper of New
York's Community Service Society, housing policy expert Chester Hartman, and sociologist Richard Appelbaum. All criticized the report on
methodological grounds, accusing HUD of making statistics out of "im-
pressions" of service providers, compiling estimates from dissimilar
sources, and a host of other methodological concerns that critics contended produced a downward bias in the report's estimates.[6] The conservative Heritage Foundation's Anna Kondratas weighed in on the side
of HUD, and criticized the CCNV study's methods and dismissed critics'
allegations as "misinformed or false" (Erickson and Wilhelm 1986:148).
The preponderance of testimony, however, was highly critical of the
HUD study's methods and results.

The CCNV, other advocates, and some government officials then took
the unusual step of filing a lawsuit against HUD Secretary Pierce in U.S.
District Court. The suit asked the court to issue an order to halt further
circulation of the study and to force Pierce to publicly disavow its findings (*Minnesota New-Tribune and Herald,* June 22, 1984). The suit stated,
"The real purpose and effect of the report are to curtail public and private
support for increased initiatives in this area and reduce the pressure on
the administration to respond to the needs of the homeless at the federal
level" (*WP,* June 22, 1984). In the same article Pierce retorted, "We went
through a totally scientific approach of determining those figures. I say
they're right."

The criticisms became worse. By the end of the summer, advocates
and service providers interviewed by HUD for the study began to claim
that they had been misquoted or misreported in the HUD study. For
example, Phoenix advocate Louisa Stark claimed that she had told HUD
that the local homeless numbered 3,000, but HUD had reported 1,500 for
Phoenix. In Kansas City, shelter manager Reverend Bill Pape had estimated 1,400–1,500 local people were homeless and had reported being
involved in a one-night count that produced 900 staying in shelters. HUD
had reported 340–400 (*Kansas City Times,* August 16, 1984). Likewise, in
Baltimore, "the HUD report estimated the number of homeless at 630–
750, even though 11,227 individuals were housed in the city's shelters at
one time or another last year."[7] The story broke under the headline,
"Homeless Systematically Undercounted by HUD to Minimize Issue,
Critics Claim" (*Los Angeles Times,* August 11, 1984). By this time, Mitch
Snyder was publicly threatening to bring perjury charges against HUD
officials (*Kansas City Times,* August 16, 1984).

The suit was filed and dismissed in September on technical grounds. Judge Thomas Jackson held that the report was not subject to rules governing some agency actions that can be challenged in federal court. Snyder retorted that Jackson was a Reagan appointee so the plaintiffs "were not surprised that he upheld the government" (*WP,* September 7, 1984). HUD official June Koch reported that "we're delighted" but back-pedaled criticism of Snyder, saying, "I can't say it was frivolous but the suit and what's behind it tend to deflect the focus from the real problem. . . . I think [Snyder's] motives are high motives, but I disagree with his numbers" (*WP,* September 7, 1984). Nevertheless, the HUD report had been so thoroughly discredited that its numbers, though sometimes cited as a low estimate by the national media, never became "facts." The *Village Voice* summed up the attitude of many of those who cared about homelessness toward HUD and the Reagan administration:

> What irritated HUD officials was that the little Western minds of the media had, by early 1984, latched onto Snyder's figure and used it in editorials, in news stories, on TV and radio. One way or another these stories all posed the same question: If there are two million homeless, why isn't the government doing more to help them? The HUD report was Washington's answer: turn the debate about what to do into a dispute over numbers. (*Village Voice,* December 3, 1985)

Instead, national newsmagazines mostly reported CCNV-generated figures when they published articles about homelessness: "3 million" (*US News and World Report,* January 14, 1985), "up to 2 million" (*Time,* February 4, 1985). *The Progressive,* a left-leaning investigative magazine, characterized the estimate this way: "HUD says 250,000–350,000 but this figure has been widely criticized" (March 1985). The democratically controlled House Government Operations Committee characterized the population as being between three hundred thousand and three million and increasing (*WP,* April 20, 1985), though the conservative Heritage Foundation unsurprisingly preferred HUD's count to the CCNV's (*WP,* April 28, 1985). The advocate argument that the HUD study minimized the numbers of homeless people for political reasons continued to receive publicity. Jack Anderson, a columnist with the *Post,* headlined his story with "HUD Cooked Statistics on Homeless" (July 15, 1985), while a news story claimed, "HUD's Lower Estimate Creates Uproar" (*WP,* August 26, 1985).

In October, University of California at Berkeley social scientists weighed in on the number issue. After reviewing the HUD and advocate numbers and the difference between nightly and yearly estimates, they opined, "We will never know the precise number of homeless on a given night, or of those who experience an episode of homelessness during the year." The report continued, "Whatever the number of homeless, however, all the evidence indicates that millions of Americans experience some form of homelessness, and that the problem has increased dramatically in recent years" (Ropers 1985).

By year's end the House Subcommittee on Housing was set to hold a hearing on the veracity of the HUD study (legal documents, October 29, November 6, 1985). The *Village Voice* published an investigative report on the HUD study entitled, "Body Count: How the Reagan Administration Hides the Homeless" (December 3, 1985). The New York City count was reported as forty-five thousand (*US News and World Report,* January 14, 1985) and fifty thousand (*NYT,* January 21, 1986). Mitch Snyder, in an article critical of his publicity-seeking tactics, was quoted as saying the original CCNV two million figure was "meaningless" (*Plain Dealer,* January 28, 1986). In a subsequent fund-raising letter, however, the group stated that two to three million "eat out of trash bins and suffer and die in our streets" (CCNV fund-raising letter, April 9, 1986).

By February 1986, the CCNV announced that it would go on a hunger strike in part to get the Reagan administration to withdraw the HUD study and its estimate of three hundred thousand (*National Catholic Reporter,* February 28, 1986) though this aspect of the fast received little publicity. Even the American Bar Association's report on homelessness (published July 26, 1986) cites both numbers: "In 1983, advocates estimated the number of homeless men, women and children at two to three million. A 1984 report by HUD put the number at 250,000 to 350,000." "Homelessness remains on the rise," the report asserts, and estimates of the "annual rate of increase vary from 10% to 38%."

In August, Harvard economist Richard Freeman released a study in which, through interviewing seven hundred homeless individuals in New York City, he derived a street-to-shelter ratio of 3.23 street homeless people for every one staying in a shelter. This amounted to 350,000 nationwide, a figure in keeping with the HUD study (*Boston Globe,* September 6, 1986; Freeman and Hall 1987). The study was publicly denounced in Boston shortly after its publication by Snyder; Hayes; local advocate and shelter operator Father Frank Kelly; Richard Appelbaum, a sociologist and expert on homeless estimation; and Boston's mayor, Raymond Flynn (*Boston Globe,* September 6, 1986).

Meanwhile, the CCNV and other advocates continued to legally challenge the distribution of the HUD study. After the original civil suit was dismissed, the group filed charges claiming that the study's project director Kathleen Peroff had perjured herself before Congress and in sworn depositions taken for the civil suit (*WP,* October 6, 1986). Snyder then made an appeal directly to a federal grand jury, asking it to "investigate charges that federal officials intentionally underestimated the number of the nation's homeless" (*Washington Times,* October 15, 1986). In an in-depth article about the "homeless movement" in the *Washington Post Magazine,* the enumeration and estimation debacle was summed up by a Partnership for the Homeless spokesperson: "It has become axiomatic that the nature of homelessness prevents any scientifically reliable esti-mate of the total number of homeless in the nation" (November 2, 1986).

Articles on homelessness in 1987 continued to report a variety of fig-ures. Peter Marin's article in *Harper's* put the figure at "at least 350,000" and "perhaps as many as 3 million" (January 1987), *Time* reported 350,000 or more (February 2, 1987), and the *New York Times* cited 250,000 to 3 million (February 7, 1987). The *Post* reported that a "national survey" by HUD had concluded that there were 350,000 homeless people nation-wide in 1984. The survey, the paper stated, "was bitterly denounced by advocates of the homeless, who insisted the numbers were closer to 2 million or 3 million" (February 28, 1987). In *USA Today,* a news story about shelter aid mentioned the "USA's estimated 3 million homeless" while an editorial two days later put the estimate at between "250,000 and 2.5 million" (March 3, 5, 1987). The *Christian Science Monitor* stated that the homeless number "350,000 to 3 million" (March 9, 1987), while *Black Enterprise* magazine said, "Most estimates indicate the homeless population is well over three million and increasing at a rate of 20% a year" (August 1987). In June, the Neighborhood Reinvestment Corpo-ration, a nonprofit group funded by Congress, released a study on low-income housing loss predicting that eighteen million would be homeless by 2003 (*WP,* June 3, 1987). By the time the McKinney Homeless Assis-tance Act was signed into law on July 23, 1987, Congress had allocated over $1 billion in federal assistance to ameliorate a social problem, the extent of which remained in contention. But most Americans judged it a problem of significant size about which something should be done, and judging from press accounts, Americans who paid attention might well believe that there were millions of homeless people in America.

THE CONTEXT OF THE NUMBERS GAME

The story of "how many homeless" has been extracted, of course, from a complex context of ongoing social activities. Claimsmaking about homelessness also consisted of a multifaceted array of other activities I have described elsewhere. In this section I examine the interplay of problem-specific or homelessness-related elements of context as well as relevant aspects of the general context with the goal of teasing out why social life was elaborated in this way, rather than in some other way. An additional goal is to determine what role "experts" played in constructing homelessness. Finally, I fit the story about how many homeless back into the larger context to answer, at least provisionally, how this particular story influenced "the outcome" (by this I mean subsequent events, and specifically here, the McKinney Act) of homelessness as a social problem. I again employ the analytic categories of environmental and interpretive aspects of context and use a comparative structure, in this case, between the numbers story in New York and the nation as a whole.

THE ENVIRONMENTAL CONTEXT

Estimating the size of a social problem seems like it should be the natural domain of social science experts. But in the case of the national estimate it was CCNV activists who initiated the first effort to count the homeless. In New York, the situation was more mixed. Baxter and Hopper, both graduate student anthropologists at the time, were "experts" of a sort. This status was undermined by the fact that they worked under the auspices of the Community Service Society (CSS), an established Protestant charitable organization with well-known sympathies for vulnerable groups. In neither case, however, were these initial estimates of homeless people the direct products of universities, government agencies, or "think tanks"—the secular organizations usually associated with social science "experts" and their products.

In both the New York and national cases of estimating the size of the problem, constructing the estimates took similar paths. First, each estimate was legitimated by linking it to a political authority, and second, the estimates were publicized widely in the media. These aspects of the environmental context, however, were handled somewhat differently by the two advocacy groups and were reacted to somewhat differently by counterclaimsmakers. Moreover, the legal, political, and economic contexts that directly affected the reception of each estimate differed markedly.

Legitimating the Estimate

The CSS in New York and the CCNV in Washington both realized early that compiling statistics and facts could aid in legitimating homelessness as a pressing social problem, one that therefore required government intervention. The CSS, perhaps to lend its own study legitimacy and certainly also because its were the only numbers then existent, began its study with the New York State Office of Mental Health's estimate for men. This was joined with an estimate for women generated by the Manhattan Bowery Corporation—a service provider for homeless women. Both originating organizations had legitimacy, one because it was a government agency, the other because it had street-level experience. These figures, repeated by a respected charity organization, the CSS, had instant authority with the media—they had been generated by familiar and appropriate sources for this type of information. Moreover, the number was dramatic—a small city's worth of homeless people within the larger metropolis. Finally, the estimate confirmed the "person on the street's" experience. Street dwellers were becoming a persistent and uncomfortable reality, as any Manhattan passerby could attest. It was unsurprising then, that the thirty-six thousand figure became an instant "fact."

The CCNV discussed the need for national statistics with various government agencies including HEW (later to become Health and Human Services, HHS).[8] HEW/HHS was a broad-based agency with a purview over many of the problems (aside from, importantly, housing) with which destitute people needed help. It made sense to build a working relationship with a bureaucracy with such a broad mandate. As it happened, HEW/HHS during the last months of the Carter administration found it within its interests to mildly support or at least not contradict the "1 percent of the nation" figure. And even HHS under Secretary Margaret Heckler (who had much sympathy for the issue: see Chapter 6) had cited the number as late as 1983. At the same time, the sporadic support HHS showed for the CCNV numbers added legitimacy to the advocacy groups' claim that destitution affected 2.2 million Americans. As homelessness became legitimated as an issue of concern, however, the Reagan administration's attitude toward the question changed dramatically.

It is interesting that the Reagan administration directed its Department of Housing and Urban Development (HUD) and not another federal agency (especially HHS, which had shown some concern) to undertake an enumeration of homeless Americans. First, the Reagan administration, to the extent that it had commented on homelessness at all, had maintained that homelessness was not a housing problem and that the housing stock was sufficient. Second, the administration was trying to get out of the housing business by privatizing housing and housing development wherever possible and thus had little interest in finding a new group for which public housing provision might be appropriate. HUD, under Secretary Pierce, advocated market-based solutions to housing concerns. Moreover, admitting that substantial numbers of Americans needed housing assistance clashed with the veneer of "Morning in

America" economic recovery and individualism that were hallmarks of the administration. By charging HUD with this task, even when it was largely FEMA that had mostly engaged with the issue at a federal level thus far, the Reagan White House seemed to be tacitly conceding that homelessness was a problem that had to do with the lack of housing. The mission of HUD during the Reagan years, combined with administration rhetoric that mostly denied homelessness was a social problem of import, provided grounds for calling into question the study's findings from the first.

The estimates of New York's homeless and the nation's were products of different processes. In the New York case, the numbers the CSS used were simply taken directly from well-known and legitimated local sources. In the national case, the CCNV conducted the research from which the estimate was derived. This may well have led to different amounts of investments in the estimates by the two advocacy groups. When the Koch administration started to successfully undermine the New York estimate, the CSS had little incentive to defend it. Hopper and Baxter, had, after all, discounted the estimate's accuracy in the original report in which it appeared. In contrast, the national number was the CCNV's own invention. Even though Mitch Snyder had occasionally been quoted saying that 2.2 million was a "meaningless" number, the group still had the only research-oriented estimate in existence for a time and it was a large enough figure to justify claiming that homelessness was pressing national problem.[9] These factors made Snyder and others interested in defending the figure and pressing for its legitimation, at least against the HUD estimate, which seemed to minimize the issue. Though the CCNV estimate was never exactly accepted as "fact," it was repeated often enough to attain some legitimacy—at least enough to call the government estimate into question.[10]

Managing the Relationship between Housing and Homelessness Policy

The perception of housing needs also affected the reception of each estimate. In New York, the gentrification of housing formerly used by the poor was viewed by local power brokers, including news media such as the *New York Times*, as necessary if the city were to recover from the economic slump. Though the CSS estimate was dramatic and at first reported widely in the press, there was little support for a massive public housing effort to counter homelessness. The city was in debt and increased investment in bringing business to the area was widely viewed as the solution. If new businesses and their professional workforce were successfully wooed, sufficient housing at a level commensurate with professional expectations must be created. All the while homelessness brewed as a public issue, the Koch administration continued to support policies that favored landlords who upgraded their apartment units. Much of the SRO capacity of the city was lost during the 1980s (Blau 1992; Burt 1992).[11]

The perceived need for more middle-class housing helped to eventually make the Koch administration's counterclaims persuasive with the media. The Koch administration took an essentially unconcerned stance toward the estimate. The mayor could not counter the CSS estimate with one produced by the mayor's office (the office was quoted as saying it suspected about twelve thousand homeless in the city), but Mayoral Aide Trobe and Mayor Koch did not expend much effort countering the estimate either. They let the thirty-six thousand number stand from March 1981 until the following December. Then they announced the city would do its own count. Some months later, this idea was retracted. Meanwhile, the mayor's office occasionally made statements that attempted to undermine the number, all the while pursuing a progentrification housing policy that was never really effectively posed by local advocates as a cause of homelessness. Thus the question of how many homeless in New York was never tied to how many fewer SRO units there were in the city's housing stock nor any other issue related to housing affordability.

Instead, homeless advocate and attorney Robert Hayes did what lawyers do, he pursued class-action lawsuits demanding that the city meet the terms of a Depression-era state constitution clause which mandated that all New Yorkers be provided with shelter. The original suit, *Callahan v. Carey,* was successful early on, though the Koch administration stalled for as long as it could before agreeing to the court-ordered decree to provide shelter. The policy implications of this lawsuit, however, were obvious as early as December 1979, when Hayes won his first victory for the homeless. Emergency shelter would have to be supplied "on demand" to anyone who asked the city for it. While a private estimate of those likely to seek shelter might have helped city service providers open sufficient shelter space, keeping a vague notion of the number of beds that would be needed probably served the city better. Aside from the obvious methodological difficulties of counting homeless people, it was more cost-effective to come up with emergency shelter space as needed than to meet the needs of a large and specified number of homeless people. Since the Koch administration had wrung concessions from advocates that resulted in the city only having to provide the barest minimally acceptable emergency housing, this would be the policy the city pursued (at least until family homelessness spun out of control some years later).

Studies demonstrating how many homeless people there were and what services and housing they needed were not directly relevant, and were potentially damaging, to a city homelessness policy based on providing for a homeless person's minimum shelter needs only when someone demanded help. Comprehensive documentation of the problems and numbers of homeless people risked creating conditions for inciting more of a public outcry for comprehensive treatment for the homeless poor. New York officials instead concentrated on reducing the numbers of visible street people by providing minimum shelter for them. This suggested that homeless people were being cared for by the city. The mayor's office thus could portray itself as acknowledging that homelessness was a serious social problem and that it had implemented policy to mitigate it. The mayor's role as a major claimsmaker about homelessness likewise reinforced the notion that, whatever the number, the city was taking decisive steps to ameliorate the problem. Meanwhile, the city could continue to pursue its gentrification program.

The national case was quite different. One of Ronald Reagan's favorite slogans about poverty after all was, "We waged a war against poverty and poverty won." The special symbol of the supposedly failed War on Poverty of the Johnson administration was the public housing high-rise apartment building, "projects" held in contempt by the Reagan administration. Federally provided housing for the poor, the Reagan administration argued, had been a colossal failure and one that would not be repeated on his watch. HUD, under Reagan's Samuel Pierce, instead pursued tax breaks and incentives for landlords to develop housing, often not specifically designated for the poor. Although in both the New York City case and the national case, housing for impoverished citizens was being undermined by deliberate policies, how these were presented to the public differed dramatically. In New York, a progentrification policy was matched with an overt plan for aiding the homeless, which was constantly publicized by the mayor. In the federal case, the Reagan administration mostly denied and minimized homelessness and the need for ameliorative action while overtly promoting its market-based solutions to the problems of housing and poverty.

Thus the Koch administration could look like it was doing something for homeless people because it was providing them with emergency shelter, albeit reluctantly and under court order. At the highest levels at least, the Reagan administration continued for quite some time to ignore the issue or to argue that homelessness (if it existed) was a local problem and one not suitable for anything but sporadic federal intervention (see Chapters 6 and 7).

Differing legal and policy situations in the two administrations also had an impact. Koch and his aides and local New York City advocates were in constant contact negotiating the *Callahan* settlement and subsequent class action suits. Though the city's policy was hardly what the advocates had wanted to "solve" this social problem, homelessness was squarely on the city's policy agenda. The Reagan administration had mostly ignored the issue and when it did acknowledge it, it offered very temporary relief (use of military buildings, cheese giveaways, and one-year indirect emergency funds). This policy vacuum gave the CCNV added ability to press its version of events and its estimate. The White House's efforts at claimsmaking had been marked by an effort to minimize the problem. The White House hunger task force had concluded that hunger was not a problem. The HUD national enumeration of homeless people had found there were relatively few. This enabled other claimsmakers to continue to press their claims while charging the Reagan administration with callous inattention to these serious social ills.

Forging Alliances

Political alliances proved to be another key ingredient that shaped how the "facts" about homelessness were covered and interpreted by the press and made available to the public. New York City advocates and the Koch administration participated in a forced alliance during most of this period, as they struggled with the policy implications of the *Callahan* decision. This preeminent policy decision by the courts—that all New Yorkers had the right to shelter—made other policy options and the "facts" marshaled to support them of less relevance than they might have otherwise been. In the national case, the CCNV initially gained legitimacy from its weak alliance with HEW/HSS. The CCNV's excellent national media connections, discussed further below, also was a crucial resource. The CCNV was also able to ally itself with experts (such as Richard Appelbaum and Chester Hartman) and political figures such as Mayor Raymond Flynn of Boston, in whose interest it was to challenge the HUD estimate. And behind the scenes, Snyder and the CCNV had developed relationships with a number of important figures on Capitol Hill, including some in the Reagan administration (see Chapters 6 and 7). That did not translate into belief in the two to three million figure; but it may have helped to undermine support for the HUD figure. And of course many in the advocacy community, especially those who had felt misrepresented by the HUD study, were ready to add to the CCNV's denunciation. More importantly here, though, was the inextricable connection between very high-ranking Reagan administration officials and HUD. As I discuss in the next section, credibility proved to be a decisive element of the argument about the "facts" of homelessness on a national scale. In the case of counting the homeless, it was the advocates and not the government who were able to retain credibility.

THE INTERPRETIVE CONTEXT

In the realm of the symbolic the reputation of claimsmakers and their sincerity is crucial. In this comparison, the credibility of political author- ities differed sharply, while the advocates, especially in the national case, were able to use their good reputation and sincere commitment to the issue to successfully press their claims. Advocates and policy activists, whether insiders or outsiders, had framed the issue in a way that reso- nated better with the public than had the Reagan White House. Home- lessness was an issue that shocked the public and pulled at its heartstrings. Once established as a social problem of a particular kind, it was one in which sizable majorities of the public wanted their govern- ment to take action.[12] Advocates, who shared this opinion, had a natural ally in the sympathy of the public. Additionally, homelessness was a social problem that lent itself to dramatic representation, which in turn made the media eager to cover it. These interpretive aspects of context quite clearly favored the advocates and their position, especially in the case of the CCNV versus the Reagan administration.

Credibility and Sincerity as Symbolic Capital

From the late 1970s onward, the CCNV had worked continuously to bring homelessness (and its related concerns of poverty and hunger) to the fore of the nation's conscience. Even as early as 1980, the group was recognized as advocating for the poor and homeless locally, which in this case also happened to be the seat of the federal government. Though people might disagree over whether the group used worthwhile tactics, even Mitch Snyder's detractors admitted he and his group had shown an unwavering interest in and commitment to the issue of homelessness. The CCNV was also the most vocal group attempting to make home- lessness a public issue (though the Catholic Workers, Salvation Army, and other groups had long made serving this group a priority). Thus the CCNV had one powerful symbolic tool at its disposal—credibility.

The CCNV had another group characteristic uncommon to social problems advocates—the group backed up its advocacy with its lifestyle of self-imposed poverty. This gave the CCNV's projects a Mother Theresa–like saintliness to some portion of the public. Even most cynics and critics could see that CCNV members, including the controversial Snyder, "walked the walk" of social justice for the homeless poor. Group members had given almost all their money to the poor, had lived outside with homeless people, had offered them "night hospitality" in their home, and had dived into dumpsters and begged food from corporations to feed them. They had run shelters and food lines, had made sure the poor had a holiday meal at Thanksgiving, had lobbied politicians, initiated lawsuits, staged sit-ins, risked arrest, and had been arrested and jailed. They had even starved themselves, at times until close to death, all in a continuing concerted effort to bring attention to the plight of homeless and destitute people.

These efforts had gotten them enough publicity that a wide swath of the public and politicians in Washington recognized the CCNV's unofficial leader, Mitch Snyder. Indeed, he once bragged that he was better known than Mayor Barry and he may well have been right. The CCNV and especially Snyder were not universally liked. But their commitment was beyond dispute and this gave their activities a cachet and a symbolic weightiness that many other advocacy groups rarely achieve. Importantly, their credibility and the finesse with which they dramatized homelessness, also made them, and especially Snyder, sometimes darlings of the media.

The issue of homelessness also lent itself to construal as a social evil unconscionable in a wealthy nation. Street people made destitution and poverty visible and this proved to be a method of making middle-class and wealthy citizens aware of poverty. Homelessness was poverty taken to the extreme as it affected the daily lives and comfort levels of the better off by its visibility (Blau 1992). Homelessness made poverty real to nonpoor Americans in a way not seen at least since John F. Kennedy's trip to Appalachia in 1960. The visibility of homelessness was a symbolic resource that could be and was effectively mobilized by advocates, and later, by local politicians to urge the federal government to "do something" about homelessness. For different reasons perhaps, the diminishing numbers of visible street people was something most Americans favored. Homelessness, at least at first, was an embarrassment to Americans.

Credibility on the issue, the sincerity of the advocates, and the emotions that homelessness evoked in many Americans combined to give advocates claimsmaking advantages. The CCNV and other advocates' early claimsmaking, together with the visibility of the problem, rapidly made homelessness "real" to many Americans. By the mid-1980s, Mayor Koch realized his best strategy was to take an activist stance on the issue. Early on Koch blamed the state for releasing too many psychiatric patients and later admonished private charities and religious organizations for not offering shelter. Eventually though, especially when the *Callahan* decision refused to go away, the mayor realized that portraying himself as actively doing something about homelessness, or at least its visibility, was politically more savvy than merely shifting blame to other entities. As advocate lawyer Robert Hayes explained in an article about the Mayor's shift in policy, "From being an implacable foe, the Mayor has become a zealous advocate, in words at least. It's an about-face in some ways" (*NYT*, January 22, 1983). This was made easier because Koch was a Democrat as were the majority of New Yorkers. Democratic politicians are associated with activist stances toward policy and their constituents are used to and in fact often demand activist government from their leaders. Thus the Koch administration was able to gain some credibility with the public and media by "doing something" about homelessness, even though that something seemed sorely lacking in substance to advocates (and homeless people). This credibility and activism made "how many" and other such facts about homelessness less contentious than they might otherwise have been.

The Reagan administration, by the mid-1980s, lacked almost any credibility or sincerity on the issue. After her confirmation to HHS in 1983, Secretary Heckler had tried to establish a sympathetic government stance toward the homeless but her efforts were undermined by other top Reagan administration officials, including the president himself. Within a short period of time before the HUD study's release, Presidential Counselor Edwin Meese had expressed suspicions about the motives of soup line users, the task force on hunger had minimized the problem, and the president had expressed the opinion that most people were homeless by choice. This public track record provided a frame of denial and callousness toward the poor into which a study that found relatively low numbers of homeless people could be easily put.

The success of CCNV's fight against the HUD study, however, was in the group's multiple strategy of lawsuits, hearings, counterexperts, and media. Filing a lawsuit against the government for lying to the people through a statistical report was a novel approach in which to express disagreement with the government, one sure to spark media attention. A congressional hearing on the matter caused further media attention and garnered support from politicians who could benefit from pointing out the administration's lack of concern for the poor. Expert testimony that questioned the methods used and procedures followed in the HUD study further undermined the public perception of the study. Although studies of this sort are always subject to methodological critique, it is rare to see such a critique as part of a public and publicized hearing, as was the case here. The media was also predisposed to like the CCNV's number in any event simply because it was more dramatic than HUD's. When a fight about "how many homeless" ensued, the drama was increased, thus making coverage more likely. With such tactics the advocates used their interpretive resources to good strategic effect, garnering a lot of media attention for their issue, much of it sympathetic. In addition, they successfully forged alliances around the issue of the estimate with all of the other sectors of the iron quadrangle of claimsmakers.

The CCNV pursued a politics of outrage with regard to the HUD study. It was quite direct in its criticisms, publicly questioning the HUD report's "veracity, fairness, objectivity and reliability." It went further and contended that the real purpose of the report was to minimize the need to do anything about a serious poverty problem—and this language was used in press conferences and in hearings so that the media reported it. Unlike most other possible claimsmakers, the CCNV, as a political outsider group, was able and willing to make such overt accusations, which, regardless of the reputation of the group, did put the HUD study in doubt. Because minimizing the need to intervene on behalf of the poor had emerged as standard Reaganomics, this claim by the CCNV was made more likely to be believed.

Together the elements of this offensive resulted in transforming standard government "facts" produced by government experts into ideologically driven claims. When the media repeated the claim that the HUD study was biased, it became so tarnished that nonexperts did not know what to believe. Thus the HUD numbers were reduced to merely a competing set of claims. At the same time, the CCNV and its allies gained equity for the advocates' point of view. Just by making the argument of bias, the CCNV preserved a public forum for its viewpoint and a public position for its version of the numbers. The result was that *no one could say* how many people were homeless. Thus, the CCNV number was used by other claimsmakers alongside the HUD number, often in a range, with the HUD number forming the bottom and the CCNV number the top. Many groups were satisfied with this turn of events. The advocates wanted the importance of the problem to be recognized. The media liked the drama of the contested estimate and the drama of the high estimate. Many local and state politicians desired some federal help with homelessness, something that would be more likely to materialize if the numbers were high. Even Democratic and some Republican Congress members were amenable to the high estimate.

THE ROLE OF EXPERTS IN SOCIAL PROBLEM CONSTRUCTION

The element examined here is the construction of a number—a statistic answering the question, How many homeless people are there? Surely this part of the construction process of a social problem is the natural purview of experts. Yet in both New York and nationally, the "experts" did not play primary roles in publicizing conclusions about how many homeless there were, nor, in the national case, did they even play a role in constructing the first "viable" (from a constructionist perspective) estimate. In the New York case, the State Office of Mental Health had created an internal estimate that was cited by a charity organization conducting a study that was then widely publicized. The state agency and its "experts" had not publicized the figure originally nor did they attempt to take ownership of it when it did become widely circulated. Instead it was "advocate-researchers" Hopper and Baxter of the CSS who adopted the figure and publicized it. In some sense then, the estimate in New York was a disinterested and an "accidental" figure, one not specifically sought for the purpose for which it was later used. No experts had created it for public consumption and none defended it when it came under attack. This eventually led this estimate—at first so widely used and publicized, to fade away as the city's main homelessness claims-maker, Mayor Koch, refocused public attention on not how many there were but how many were being sheltered by the city.

In the national case, no experts, in the traditional sense at least, were involved in the original CCNV data collection process. The CCNV was comprised of amateurs, untrained in social science methods. Their final national estimate had an unclear relationship to the telephone calls to advocates around the nation from which it was derived. Experts should have been able to devise a method more in keeping with social science standards, should have been able to conduct a reputable study, and should have been able to replace the CCNV's suspect estimate with one in keeping with the rigors of science. That this did not happen suggests several things about the role of experts in the construction of this social problem.

First, this was a rather novel problem for social science. As others have pointed out, counting homeless people, because they live in no stationary place, is more akin to counting populations of animals or birds in the wild than it is to most human demographic efforts (Laska and Meisner 1993). Homelessness was also a very fluid social problem during the 1980s, making an estimate all the more difficult. Because it was a novel and difficult problem, in retrospect, perhaps a consortium of professionals with various types of expertise should have been called upon to design and carry out such an estimate.

Second, by 1984, homelessness was a contentious social problem—at least as measured by the distance between the CCNV's view and that of the Reagan administration. If doing good science had been the goal of getting an estimate, a consortium of experts with a range of affiliations might also have helped obtain a balanced and believable estimate. Or the Reagan administration might have hired a university or some other independent organization to conduct the study. Instead, both of the national estimates were overwhelmingly associated with advocates in one case and the Reagan administration in the other. Since both had already established views on the seriousness of homelessness as a social problem, both produced suspect numbers. Government had, perhaps, itself once been perceived by the public as providing objective, not partisan information such as statistics. In the post-Watergate era, however, all pretense of government nonpartisanship had begun to fall away. Numbers produced by government experts were likely to be seen as partisan products just as were the numbers produced by advocates. This made it possible for the CCNV to undermine the HUD study and gain equal publicity for its own numbers, despite the fact that one set had been produced by rank amateurs, the other by "experts."

The turn of events in this case suggests that experts closely affiliated with a political faction have little credibility as purveyors of facts, at least with the media and their audiences. Instead, data produced by affiliated experts, no matter how closely they follow the rigors of scientific method, are judged by their affiliation, not on their merits. Few reporters and even fewer members of the public are equipped to judge on any other grounds—political party or advocate group affiliation becomes shorthand for tendency toward bias in one direction or the other.

In the end, how the numbers were produced did not matter much; what mattered were the interests of those who produced them. The normal processes of scientific critique, made public through the lawsuit and hearings on the HUD study, exacerbated this tendency. Experts who legitimately criticized the HUD study on methodological grounds, because they were affiliated with the publicity and controversy caused by CCNV contesting of the study, were lumped by both press (and public) as belonging to the advocate camp. (In many cases, this was in fact the case.) Likewise, when HUD experts defended their methodology they were viewed as Reagan partisans. Indeed, few truly independent experts emerged during this period, with the possible exception of Richard Freeman. In this sense it was the role of the expert itself that was undermined.

The CCNV's suit against HUD was an early example of what is now a common trend—that of politicized competing statistics (Best 2001). In a nation that was shocked by homelessness and one in which the CCNV had more credibility than did the Reagan administration on the issue, the CCNV's statistic was viable because both statistics were viewed as biased and because the CCNV's was more dramatic.

There are several other features of expertise that make experts the "weak link" in the iron quadrangle of claimsmaking sectors. Social science experts are often the last to identify an emergent social issue such as homelessness because the very nature of the social sciences is to reflect on social processes that have already happened and social categories that are already established. Beyond this, those who practice the scientific method practice a deliberate and deliberating type of work, one marked by reflection and peer review. Research studies take time. Experts are always the "Johnny come lately's" to any construction process. In this case, developing a solid methodology was difficult if not impossible, especially given the rapid development of the social context of homelessness during the 1980s.[13] Because of the lack of federal policy and the nation's tendency to deal with emergent problems on the local level, what research was taking place was mostly concerned with homelessness on a city or state level. Since this early research was not coordinated methodologically, the results produced by these early efforts at estimation and enumeration were not comparable. The first comprehensive national estimation, conducted by the Urban Institute was published after the major federal initiative that became the McKinney Act (Burt and Cohen estimated the 1987 homeless population at five hundred thousand to six hundred thousand in a study published two years later). Policy cannot always wait for the slow wheels of science.

I have argued that following the story about the extent of homelessness is important because persuading others that a social problem is prevalent ("1 percent of the nation") is often central to convincing people to do something about it. Quantification of a social problem is especially important if the remedy sought is government funding or legal action; government bureaucracy demands documentation of need, especially, it seems, for poverty-related ameliorative efforts. In many ways then, conflict over how many were homeless can be seen as a struggle over whose responsibility homelessness was. Only an entity as large as the federal government could deal with a social problem that affects "1 percent of the nation." If homelessness was confined to a quarter or less of that figure, perhaps the efforts of charities and volunteers working on a local level were all that was needed to handle it. By not letting the Reagan administration figure stand, the CCNV and other advocates denied the president the ability to minimize the problem and made the enactment of federal policy more likely. As it turned out, experts played only a supporting role in determining "how many homeless."

NOTES

1. There are, of course, other kinds of experts such as mental health professionals and social welfare workers who participated in the construction of homelessness

as a social problem. Here, however, I am limiting the discussion to those social science professionals who had the responsibility of delineating "facts" about the dimensions and extent of homelessness.

2. The lower figure seemed to have originated with New York advocate and CSS author Kim Hopper, who had taken conservative estimates from six major eastern seaboard cities and created a homeless estimate/city population ratio. The average of these ratios indicated that an estimated 0.45 percent of these cities' populations were homeless. This multiplier was then applied nationally to cities with 100,000 population or more to arrive at the 250,000 figure. Suburban, small town, and rural homelessness was ignored in this estimate (memo to CCNV from unknown source, January 8, 1982).

3. New York finally did attempt a census of its homeless in February 2003 (*NYT*, February 25, 2003).

4. Parts of the HUD report are reprinted, along with commentary and criticism in *Housing the Homeless*, edited by Erickson and Wilhelm (1986:127–64). See also the original report (U.S. Department of Housing and Urban Development 1984).

5. For another, more detailed description of the methodology published in the popular press, see the *Village Voice* (December 3, 1985).

6. See Hopper testimony (May 24, 1984) and that of Hartman and Appelbaum (reprinted in *Housing the Homeless*; see note 3).

7. Those familiar with homeless enumeration and its many problems will recognize the mixing of "point prevalence"—one-night count with "incidence," usually a yearly figure here. For more discussion on the role of advocates in the attempt to enumerate homeless people, see Bogard (2001).

8. Education was removed from the purview of HEW in May 1980. Two new departments resulted: the Department of Education and the Department of Health and Human Services (HHS).

9. Burt (1992) points out that "1 percent of the nation" was the figure given for homelessness during the Great Depression. Thus the CCNV estimate had historical and metaphorical resonance. In addition the size of the figure alone indicated the seriousness of the problem.

10. For another view of how the media used these estimates, see Hewitt (1996).

11. Burt reports that between thirty thousand and one hundred thousand SRO units were lost during the 1970s and 1980s, which amounted to at least 38 percent of the total SRO stock for the city (1992:34). According to Hoch and Slayton "New York City lost 30,385 units in 160 buildings, between 1975 and 1981, for a decrease of 60 percent overall" (1989:174).

12. Link, Schwartz, and Moore (1995b) did a national telephone survey after "compassion fatigue" supposedly had struck in the 1990s and still found that a majority of Americans were concerned about the issue and wanted something to be done about it.

13. Burt's studies for the Urban Institute perhaps come closest but even these have many shortcomings as she freely acknowledges (see Burt 1992; Burt and Cohen 1989).

6

Building the Moral Momentum for Federal Action

INTRODUCTION

By 1984 homelessness was fully constructed as a national-level social problem of importance. Claimsmakers in state and local government and the activist/advocate community had been successful in convincing the media to pay attention to this social ill. Coverage had markedly expanded over the previous two years. In 1982, for example, the *NYT* indexed 95 articles about homelessness and the *Post* indexed 39, including those indexed under "vagrancy." In 1984 the numbers were 159 and 146. At this point in the career of homelessness as a social problem, local claimsmaking activities and local media coverage increasingly took on a supporting role, reinforcing that homelessness was a serious social problem in need of national attention. Since homelessness is no longer a local social problem but rather a national one, methodologically speaking, comparison of the cases in New York and Washington is no longer the relevant terrain. Instead, examining the national media and interactions between national-level claimsmakers is more to the point.

Members of the general public had also become convinced that homelessness was a pressing social concern. Although it seems clear that the Reagan administration would have preferred not to engage with this social problem at all, momentum continued to build starting in 1984 for federal intervention to mitigate homelessness. In this chapter, I highlight the national-level social problems work that gave homelessness the *moral momentum* to coalesce into a national problem in which the federal government was compelled to intervene. The coalition of activists and advocates, government officials including Reagan administration officials, the media, and experts who increasingly demanded that this social problem be dealt with at a national level was in part forged from a common "call of conscience" felt by people from all political persuasions. It was not merely political or legal maneuvering, nor expanded media coverage that worked to successfully construct homelessness as a social problem. Social problems work is also moral work, not merely cynical appeals to the emotions of the public in order to further agendas. Here I focus on how the moral case was made in this presidential election year.

FEDERALLY SPONSORED SHELTER VS. "HOMELESS BY CHOICE"

On January 16, 1984, the nation's first federal homeless shelter was opened with great fanfare. The event had been previewed by the *Post* in an extensive article profiling Mitch Snyder—"the Wayward Shepherd" as the paper termed him. The Second Street shelter in the old Federal City College Building, located just a few blocks from the Capitol Building, was the product of what the article stated was "an unprecedented accord between the Reagan administration, the District government, and the CCNV" (*WP*, January 11, 1984). As a national project, the shelter had already achieved success before it had opened. The GSA and HHS had coordinated to donate use of the building and pay for its rehabilitation; and Susan Baker, wife of White House Chief of Staff James Baker III, had advocated for it as had House Speaker Tip O'Neill. Even private sector developers had gotten involved and donated an old hotel for temporary shelter when the Second Street shelter could not be rehabilitated in time for Christmas. The CCNV invited a crowd to a brief opening ceremony and luncheon. James Baker, Susan Baker, and Margaret Heckler, the secretary of HHS attended, as did Democrat and Kennedy relative Sargent Shriver, District Deputy Mayor Thomas Downs, and many officials from HHS and GSA (*Washington Tribune*, January 19, 1984). About three hundred homeless people also celebrated the shelter's opening (*Philadelphia Inquirer*, January 16, 1984). The event was widely covered in the media, mostly with photographs showing Secretary Heckler and Mitch Snyder sharing a soup line meal (*USA Today, Baltimore Sun*, January 16, 1984). Heckler commented that the administration had twelve other federal shelters in planning stages but that having one in the nation's capital took priority because, "We should set an example here" (*Washington Tribune*, January 19, 1984). The shelter was soon offering nightly lodging to up to eight hundred homeless people and had opened an infirmary to meet their medical needs (CCNV shelter internal report, spring 1984).

A few days later, on the day of the annual State of the Union message, the House Subcommittee on Housing and Urban Affairs held the second

federal hearing about homelessness in the new shelter. Governor Mario
Cuomo of New York testified as did Mayor Barry and the mayors of
Denver, Chicago, and New Orleans. Mitch Snyder and Robert Hayes
were witnesses and the Coalition for the Homeless brought in representatives from various parts of the nation to testify about the nature and
extent of the problem in their regions (*NYT*, January 26, 1984). Harvey
Vieth, director of Community Services for HHS and involved in the task
force on homelessness in the department, also appeared as did Kitty
Dukakis, who chaired the Governor's Commission on the Homeless in
Massachusetts. Service providers testified and so did several homeless
people (witness list for Hearing on Homelessness in America, January
25, 1984). Representatives from the U.S. Conference of Mayors used the
new shelter as a site from which to make a plea for federal funding for
homeless services (*WP*, January 26, 1984). Though no Republican committee members attended, the hearing received press coverage in most
major east-coast dailies, in *USA Today* (January 26, 1984), the *National
Catholic Reporter* (February 3, 1984), and in papers such as the *Minneapolis
Tribune* (January 26, 1984) and the *Chicago Tribune* (January 26, 1984).
According to the *National Catholic Reporter*, "As a media event the hearing
was a tremendous success. It attracted a swarm of U.S. and foreign reporters and more than a dozen TV cameras" (February 3, 1984). Most
featured photographs of a fifty-five-year-old homeless woman, Mae Ash,
weeping as she told of the hardships she had had to endure during six
years of homelessness in New York City (*Richmond-Times Dispatch*, January 26; *National Catholic Reporter*, February 3, 1984). Many reports noted
that FEMA had allocated $40 million for homeless shelters for 1984 but
that the mayors felt this was insufficient (*Middesex News*, January 26,
1984).

On the last day of January, Ronald Reagan made a trip to New York
to appear on ABC's "Good Morning America" program. When asked
why many Americans say, "He's the nicest man and we like him but his
policies are causing misery," Reagan responded with this now-famous
quote: "What we have found in this country, and maybe we're more
aware of it now, is one problem that we've had, even in the best of times,
and that is the people who are sleeping on the grates, the homeless who
are homeless, you might say, by choice" (as quoted in *WP*, February 1,
1984). The *Times* called this comment "uninformed, if not callous" and
opined that "a civilized community is obliged to offer more" than the
poor choices we now offer homeless people (Editorial, February 7, 1984).
In a *Post* column entitled "Reagan's Grate Society," Colman McCarthy
invited the president to "open a warm unused room in the White House
and then see how many stay outside" (February 11, 1984). The *Village
Voice* called Reagan's comment and policy position an "attack on the

homeless" (February 14, 1984). The "homeless by choice" quote later would be used to demonstrate that the administration sought to minimize homelessness and therefore could not be trusted to produce an accurate estimate of the problem's size and scope (see Chapter 5).

Behind the scenes, the National Coalition for the Homeless was moving forward with its plan for national coordination of homelessness advocates. Beyond supplying witnesses and helping to coordinate the congressional hearings, the group planned to register homeless voters, hold another national conference, and press for national hearings on a federal right to shelter. In addition, it had forged a "statement of principles" for the organization which in part stated, "The production and distribution of social goods according to a culturally accepted standard of decency is basic to the definition of a just society" (Coalition for the Homeless letter to supporters, February 10, 1984). The group's purpose according to the statement was to "increase the quantity and alter the character of the resources available to the homeless, empower the homeless themselves, and to challenge the institutional mechanisms which presently contribute to homelessness." The *Times* ran an editorial criticizing the Reagan administration for refusing to release $100 million in emergency shelter aid that had been appropriated in 1983 by Congress (February 28, 1984). Senator Daniel Patrick Moynihan (D-N.Y.) wrote a letter to the *Times* agreeing with the editorial and stating that he was working to get more funds released for emergency shelter use (March 6, 1984).

This year also marked a return, of sorts, to detailing the types of people who were homeless. *Newsweek* featured a white homeless family on the cover of its first issue of the year (January 2, 1984). The extensive feature story stressed the diversity of the homeless population, as children and adults, and white and Black men and women from a variety of regions throughout the nation were profiled, photographed, and interviewed. The article additionally emphasized the range of approaches taken to deal with the "crisis" around the nation and mentioned that federal aid had been limited to $140 million from FEMA distributed over two years in a "one-time effort." HUD was said to be in the process of deciding whether to subsidize shelters directly. The inadequacy of the housing stock and wages were cited as causing homelessness, while the solutions, the article stated, were difficult to come by. Homeless youth were examined in a *Philadelphia Inquirer*'s Sunday magazine cover story (February 19, 1984), Jewish homeless people were featured in *Washington Jewish Weekly* (February 16, 1984), and mentally ill homeless people were emphasized in two popularized science magazines, *Psychology Today* (February 1984) and *Scientific American* (July 1984). Homelessness was also acknowledged to be spreading to suburban bedroom communities in New York's surrounding counties (*NYT*, July 15, 1984).

The nation's first federal shelter continued to receive coverage. The *Philadelphia Inquirer* called it "a little bit of heaven" for many homeless people (March 3, 1984) while the *Post* featured a story about the outreach necessary to get "grate people" to try the CCNV-run shelter (March 8, 1984). At the end of March, the CCNV planned a march from the shelter to Lafayette Park to protest the planned spring closing of the shelter and four others in the District. The marchers said they would wait until the president intervened to insure that the shelters remained open (CCNV letter to supporters, March 20, 1984). The CBS investigative news program "60 Minutes" was in the process of filming a segment on Snyder and the CCNV at the time. The protest was planned for April 1, but on March 31 Reagan himself ordered the postponement of the closing of the shelter (*WP,* March 31; *NYT,* April 2, 1984).

In April, Colman McCarthy called Mitch Snyder "the capital's hottest power broker" (*WP,* April 8, 1984). Snyder had succeeded, McCarthy stated, "in rallying the White House, Congress and the Department of Health and Human Services to come across with money and concern for the homeless. With a case pending before the Supreme Court, he has penetrated all three branches of government." [The Supreme Court had started to hear arguments regarding the right to protest by sleeping in Lafayette Park in March (*WP,* March 16, 22, 1984).] The CCNV's most recent victory, McCarthy stated, had been to get the Reagan administration to rethink its idea of closing the new federal shelter now that the weather had improved. The building originally had been slated for auction at the end of March. McCarthy then proceeded to interview Washington's political elite, including HHS Secretary Margaret Heckler, House Speaker Tip O'Neill, Susan Baker, and the wife of the vice president Barbara Bush; each had a good word to say about Snyder in print. "His heart is in the right place," said Heckler. He's an "able and talented man who cares about his cause," said O'Neill. Susan Baker stated, "He's somebody who's really living out his commitment," and even Barbara Bush said, "We agree on the very important subject of the poor and hungry." With the opening of the federal shelter, homelessness was clearly on the minds of Washington's powerful and well-connected.

LOCAL ISSUES AS NATIONAL MODELS OF COMPASSION

Like the opening of the federal shelter, the CCNV's next project was a local campaign that could be used as a national model. This campaign was squarely in keeping with the agenda set by the Coalition for the Homeless and indeed, the two groups were in regular contact. The CCNV decided to pursue the civil rights of homeless people by pressing the issue of whether those without addresses could be allowed to vote. The group initiated this effort by holding a "registration luncheon" at the shelter during which members registered five hundred homeless voters (*Washington Times*, June 5, 1984), and thus pressed for a ruling on the status of homeless voters. In an early ruling, the D.C. Board of Elections and Ethics decided that sheltered homeless people may register to vote but grate sleepers and other street people would not be allowed to register (*WP*, April 10, 1984). The CCNV decided to challenge this ruling with a lawsuit, arguing that all homeless people should have the right to vote.

The voters' rights lawsuit in turn was linked to a petition drive to get what would become known as Initiative 17 on the 1984 November District ballot. The initiative would make it the official policy of the District government to provide sufficient overnight shelter for any homeless person who asked for it. In other words, the CCNV decided to press Washington to adopt a similar policy to the one that mandated that all homeless New Yorkers be offered shelter (*Coalition for the Homeless Newsletter*, Number 3, June 1984). If homeless people were denied the right to vote because they had no residence and if the right to vote was an inviolable one, then the solution would be to offer all citizens shelter so that they could then be reenfranchised. On May 1, the CCNV would start collecting the twenty-one thousand petition signatures needed to place the initiative on the ballot on November 6 (CCNV letter to supporters, April 11, 1984; and CCNV "Right to Shelter" brochure on the initiative, spring 1984). This project dovetailed nicely with efforts among advocates in many locations across the nation to encourage poor people to register to vote (*Nation*, April 21, 1984).

On May 1, the day of the city's presidential primary, the drive to collect signatures for Initiative 17 began (*USA Today*, May 2; *NYT*, May 1, 1984). Shortly after voting in the primary, Mayor Marion Barry signed the petition, indicating his willingness to support shelter on demand for homeless citizens of the District (*Washington Times*, May 2, 1984). The next day, the HUD study was released (*WP*, *NYT*, May 2, 1984; see Chapter 5). By June, a lawsuit brought by five homeless street men had been filed. The D.C. Board of Elections and Ethics reversed itself and ruled that homeless people who lived out of doors could register to vote (*Washington Times*, June 5; *NYT*, June 6, 1984). The unanimous decision held that homeless people who had demonstrated intent to remain in the District, who had a mailing address in Washington, and who habitually returned to the same place—even if that was an unconventional place—could register and vote (*WP*, June 5, 1984). The *Post* reported that the decision was the nation's first and would likely fuel efforts elsewhere to protect the rights of the "estimated 1.3 million homeless people in the

United States" (*WP*, June 5, 1984). A follow-up article profiled several homeless African-American men who were reported to be savoring the right to vote in their hometown (*WP*, June 6, 1984). The *Post* also ran an editorial on the issue applauding this expansion of the democratic franchise (June 12, 1984). The lawsuit was later replicated in New York. A U.S. District Court judge similarly ruled that homeless people must be given the right to vote if they had a local mailing address and a habitual place to sleep, even if it was out of doors (*Newsday*, September 27, 1984).

MORALS AND LAWS

As the petition drive neared completion in June, the CCNV started planning for a new fall campaign. Rader (1986) reports that this effort was a contentious one within the CCNV membership as many members were exhausted from the grueling work involved in feeding and sheltering eight hundred homeless people every day. As was usual during this period, however, Mitch Snyder's agenda prevailed and the group sent out a planning letter describing fall's Harvest of Shame campaign. The letter called Reaganomics "little more than legalized and systemized rape" and urged that people come to Washington in October as advocates of many issues, in a collective protest against the Reagan administration and its policies. The plan was for a month of protests and acts of civil disobedience culminating on November 3 with a more massive act of resistance (CCNV letter, June 18, 1984). The CCNV also wrote President Reagan a letter during this period, thanking him for allowing the shelter to remain open but warning him that the group felt it had "allowed our relationship with your administration to temper and dilute our responses" and that this was now at an end. The letter closed with an announcement that the Harvest of Shame activities would commence in October and that the group thought the administration had the right to know what was planned and have a chance to plan accordingly itself (CCNV letter to Reagan, mid-summer 1984).

Mid-June also was marked by the release of a U.S. Conference of Mayors survey reporting that the economic recovery under way had not improved the plight of urban homeless people (*NYT*, June 15, 1984). At the end of the month, the Supreme Court voted 7–2 that the Park Service ban on sleeping in Lafayette Park as a form of symbolic protest did not violate free speech rights. The majority opinion written by Chief Justice Warren E. Burger said that the "tent city" "trivializes" the First Amendment. Dissenters Thurgood Marshall and William J. Brennan, Jr., argued that the Court had not taken the plight of the homeless nor the actions of the demonstrators seriously (*WP*, June 30, 1984). The *Post*'s July 3 editorial on the ruling agreed with the court. A letter published in the paper a week later noted that the CCNV was not desiring to "camp" but rather to "awaken the consciousness of the complacent to the fact that so many people have nowhere to go at night" (*WP*, letter, July 10, 1984). The HUD suit also proceeded through the courts during the summer (a federal judge dismissed it in early September; see Chapter 5) as did the process of generating momentum for the passage of Initiative 17 (*City Paper*, July 27, August 24, 1984). Mitch Snyder was reported as stating the initiative had a reasonable chance of passage and that the group had accomplished its main objective—to get District residents to discuss the plight of the homeless in their community (*WP*, *Washington Times*, August 2, 1984).

FASTING AND HARVESTING

By the summer's close, the CCNV had reerected Reaganville in Lafayette Park. On this occasion, however, the group was protesting the deplorable conditions in the federal shelter it ran and asked the Reagan administration for $5 million to renovate the shelter. The administration replied that it had only opened the shelter on an emergency basis the previous winter and had never promised to upgrade the building (*WP*, August 16, 1984). Snyder countered that the group's tents would remain empty in protest at Lafayette Park for one month. Then some CCNV members, including Snyder, would begin a fast on September 15 if the Reagan administration did not improve conditions in the shelter by then (*Guardian*, September 5, 1984). The administration had promised to find another more habitable building but Snyder vowed to fast to get the administration to repair the current shelter, saying "We ain't letting go" (*WP*, August 16, 1984). The city government said that this disagreement was completely between the CCNV and the Reagan administration. The *Times* ran a First Amendment story mentioning the tents as one of several protests taking place across from the White House. In this story, Snyder refashioned the tents' symbolism to put a positive spin on the Supreme Court decision banning sleeping in the park. "The tents are empty, just like the president's promises," said Snyder (*NYT*, September 7, 1984). A few weeks later the *Post* reported in an editorial that congressionally appropriated funds that were supposed to be used to convert military surplus buildings into homeless shelters were instead being used for routine military maintenance (October 5, 1984).

During its first few weeks, the Harvest of Shame received little press coverage, though coverage of Initiative 17 continued. In one article city officials warned, "Costs could exceed $20 million the first year" if the initiative was passed (*Washington Times*, September 30, 1984). The *Post* gave Mitch Snyder a spot to make a case that offering shelter should be required by the city. This opinion was countered by a Coalition for the Homeless Board member. She argued that Initiative 17 was not the best way to meet homeless people's needs and that a "partnership of business, labor, religious and government leaders and individual residents" was the only thing that would result in a comprehensive response (October 14, 1984). Indeed, the initiative, if passed, would only give people the right to "overnight shelter" and not something more permanent. Snyder argued that bringing people in from the cold was the first step in providing more comprehensive help and that cost should not matter because sheltering people was the "just and necessary thing to do."

While the CCNV pursued Harvest of Shame activities, D.C. police officers pursued homeless people. Between October 10 and 19 they arrested fifty-seven CCNV shelter residents for various infractions. On October 20 they surrounded the CCNV shelter and served eighty-seven felony and misdemeanor bench warrants to residents and arrested eleven more. CCNV member Carol Fennelly called the arrests "harassment" and linked them to the group's Initiative 17 efforts (*WP*, October 20, 1984). Indeed, the mayor had changed his mind about the initiative and the city had filed suit in D.C. Superior Court in an attempt to knock the initiative off the ballot (*WP*, October 12, 1984). Fennelly charged that the arrests were part of the city's attempt to "discredit us as a community." The court ultimately decided to let the initiative stand, with the judge stating that the issue was too important to be decided so close to election day (*WP*, October 30, 1984).

By late October, Harvest of Shame activities had begun to receive press coverage, such as that of nuns being arrested for various protest activities (*Daily News*, October 20, *Associated Press*, October 19, 1984). As arrests increased, so did press coverage (*USA Today*, *Houston Chronicle*, October 25, 1984). The *Post* first covered the events on October 25, near the end of the month's activities. The civil disobedience activity for that day entailed over two dozen supporters taking the White House tour, breaking away from it and praying on the White House lawn. Twenty-four protesters were arrested for what spokesperson Fennelly described as "praying for a change of heart and policy on the homeless in America, particularly as it relates to the Federal City College and the HUD Report" (*WP*, October 25, 1984). Some protesters had refused to move and had to be carried away. Among them was Mitch Snyder, who, along with eleven other people, was in the fortieth day of his fast to get the Reagan administration to change its policies. The group's handout cited three reasons for the fast: the misuse of Defense Department funds appropriated for homeless shelters; the "waste" of HUD study funds on a report "intended to minimize and trivialize" homelessness; and the administration's refusal to renovate the CCNV shelter (CCNV brochure, late October 1984).

By day forty-seven of the fast, both the *Washington Times* and the *Post* ran lengthy stories about the fast, Mitch Snyder and his mission, and photographs of the activist looking weak (*WP, Washington Times,* November 1, 1984). The fast also had gotten the attention of Reagan administration officials. Harvey Vieth, the chair of HHS's Task Force on Food and Shelter, had asked Snyder to stop fasting several weeks earlier. Vieth said his department could not do anything about the HUD report and that the only way the military appropriation could be used to renovate the homeless shelter was if it would be declared a military facility (*WP,* November 1, 1984). *USA Today* asked Mitch if he was scared to die. No, replied Snyder. "It's painful, but I have a greater fear of allowing people to languish like animals, and sometimes I'm afraid I'm not doing enough" (November 1, 1984). The *Philadelphia Inquirer* stated that Snyder had lost fifty-seven pounds and that doctors who had examined him told him that he could die within days (November 2, 1984). HHS had made an offer to do some repairs to plumbing in the building and urged Snyder to quit his fast, but Fennelly responded that the offer was "insufficient." Meanwhile, the Harvest of Shame was winding up. The CCNV put a successful face on the series of actions, which had not been much covered by the press. It had been a goal to have at least one person a day arrested during the protest. The group had managed forty-two arrests on the White House grounds and eighty-eight in front of the mansion (*Philadelphia Inquirer,* November 2, 1984).

The following day, day forty-nine of the fast, Harvey Vieth visited the shelter again to urge Snyder to cease his hunger strike. Earlier in the day House Speaker Tip O'Neill (D-Mass.) and Representative Henry Gonzales (D-Tex.) had urged the Reagan administration to allocate money to repair the shelter. They had also urged Snyder to put an end to his fast, a request that the activist refused. O'Neill then sent a telegram to HHS secretary Margaret Heckler, asking her to intervene in the dispute. Gonzales told reporters, "I certainly hold the president responsible for anything that happens to Mitch." White House officials declined to comment on the fast or on Gonzales's statement (*WP,* November 3, 1984). It was now Saturday, three days before the presidential election. On Sunday evening, CBS was planning to air the "60 Minutes" segment on Snyder, and investigative reporter Mike Wallace had come to Washington, in case a live update of the activist's story was needed. The *Post* ran a "preview" of the show, in which it stated that Wallace had spoken to Snyder briefly on Friday. "I like him," Wallace was reported as saying.

"He's a fascinating man. I think he believes deeply in what he's doing." The *Post*'s review of the show was positive and stated, "Too seldom . . . does *"60 Minutes"* air pieces that really have the capacity to cause the middle class audience productive discomfort. This one does" (*WP*, November 3, 1984).

The following day, the Sunday before Tuesday's presidential election, the *Post* published a story covering the finale of the "Harvest of Shame," including photographs of a protester praying outside the White House and another being arrested (November 4, 1984). The paper reported that seventy-four people had gotten themselves arrested, bringing a total of 228 arrests during five weeks of daily protests. The same day, the paper ran a profile of Harold Moss, a longtime member of CCNV, and in a third CCNV-related story, described the group's food scavenging efforts and feeding program (*WP*, November 4, 1984). The paper also covered Initiative 17 and interviewed a CCNV spokesperson for the story (*WP*, November 4, 1984). A lengthy article entitled, "A Life Style Dedicated to Poverty" profiled the CCNV and its history on page one of the local edition of the paper (*WP*, November 4, 1984). The Harvest of Shame finale was covered in many newspapers around the nation, some including photographs of those arrested being carried away by police officers. Many papers merged this story with coverage of Snyder's fast, its purpose, and his near-death condition (*Cleveland Plain Dealer, Hartford Courant, Miami Herald, Philadelphia Inquirer, Seattle Times/Seattle Post-Intelligencer, State Journal-Register* [Springfield, IL], November 4, 1984).

Finally, on the weekend before the election, President Ronald Reagan told Chief of Staff James Baker to put in a call to Secretary Heckler about the shelter. Negotiations commenced and Snyder and Fennelly received several calls from Harvey Vieth, Secretary Heckler, and even James Baker (Rader 1986). At first the administration attempted to get the CCNV to accept "repairs" and refused to commit to a model shelter. The group held out. Eventually Baker ordered Heckler to agree to "upgrade the facilities" and to "make it a model for the homeless," according to presidential spokesperson Larry Speakes (*Washington Afro-American*, November 6, 1984). The administration eventually promised to provide the shelter with locker facilities, space for separate men's and women's quarters, a new kitchen and laundry room, an emergency first aid station, and a fire protection system. Snyder agreed to drop his demand that the HUD study be withdrawn. Four hours before "60 Minutes" went on the air, the president signed on to the agreement and Mitch Snyder ended his fast (*Washington Afro-American*, November 6, 1984).

The agreement received widespread news coverage on the day before the election (*Boston Globe, Chicago Tribune, Commercial Appeal* [Memphis, TN], *Dallas Morning News, Detroit Free Press, Gardner Massachusetts News,*

Los Angeles Times, Milwaukee Journal, Philadelphia Inquirer, Pittsburgh Press, San Francisco Chronicle, Baltimore Sun, USA Today, Winnepeg Free Press [Canada], November 5, 1984). The *Washington Times* headlined, "Snyder's Fast Ends in Success," while the *Post* ran "Reagan Agrees to Refurbish Homeless Shelter" on page one (November 5, 1984). White House spokesperson Larry Speakes said that the president had seen *Washington Post* stories about the fast and the CCNV and had known that the "60 Minutes" segment was to be shown on November 4 (*Kansas City Times,* November 5, 1984). The CBS show had included an updated segment showing a pale and bedridden Snyder and reported the agreement with the president (*Los Angeles Herald Examiner,* November 5, 1984). Snyder said he was "grateful to the president for taking time, two days before the election, to do what he did to create a model shelter in the nation's capital" (*NYT,* November 5, 1984). On election day, the *Post* followed up with a report of Snyder's hospital room press conference in which he said, "The hardest time is when things begin to happen. . . . I wondered if I was going to die before seeing it work out" (November 6, 1984). Harvey Vieth was interviewed for the same story and said that exterminators and plumbers had already been dispatched to the shelter. In an editorial entitled "Mitch Snyder's Victory," the *Post* called him "a zealot" and someone who "took full advantage of the media and of the timing of the presidential election to press his demands." The paper's editorial page editors also opined that they found "many of his positions unreasonable" and that his tactics "generally strike us as a bad idea." But, the paper concluded, in a note of grudging respect, Snyder had won an important victory for homeless people and "succeeded in this one instance in reminding the country that the homeless ought to be a national concern" (*WP,* November 6, 1984).

Securing approval for renovating the shelter was not the only CCNV victory that week. Initiative 17 was approved, with 72 percent of the voters casting a vote in favor of the referendum (*Baltimore Sun,* November 7, 1984). A CCNV spokesperson said, "It's a clear and powerful statement and a clear message to the city that despite their campaigning against it, the majority of voters think shelter is a good thing." Estimates of the city's costs, as reported in the article announcing the victory, had risen to $65 million—ten times the amount currently allocated (*WP,* November 7, 1984). In an article the next day, however, the city was said to be softening its opposition to the initiative. Mayor Barry stated that the plight of the homeless stirs "human emotions even the best politician can't fight against," and admitted that Snyder's hunger strike "even grabbed me" (*WP,* November 8, 1984). Even the *Post,* which had strongly opposed the initiative, editorialized that since the voters had spoken the mayor and district council were obligated to come up with "the most reasonable, workable, fair—and financially responsible—answer it can" (*WP,* November 9, 1984).

In a matter of a few days, the CCNV had received tremendous national press coverage for homelessness as a social problem. The group seemed to have captured the attention of both of the nation's "national newspapers," the *Times* (four stories in early November) and the *Post* (fifteen stories between November 1 and 11, 1984). The CCNV had seen its Initiative 17—the first time voters had directly expressed their views about sheltering homeless people—achieve a resounding victory. And, against all odds, the group had gotten a reluctant president of the United States to accede to its demands about the creation of a federal model shelter. Perhaps most importantly, the CCNV had finally gained the moral momentum the group had worked so hard to achieve.

CONSTRUCTING MORAL MOMENTUM

If this were a made-for-TV movie about homelessness, the narrative would end there, with a major victory for the CCNV and for homeless people against an indifferent president. In fact, this is how the David and Goliath story did end in the television movie made about Snyder in 1986 (*Samaritan: The Mitch Snyder Story,* CBS), although the film had been watered down so the victory had been against "faceless bureaucrats" rather than the president. But real social life is an ongoing process and is not so neatly concluded. Reversals to these victories followed in short order. The week following the election the *Post* ran an "Insight" column by Michael Berenbaum and Judith Rosenfeld entitled, "Snyder's Suicide Tantrum: What Does He Do for an Encore?" (November 11, 1984). The Reagan administration reneged on its agreement and for a time tried to close the CCNV shelter, which led to more protests and more lawsuits (*WP,* June 15, *NYT,* November 5, *WP,* November 15, 1985; see also Chapter 7). The city almost immediately sought to short-circuit the intentions of Initiative 17 through filing a suit challenging the legality of the initiative (*WP,* November 17, 1984). Still, in terms of the construction of homelessness as a social problem, 1984 was a pivotal and victorious year for the CCNV as the nation's central "moral entrepreneurs" of homelessness (Becker 1963). If social problems are what relevant actors and audiences *recognize* as social problems, then this time period is when homelessness was definitively typified as a serious national social problem of a particular type, even against the wishes of a popular president. Moreover, this period of social problem construction created the moral momentum that was needed for homelessness to be put on the national social policy agenda. In this case, the actors who had to accede to the problem's seriousness if something was to be done about homelessness included an administration devoted to minimizing aid for the poor. Momentum on the issue had to overcome this obstacle as well as mobilize significant portions of the iron quadrangle and the general public. Regardless of how transient the "actual" victories of the 1984 campaigns were, they did achieve moral momentum along several dimensions.

In explicitly examining the moral terrain of how homelessness was elaborated during this time period, I rely on distinctions made by Donileen Loseke (1999). She distinguishes between "types of moralities" within which to pose claims (ibid.:49) and categorizes these as religious, humanitarian, and organizational. Within these moral types, claimsmakers pursue various strategies to create moral momentum when attempting to a construct a social problem. These Loseke defines as (1) constructing indisputable moralities, (2) constructing multiple moralities, (3) constructing cultural worries, (4) constructing moralities for mass media presentation, and (5) remembering the audience (ibid.). I do not use a comparative framework here (nor do I explicitly distinguish between environmental and interpretive contexts). I do, however, continue to rely on these distinctions as a framework within which to examine the kinds of moral momentum building work undertaken by the CCNV and others during this phase of problem construction.

CONSTRUCTING MULTIPLE MORALITIES

Religious Moralities

The CCNV, as an experienced activist group, was by this time adept at constructing homelessness as a phenomenon that could be viewed as problematic through multiple moral lenses. Since the group had its roots in radical Christianity, homelessness had been constructed from as far back as the Holy Trinity campaign as an affront to the Christian values of generosity to the poor and the moral imperative of acting as "my brother's keeper" in relation to the less fortunate. Although evoking overtly Christian values had diminished as the group cooperated with secular claimsmakers to press its claims, a specifically *religious* morality was never far from the center of the group's claimsmaking activities. In this period a Christian moral approach to the problem of homelessness (and other Reagan policies) was most in evidence in the Harvest of Shame campaign, when activists' acts of civil disobedience frequently involved kneeling in prayer on the White House lawn. When members of the group were quoted in the press, they at times specifically cited religious motivations or ends as the reasons why they pursued certain actions or had faith that these actions would be resolved in the "correct" fashion. For example, Carol Fennelly of the CCNV said that the protesters in her group "were praying for a change of heart and policy" (*WP,* October 25, 1984). When asked by the press if his death from fasting would be meaningful, Snyder replied, "That's not my concern. I'm doing what God tells me to do" (*Washington Times,* November 1, 1984). Snyder is quoted as thanking "God and the president" for the successful resolution of his hunger strike for shelter renovation (*Pittsburgh Press,* November 5, 1984) and termed the homeless "God's children all" in a guest editorial in favor of Initiative 17 (*WP,* October 14 1984). Snyder was often referred to by the press in terms such as "crusader" and "wayward shepherd," which suggested Christian motifs (*Los Angeles Herald Examiner,* November 5, *WP,* January 11, 1984). And the CCNV in general was referred to by the press as a "radical Christian" community. On a symbolic level, Mitch Snyder's body itself, often photographed shirtless during his various fasts, evoked Christ-like suffering. Its emaciated appearance doubtless reminded all Christians of Christ as he is typically portrayed on the cross. Although evoking a specifically religious morality was no longer front and center by this phase of problem construction, there was enough reinforcement of specifically Christian values that believers among the public understood what moral message was being promoted.

Humanitarian Moralities

More prominently on display during this period was the call to do something about homelessness for humanitarian reasons, an appeal to audience *emotion* (as opposed to reason) (Loseke 1999). At this point in the history of "new" homelessness, the public could still be shocked at seeing people dressed in rags wandering the streets of America's cities. In part, homeless people, by their very presence, engaged in effective claimsmaking and suggested to some members of the public that "something must be done" on humanitarian grounds. The visibility of homeless poverty enhanced its appeal as a humanitarian issue—a case of easing pain and suffering that Americans could and should do something about. This was a prominent theme among advocates and homeless people themselves when members of the Coalition for the Homeless and homeless people testified at the 1984 congressional hearings on homelessness.

Evoking this moral framework was a prominent theme of CCNV claimsmaking. Whether pursuing the Reaganville actions, feeding people in front of the White House, engaging in Harvest of Shame activities, or pursuing the right to shelter, the CCNV consistently evoked humanitarian themes as a central reason why the government should act on behalf of the homeless. The three campaigns the group concentrated on during 1984 all centered on acting on behalf of homeless people for humanitarian reasons. The first step in easing pain and suffering in the CCNV's view was to provide people with immediate shelter. This the group did by getting the government to donate the Federal City College Building for a temporary shelter. When that failed to be immediately available, the group sought and found a temporary replacement for it from local developers. In early 1984 the CCNV did open the Federal City College Building as a shelter. Moreover they saw to it that people were actually provided shelter by staffing it themselves. In addition CCNV members roamed the streets urging homeless people to come to the shelter. The group provided shelter on terms most homeless people could live with, as it did not have excessive bureaucratic requirements or a religious agenda (*WP,* March 8, 1984). Thus the CCNV served a segment of the homeless that few other shelters sought to serve—the segment most distrustful of assistance, which included people with mental health problems. It was on humanitarian grounds that the group requested permission from the president to keep the shelter open even after the spring weather had returned. It was also on humanitarian grounds, at least in part, that CCNV members demanded that repairs be made to the shelter. Initiative 17 was also grounded in the humanitarian claim that, as one CCNV brochure slogan put it, "All God's Children Gotta Sleep" (photograph of protest sign in CCNV Initiative 17 brochure, Spring 1984). Initiative 17 sought to extend the right to shelter to all of the District's residents, surely a humanitarian policy. The Harvest of Shame campaign (which pursued a variety of poverty, health, and environmental issues) also protested Reagan administration policies on humanitarian grounds, stating the president's policies "were setting new records for barbarity and abuse" (CCNV letter, June 18, 1984).

CCNV members were not the only ones who took a humanitarian approach to claimsmaking about homelessness. Most government officials in both parties who weighed in on the issue did so, at least in part, from a humanitarian perspective. When New York Governor Mario Cuomo and Chicago Mayor Harold Washington testified before Congress in the January hearing on homelessness, it was on humanitarian grounds that they demanded federal action. Mayor Washington, for example, denounced homelessness as a "spreading plague" (*Chicago Tribune,* January 26, 1984) while Representative Henry Gonzalez (D-Tex.) said the homeless had become "the ultimate throw-away of a throw-away society" (*Baltimore Sun,* January 26, 1984). Though perhaps federal financial aid and political advantage were foremost on their minds, they nevertheless made their claims for aid from a humanitarian moral perspective (see, for example, *National Catholic Reporter,* February 3, 1984).

Republicans Heckler, Vieth, and Susan Baker used the HHS-sponsored Task Force on Homelessness as a venue from which to pursue policies that would aid homeless people and all seemed to have a genuine concern for this segment of the population. In part, this can be seen through their willingness to collaborate and cooperate with the CCNV. Though the radical anarchist CCNV and the members of a conservative Republican administration were at odds politically about most everything, their common humanitarian commitments (and in some cases, a shared Christian ethic) enabled them to act in concert at times when it came to homelessness. It was upon humanitarian grounds that the strongest relationships were built between these two claimsmaking groups and these relationships in turn enabled homelessness to become prominent as a social problem. Reagan himself might have been most concerned about the political fallout of an unfavorable "60 Minutes" portrayal of his administration so close to the election. But Vieth, Susan Baker, and Heckler, at least in part, chose to intervene to get Snyder to cease his fast because he and other fasters had touched these members of the Reagan administration with previous humanitarian claims for which they knew the CCNV would be willing to die. Thus do the moral activities of one group multiply to become moral momentum.

Newspapers too often spoke out about homelessness in humanitarian terms. The very fact that Sydney Schanberg of the *Times* and Colman McCarthy of the *Post* were employed as "conscience columnists" acknowledges these national newspapers' self-perception as vehicles for the promotion of moral claims. Both of these columnists made an effort during the early 1980s to bring homelessness to readers' attention and to state that something had to be done about homelessness on humanitarian grounds. The two papers' editors also made humanitarian (among other) moral claims in their corporate editorials. The *Times,* for example, criticized Reagan's "homeless by choice" statement with a humanitarian suggestion that "a civilized community is obliged to offer more" than unappealing and insufficient shelter to the homeless poor (Editorial, February 7, 1984). The paper also encouraged the administration to release appropriated funds for shelter use (*NYT,* February 28, 1984). The *Post* was an early humanitarian claimsmaker when it ran its seven-part editorial series on "America's Dispossessed" (December 25–31, 1981). At the end of 1984, the *Post* editorialized that despite Mitch Snyder's tactics, they agreed with him that homelessness "ought to be a national concern," presumably a humanitarian one (*WP,* November 6, 1984).

Organizational Moralities

Loseke defines organizational moralities as being based on secular values that appeal to *logic* (1999). Examples of these include appeals to nationalist values, capitalist values, individualist values, family values, and the value of "fair play." Some of these were used by various claimsmakers in constructing homelessness as a moral problem. The CCNV and other claimsmakers, especially Democrats, obliquely invoked patriotism or nationalism in some of their statements. For example, Mayor Ernest N. Morial of New Orleans asked at the congressional hearing, "How large does the hunger or homeless problem need to be before it elicits a federal response?" (*USA Today*, January 26, 1984). Some said that it was "unconscionable" that a wealthy nation like America would let some of its citizens go without something as basic as shelter. Mayor Harold Washington of Chicago stated, "This is the richest society in the world, and one person without a place to live is a tragedy" (*Chicago Tribune*, January 26, 1984). In some sense these types of appeals were intended to call forth "American values" such as the generosity of a wealthy nation. Governor Mario Cuomo of New York stated that nothing "can allow us to feel ourselves justified as the great American union while so many of our brothers and sisters are refused any share of our abundance" (*Daily News*, January 26, 1984). Secretary Heckler implied that such values were at work in her decision that the nation's capital should be the first place to open a federal shelter (*Washington Tribune*, January 19, 1984).

Capitalist values which state that the market will provide for those who participate show up repeatedly in the Reagan administration's proposals to deal with homelessness. The contentious hunger study "demonstrated" that the marketplace did work and that people mostly were well-fed. The cheese giveaways were said to threaten the right of cheese producers to profit from their labor. Homelessness, like most other federal expenses, was said to be better handled through "private sector initiative." And Presidential Counsel Edwin Meese believed that people chose to eat soup line food because it was "a better deal" than paying for food themselves. At this point in the development of homelessness, there were not many statements implying that it would be cheaper to shelter homeless persons than to rehouse them. But of course this was the underlying reason that the Koch administration had demanded that advocates give up the push for a right to housing in favor of a right to emergency shelter when the *Callahan* lawsuit was won. And the Barry administration expressed fears that Initiative 17 would mean that people would have the right to demand public housing paid for by the government. These were all ways in which the capitalist values of the market and the bottom line influenced claimsmaking. Largely, in this case, the expression of capitalist values mostly worked as counterclaims against which claimsmakers with religious and humanitarian aims could contrast themselves. Moral momentum was maintained by arguing that in the case of homelessness, capitalist values were inappropriate and callous.

Individualism argues in part that people are free to choose their own lives and that individuals are responsible for themselves. Surely the president's strong belief regarding the efficacy of individualism was at work when he made his famous "homeless by choice" statement. People in various sectors including members of the public made variations on individualist moral claims when they expressed their displeasure with homeless street persons and their unsavory dress and behavior. Romantic images of homeless men as hobos and eccentric but kindly vagrants that dominated the construction of homeless people earlier in the decade also were framed from an individualistic perspective, one in which homeless people were presumed to have adopted homelessness as a lifestyle. In these claims, society's obligations to homeless people were minimized or absent and homeless people's freedoms and (often unfortunate) choices were emphasized. The CCNV also participated in claims in this moral register, largely when it expressed its desires to keep regulations at a minimum at the group's shelter so that homeless people's freedom would not be further abridged than it already was by their destitution.

Though "family values" were not much in evidence as a moral framework at this stage in the construction of homelessness, they did appear in a few cases. The early 1984 *Newsweek* issue on homeless featured a homeless family on its cover and from time to time others invoked the existence of homeless families as a moral evil when making claims that something must be done about homelessness. For the most part, however, the impact of homeless families was not yet part of public claimsmaking about homelessness. Governor Cuomo used the concept of family values in a unique way to make claims about homelessness. In comments to the *Post* during the congressional hearing, the governor stated that he had sold his state on the "family" concept of government and, in invoking this public sense of family, had raised money to open numerous shelters in New York State (*WP*, January 26, 1984).

The moral framework of fair play was used frequently by all sectors of claimsmakers. This was the frame in which voting rights for homeless people were put. They, like their housed peers, should have an equal opportunity to cast a vote like any other citizen. Homelessness had become a problem, according to some claimsmakers, exactly because fair play was not in operation in Reagan's America. Reaganville was one visual way in which the lack of fair play was expressed by advocates, as was the soup line Thanksgiving dinner. Early claims about homelessness, somewhat muted by this period, lay the blame squarely on the unfairness of Reaganomics. Fair play was used to invoke support for homeless people as individuals too. For example, Heckler spoke directly to homeless people in comments she made at the opening of the CCNV shelter: "You have as much right to dignity and respect as anyone" (*WP*, January 16, 1984).

CONSTRUCTING MORALS STRATEGICALLY

The CCNV had from the first acted out of a sense that its construction of homelessness—as unnecessary and inhumane—was beyond dispute. The shelter was negotiated for, opened, operated, and its use extended, all based on an unwavering presumption that to do otherwise—to allow people to freeze and die on the streets—was morally intolerable. Initiative 17 and the extension of voting rights to homeless people were pursued on the same grounds, as demands that were morally unassailable. The force of the group's convictions and the credibility and sincerity with which members had pursued them was effective strategically as well, as evidenced by the fact that 72 percent of District voters agreed that all who asked should be offered publicly financed emergency shelter. During this period, and for the most part throughout its efforts to construct homelessness as a social problem, the CCNV's main strategy was *constructing an indisputable immorality* around the issue. To term this a strategy implies that this was a position pursued for its potential for success. Although the CCNV did "strategize" in this fashion when the group pursued particular campaigns, terming its overall orientation to the issue "strategic" is misleading. CCNV members believed what they preached and it is perhaps for this reason that they were as successful as they were.

The CCNV's pursuit of homelessness as an issue also benefited from particular *cultural worries* that characterized the Reagan era. The economy was going through a marked transition from one based on manufacturing to one primarily oriented to the provision of services. An appreciable portion of the family-wage-paying manufacturing jobs primarily held by working-class men were moving overseas and these jobs were not being replaced. The early 1980s were characterized by rampant joblessness, especially for minority men. What few jobs were available were the low-quality and low-paying impermanent jobs of the new service sector. Homeless people in rags wandering the streets of those uncertain economic times were specters of what many at the economy's bottom most feared. Even the comfortable classes that relished Reaganomic's laissez-faire capitalism were not yet so far removed from memories of a more generous welfare state that they were beyond being shocked by homelessness. They were also dismayed at having poverty so blatantly displayed. Whether rich or struggling, Americans had seldom been so privy to the excesses of poverty (or mental illness or substance abuse) and were uncomfortable, at this early stage, with accepting street dwellers as aspects of everyday urban existence. These conditions of context made for cultural worries that could be transformed into moral imperatives to recognize and ameliorate homelessness. Homelessness was constructed through the activities of many different claimsmakers and, as a result, it became a problem of *multiple moralities*. To Robert Hayes and the Coalition for the Homeless, homelessness was constructed on the grounds of fair play and enforcement of the law. To Governor Cuomo, homeless people were a part of New York's "family" and should be cared for accordingly. To some Democrats and Republicans and to some members of the Reagan administration, homeless people deserved aid on humanitarian or religious grounds (while others saw them as victims of their own poor choices). Homelessness was a problem that could be and was constructed on overlapping religious, humanitarian, and organizational moral terrain. The CCNV itself constructed the problem on religious, emotional, and rational-secular grounds. According to most members' beliefs, it was one's duty to serve God and serving the poor meant that one was serving God. To ease others' pain and suffering was the humane thing to do, a notion the group held and promoted not just on religious grounds but because of the social justice influences of Gandhi and Martin Luther King. Helping homeless people was rational and reasonable according to the secular values of a democratic society, in whose interest it was to promote equality. Homelessness was constructed by the CCNV as a problem of not serving God when that strategy was appropriate (such as in the Holy Trinity campaign), as a problem of inhumane treatment (when urging the president to provide resources), and as a problem of fair play (Initiative 17 and voting rights). I have argued that coalitions between the sectors of claimsmakers aided the construction of homelessness by having "many voices" speak about the issue, even if they were not always singing the same tune. Likewise "multiple moralities" broadened the warrants under which homelessness could be viewed as problematic. Homelessness was constructed as a moral problem on many fronts and this shored up its importance as a social problem.

To make the national case that homelessness was a serious social problem, a national audience was needed. As we have seen in previous chapters, the CCNV made involving the national media in the issue a priority. The group's claims were deliberately packaged in dramatic ways, hoping to lure media coverage. Once the CCNV had formed initial relationships with this all-important member of the iron quadrangle, the group cultivated them by continuing to provide coverage-worthy events. The CCNV purposely involved government "celebrities" such as senators and representatives so that the media would be more likely to cover the group's issues. And always it *constructed a moral message for mass media consumption.* The media were often appreciative of these efforts as moral content is a regular part of any major newspaper in its editorial section. Televised media often do "investigative reports" or holiday specials that take on a moral issue. And some programs, such as "60 Minutes," are largely concerned with the moral terrain. By providing dramatic content with a moral message, the main claimsmakers of homelessness successfully lured the media to cover the issue regularly and demonstrated one moral approach the media could adopt. Most Americans had already been made aware of the issue through previous media coverage. During 1984 homelessness became a "media sensation" of an issue through Snyder's fast and confrontation with the president and the profile of CCNV on "60 Minutes."

By constructing homelessness through multiple moral lenses, by urging people to see it as an indisputably important social issue, by playing up the cultural worries of average Americans, and by presenting compelling moral material to the media, the CCNV *remembered its audience.* The audience for this social problem ultimately became "the American public" and the president. But on the way to those audiences, the CCNV attempted to get the attention of lower-level politicians and the media by constructing moral stories that members of these groups would find appealing. By giving these sectors "something they could use," the CCNV was often successful at wooing these initial audiences. Democrats wanted issues to use against the Reagan administration. Some Republicans wanted to demonstrate a charitable side to their party.

The CCNV's multi-issue, multiple-morality approach allowed for both. The media wanted moral messages packaged dramatically. Snyder's "David and Goliath" motif in confronting the Reagan administration was bound to appeal to "60 Minutes"—and much of the public. The CCNV did not explicitly make appeals to the public (though of course they privately sent out fund-raising letters to some small portion of that public regularly). Instead, the group mostly appealed directly to powerful people (mostly politicians) who it thought could take action to ameliorate homelessness. But everyday Americans wanted to feel morally good and just. And the way the CCNV framed homelessness as an unassailable moral issue made coming out in favor of helping the homeless easy for the public. Later there would be talk of "compassion fatigue" (see Link et al. 1995b). At this point in the construction of homelessness as a social problem, however, the CCNV and fellow claimsmakers had succeeded in making a morally compelling case that homelessness was indeed a serious social ill and that something must be done about it. This was an impressive accomplishment during a presidential administration rife with attacks on the poor.

7

"Something Must Be Done"
The Outcomes of Social Problem Construction

INTRODUCTION

Social problems claimsmakers almost always have two agendas. First, they aim to convince others that a social problem exists and is important. Second, they urge that "something must be done" about the problem in question. Mostly these agendas are pursued simultaneously but they usually are not accomplished at the same time. Most often claimsmakers must first typify the problem and demonstrate its importance before relevant audiences are willing to entertain "doing something" about the issue. In New York, for example, the problem was typified and action was taken to ameliorate it very early on when Robert Hayes undertook to bring a lawsuit that demanded that the constitutional provision that required the State of New York to house every citizen be enforced. In a sense, the *Callahan v. Carey* case both defined the problem (undomiciled men) and the solution (state-mandated offer of shelter). This is frequently the attitude of claimsmakers, who construct conditions as problematic *because* they desire a solution. Often, as in this case, they have a desirable outcome in mind when they undertake claimsmaking activities in the first place. Even in this rather straightforward case of social problem construction, however, it took several years for the relevant "audience" to undertake to do something about the problem. The case was decided quickly enough, confirming in law both Hayes's problem definition and proposed solution. But for the first two years after the 1979 decision the Koch administration tried to suppress or reconstruct the problem (as one of deinstitutionalized mental patients). By the time negotiations between advocates and the city government were complete, they bore only faint resemblance to Hayes's and other advocates' initial ideas for a solution to the problem of unhoused men. Instead of housing as the solution to homelessness, the Koch administration offered to provide only emergency shelter. Because claimsmakers' activities take place in a complex social context, the results of both problem construction and problem solution remain somewhat unpredictable.

In the case of homelessness, I have argued that by the end of 1984 the problem had been "successfully" constructed. That is, audiences of all sorts (with the possible exception of high-ranking Reagan officials and the president himself) had agreed that homelessness was a problem and that it was an important problem that deserved a solution. A telling editorial in the *Post* acknowledged the rapid and successful construction of homelessness as a social problem.

> The problem of homelessness has arrived in our midst with what has to be called unnatural speed. Five years ago, if headlines are the measure, it hardly existed. Now it pervades the society. To what extent has reality changed, to what extent is this a genuine public discovery of wretchedness previously ignored, to what extent is it a media artifact? No one quite knows. (*WP*, March 4, 1987)

By 1987, homelessness had "arrived" as a prominent social problem regardless of its "actual" extent. In this first goal, the combined activities of the iron quadrangle of claimsmakers had been quite successful.

Successfully achieving the second goal of social problems claimsmakers, "doing something" to address the problem, is usually more difficult.[1] As American society is both large and diverse, it can accommodate a variety of social problems, only a few of which get much public attention at any one time. In order to get those in power to enact legislation, change social policies, or otherwise alter social behavior, it is necessary to successfully argue that something must be done *now* about the social problem in question because this problem is more important than the many others competing for attention. As soon as claimsmakers argue that established social behaviors must change, those who benefit from current practices will make an effort to minimize the problem or shift attention elsewhere. Those who have an interest in the status quo may also counterclaim that the problem is a different one than what is claimed.

Homelessness, however, in part because of the continuous and concerted efforts of the CCNV and other central claimsmakers including Mayor Koch and many other big-city mayors, proved remarkably durable as a central social problem during this period. A problem that persists is one that is likely to be paid attention, if for no other reason that society's powerbrokers desire to take it off the agenda. If demands for action to "solve" the problem will not go away, eventually something is usually done to enable the problem to lose saliency as a central issue of concern. In this chapter, I focus on discerning how persistence on the part of claimsmakers and what the *Post* describes as "the strange glamorization of this issue" (March 4, 1987) ensured that something would be done about homelessness. Whether that "something" was what advocates or homeless people wanted or needed is another matter.

PERSISTENCE

When the cold season of 1985 had ended, the CCNV planned to close and begin renovations on the Federal City College Building, armed with architects' plans and the promise of $5 million from the federal government. That figure had originated the previous spring with New York architect Conrad Levenson, who had toured the building and had estimated that $5 million would be needed for repairs. But by the end of April 1985, no specific arrangements for the transfer of funds had been made and the building's renovation designers were insisting that the project would cost much more than the funds the Reagan administration had agreed to under duress the previous autumn (*WP*, April 23, 1985). Harvey Vieth, the chair of HHS's Federal Task Force on Food and Shelter, insisted that the administration was fully committed to the project and that details of the funding transfer would be forthcoming shortly. Snyder warned that unless the project got under way soon, it would not be completed in time for the following winter and homeless people's lives could be endangered.

By June, Snyder was proclaiming that the government had reneged on the agreement and federal officials were charging that "Hollywood" Snyder was more interested in self-promotion than in housing the destitute (*WP*, June 9, 1985). Snyder had stormed out of a meeting with GSA and HHS officials over a dispute between the advocates and government officials concerning the meaning of a "model physical shelter." Architects attending the meeting said the government wanted to renovate the shelter in a warehouse style, "which everyone agrees is inappropriate" (*WP*, June 9, 1985), while GSA officials claimed that the submitted plan would cost $10 million, double the original agreement figure. Levenson said that his design was based on the agreement to build a model shelter as the government had promised and that the original figure was only to cover minimal repairs. There were other issues as well. Snyder claimed that the government plan would result in "absolutely no security for women" and that it would leave the CCNV with a "completely unmanageable building," which would be unacceptable to the group (*Washington Times,* June 12, 1985). Vieth said it was the government's position that women should not be housed with so many men at all but also said the government plan was not final. Things could be discussed, he continued, "but Snyder is not prepared to listen" (*Washington Times,* June 12, 1985).

By this time, government officials were considering alternatives to the CCNV shelter, while CCNV members had held a press conference announcing that "the promise that the president made on November 4 has been broken" (CCNV press release, June 13, 1985). A letter had been mailed to the president on June 4 asking for a meeting to discuss the matter and no response had been received. A several-page press release detailed the history of conflict between the government and CCNV members over the shelter. The press release also announced a "sit-in." Mitch Snyder and Carol Fennelly would bring chairs and sit outside the entrance to the White House and wait for the president to meet with them about the shelter's future. In addition, if no movement on the government's part was forthcoming, a lawsuit would be filed.

The following day federal officials stated in the press that the agreement between Snyder and the government had been rescinded and that they were considering making the CCNV vacate the shelter and shutting it down. They were also considering, said a HHS undersecretary, giving the money to the D.C. government for the provision of alternative housing for those now staying at the shelter. Officials had first attempted to interest the city or private agencies to take over operation of the shelter from the CCNV but no one was interested in continuing the operation of the eight-hundred-bed shelter in what the paper described as a "rat-infested" building (*WP,* June 14, 1985). The city was said to be interested in receiving the $2.7 million the federal government was now prepared to spend on repairs to the shelter, especially if the federal government did not mandate any particular number of beds. By the time Snyder and Fennelly began their sit-in outside the White House, HHS's Vieth had publicly stated that his department was through negotiating with the CCNV and that "to continue to talk to Mitch Snyder is a dead end" (*Philadelphia Inquirer,* June 14, 1985). Snyder and Fennelly were arrested for putting up an "illegal structure"—three chairs—on the sidewalk outside the White House (*WP,* June 15, 1985). On June 18, the CCNV filed a lawsuit to "force the Reagan administration to authorize the renovation of a downtown Washington shelter" or assume its operation themselves (*WP,* June 18, 1985).

The press was not shy about weighing in on the impasse. The usually friendly *Washington Times* blamed Snyder for trying to force the issue while Reagan was dealing with a hostage situation in Beirut and titled the editorial, "A Slide from Grace" (June 19, 1985). The *Post*'s Courtland

Milloy said Snyder had become a "personality" and, "Starstruck, Mitch suddenly ups his demands" (June 20, 1985). Another *Post* writer, Benjamin Forgey, however, termed the administration's "so-called plan" for the shelter—three sheets of paper showing the most minimal disposition of various functions—"as stupid and brutish as the CCNV documents are intelligent and humane" (June 29, 1985). *Newsweek* headed its report on the conflict, " 'Holiday Inn' for the Homeless?" (July 8, 1985). The news weekly reported that there was "no compromise in sight" and said that even Snyder's friends "fear his demands may be unrealistic." The federal government then ordered the shelter (which it owned) closed and the CCNV responded by taking the government to court once again (*WP,* June 22, 23, 1985). This forestalled closure and evictions as the federal government decided it had to wait until the court ruled on the renovation plan issue (*WP,* June 26, 1985). The CCNV took to the streets and two hundred people, most of them residents of the shelter, protested the threatened closure (*WP,* June 28, 1985).

In July, Federal District Court Judge Charles Richey ordered the Reagan administration to reconsider its decision to close the shelter (*WP,* July 17, 1985). Ten days later the judge ordered the shelter to remain open until the renovation lawsuit decision was issued (*WP,* July 27, 1985). In between these two events, Initiative 17—the ballot referendum mandating the city to offer homeless people shelter and approved by 72 percent of District voters—was invalidated by a local court. The judge in that case said that the scope of ballot initiatives had been exceeded in this case because the initiative had required the appropriation of funds, a power not granted to the voters. At this juncture, the CCNV acquired some much-needed allies in the District's Board of Elections and Ethics. The body decided to appeal the Initiative 17 decision (*WP,* July 31, 1985).

At the beginning of August, the Reagan administration reaffirmed its decision to close the CCNV shelter and sent in a team of health inspectors to document the many admitted health hazards. They filed a plan with Judge Richey outlining plans for closing the shelter at the end of August. Among the reasons cited by the government was that the shelter was "in deplorable condition" and "simply not fit for use as a shelter for the homeless" (*Washington Times,* August 1, 1985). Moreover, a HHS official said it was "totally inappropriate" for the federal government to be involved in running a local shelter. This of course, was a complete about-face in HHS policy, which had only a year earlier claimed that the shelter was the first of twelve federal model shelters. The attorney for the CCNV countered that displacing eight hundred homeless people was "a cruel, inhumane and wicked thing to do" (*Washington Times,* August 1, 1985). The attorney also stated that the administration had been looking for someone else to shoulder the homeless burden in the District since

October 1984 and no one had as yet stepped forward. The judge had also asked HHS to accept public comments on the shelter closing and the agency had received 707 comments, all but 37 in favor of keeping it open. About half had come from shelter residents and staff. At this juncture, the CCNV again picked up some allies, this time in the House of Representatives. A House panel heard Snyder document why $10 million would be needed and that many people would be completely without shelter if the CCNV shelter was closed (*WP*, August 2, 1985).

On August 20, Judge Richey decided that the shelter could be closed if all residents were relocated and a plan was in place for "eliminating homelessness in the nation's capital." Secretary Margaret Heckler, once an ally of Snyder, stated that HHS would "immediately pursue with Mayor Marion Barry . . . and others, arrangements for the transfer of the shelter residents to alternative sites" (*WP*, August 20, 1985). The department also stated that it had pledged $2.7 million to find homes and health care facilities for the shelter's residents (*NYT*, August 20, 1985). The White House said that Reagan believed he had met his obligation to Snyder, that HHS had tried its best to work with him, and, "It's most unfortunate that for some reason that process broke down" (*WP*, August 20, 1985).

In his ruling Judge Richey implored the Reagan administration to "find and implement a solution to this disgraceful problem" (*Washington Times*, August 20, 1985). He also wrote, "No less than the President of the United States should treat this as a national emergency in order that the full impact of the nation's resources can be brought to bear to eliminate this national disgrace" (*NYT*, August 20, 1985). Snyder, at least to the press, expressed confidence that the shelter would remain open. "There are no solutions. This building has been the only solution, and renovation is the only solution" (*Washington Times*, August 20, 1985). A spokesperson for the mayor seemed to concur with Snyder's opinion. "I cannot give you any specifics about where these people will go; I do not have them," she said (*Washington Times*, August 20, 1985).

Four days before the shelter was to close, the GSA sent in the electric company and turned the power off. CCNV staffers claimed that no one had notified them of the power cut. The mayor's Command Center arranged for food to be brought from another shelter to feed residents and the D.C. fire department provided a power generator so there would be lights at dinner (*WP*, August 26, 1985). Though shutdown seemed imminent, behind the scenes, alliances were being forged. The assistant majority whip in the House, Michael Barnes (D-Md.), dashed off a letter to Secretary Heckler urging her to delay the closing because he was "not aware of any proposals that would provide a satisfactory alternative to the present facility" (letter from Representative Barnes, August 28, 1985).

He also requested that the administration honor its commitment to provide a model shelter for District residents.

During a U.S. Court of Appeals hearing two days later, the federal government did agree to delay closing the shelter. As the *Post* reported, HHS had failed to gain cooperation from the D.C. government and a private initiative to use a building owned by Catholic University had also fallen through (August 30, 1985). HHS was in the process of locating alternative sites owned by the federal government. A report issued by the National Coalition for the Homeless had located two alternative buildings but together they would house only two hundred people. About seven hundred were in need of relocation in August and the cold season would swell numbers of shelter requesters. Robert Hayes, the New York City advocate who had authored the National Coalition report on alternatives in the District, commented, "I can think of no other city that is closing down a shelter on the eve of what's promised to be the worst autumn and winter for the homeless in 50 years" (*Washington Times,* August 30, 1985).

As federal officials had noted, the city was not cooperating in shutting down the shelter. In an editorial entitled, "Where is the Mayor?" the *Post* took Marion Barry to task for standing by instead of helping to find a way to relocate the CCNV shelter residents "as though the dispute were taking place on another planet" (*WP,* September 3, 1985). Barry, however, repeatedly said that it was the responsibility of the federal government and not the city to honor the pledge made by President Reagan (*WP,* September 7, 1985). Meanwhile, HHS floated an idea to use "forty temporary trailers" as replacement shelters but acknowledged that a private local fund-raising effort would be needed to provide enough money for the facilities. In addition, the federal government in cooperation with the D.C. Coalition for the Homeless had identified about a dozen other buildings for possible shelter conversion (including a wax museum). Many of these, however, had come under opposition from local community groups as soon as they were proposed (*WP,* September 7, 1985). In another editorial on the subject, the *Post* urged the mayor to cooperate with this federal plan (*WP,* September 14, 1985).

A few days later, Mayor Barry sent a scathing letter to Secretary Heckler that outlined the city's position. Barry placed blame on the federal government for not taking his advice in the first place as he had originally advised against opening the CCNV shelter. He also stated that he was holding the president to his word and that it was "the sole responsibility of the Federal government to solve this specific problem" (letter from Marion Barry to Margaret Heckler, September 19, 1985). In great detail, he then outlined how infeasible it was to pursue the trailer plan. The city did not allow trailers within its borders and accommodating them would at the very least require expensive electrical, sewer, and plumbing work that would add costs and time to the proposed plan. Moreover, some of the buildings specified for shelters were no longer available: one had been sold, another converted to an office building, and the wax museum was slated to be converted into permanent housing. In summary, concluded the four-page letter, "The city cannot participate in the 'plan' because of its inadequate, partial treatment of the problem and because by no means does it begin to fulfill the federal obligation as promised by the president or as ordered by Judge Richey." A few days later, Barry's opposition became public and he was quoted as suggesting that the federal government put the forty trailers on federal property such as the National Arboretum and the U.S. Naval Observatory (*WP*, September 21, 1985). Marion Barry, for his own reasons, had become an ally of the CCNV.

The shelter saga continued through the fall. The D.C. Coalition for the Homeless was now being seriously considered as an alternative group to fund and to run the large alternative shelter that was gradually becoming the main plan at HHS. In a letter to the *Post*, a longtime member of the Coalition contended that the "current board is simply not up to the task of managing the implementation of a plan as politically and logistically complex as the 40-trailer scheme" (*WP*, September 20, 1985). He contended the coalition was broke and suggested that the CCNV continue its work as it was the only group in the city with experience at managing a large shelter. In addition, he stated that the homeless were not served by the president's reneging on his original agreement nor was the *Post* helpful in its support for the federal trailer plan.

In a brief filed with the U.S. Court of Appeals to counter the CCNV's suit to overturn the Richey ruling, lawyers for the federal government argued, "When a statement of policy is made by agency officials [it] was not a legally binding commitment on the government" (as quoted in the *Post*, September 20, 1985). In an article the next day, Snyder expressed confidence that the courts would find in the CCNV's favor, and if they did not "the government would be free to shut the shelter down and throw everybody out in the street" (*WP*, September 21, 1985). A few days later HHS signed an agreement with the D.C. Coalition for the Homeless granting them $2.7 million for shelter and an additional $1 million for services. The residents of the CCNV facility would be moved to the 1985 Inaugural Committee Headquarters, according to the plan (letter from U.S. Attorney Joseph Digenova to George Fisher, clerk of the U.S. District Court of Appeals, September 26, 1985). The building had also formerly been used as the Department of Defense Intelligence School (*Washington Times*, November 5, 1985). The next day, this agreement was announced in the press, paving the way for the CCNV shelter's closing. Once the inhabitants of the CCNV shelter were moved to the new large shelter in the Anacostia section of the city, the Federal City College Building would be immediately demolished, according to federal officials (*Washington Times,* September 27, 1985). The replacement shelter on Anacostia Drive SE was far to the east of Capitol Hill, across the Anacostia River. It looked like Mitch Snyder had lost his long struggle for a shelter close to the Capitol, one that would be a constant reminder that homelessness must remain on the nation's agenda.

HHS officials, however, had possibly underestimated Anacostia community opposition to the relocation. In early November, on the anniversary of Reagan's 1984 pledge to build a model shelter, about one hundred residents of the already poverty-stricken Anacostia neighborhood organized a protest motorcade to the White House to object to the shelter opening, which they termed another "invasion" of their neighborhood. "Everything that isn't wanted is put in Anacostia," complained one neighborhood resident. The group was led by comedian and activist Dick Gregory, Mayor Marion Barry, several other local politicians, and Mitch Snyder. Barry reiterated that the president had made a social contract with the city and "he should keep it" (*WP,* November 5, 1985). He also called on the president to keep his word to renovate the CCNV shelter (*NYT,* November 5, 1985). Gregory charged the administration with indifference to poor and Black people and threatened to fast until the matter was resolved to residents' satisfaction. The shelter was slated to open later that week, according to the D.C. Coalition for the Homeless (*Washington Times,* November 5, 1985).

Snyder then wrote a scathing letter to the president of the Coalition rejecting her request to allow the Red Cross to come to the CCNV shelter and do a "needs assessment" of the soon-to-be transferred residents. In the letter, Snyder likened the Anacostia shelter to the "tribal homelands" forced moves of South Africa's apartheid system (letters between D.C. Coalition for the Homeless and the CCNV, November 5, 6, 1985). A few days later Representative Barnes held a press conference reiterating what Gregory and Mayor Barry had said. HHS officials responded by outlining the shelter resident transfer procedure to the press and stating that the CCNV shelter would soon be closing (*Washington Times,* November 8, 1985).

As time came to get on the bus for transfer to the Anacostia shelter, CCNV shelter residents began to protest. An evening demonstration attracted about fifty residents who yelled, "Hell no, we won't go," and waved homemade signs. Although HHS officials stated, "We expected Mitch Snyder to stage this demonstration," it probably accurately reflected the majority of shelter residents' opinions. On the first transport day, only eleven residents had agreed to be transferred to Anacostia, while five hundred remained at the CCNV shelter (*WP,* November 15, 1985). Both the shelter's relaxed rules and the surrounding resources of the Capitol area made the CCNV shelter more appealing to many homeless residents compared with the Anacostia site, with its limited resources and much more bureaucratic structure. Snyder promised an "occupation" of his shelter. The following day the *Washington Afro-American* reported that federal officials were threatening to delay construction on the southeast segment of the District's METRO subway system if Mayor Barry continued to resist a permanent solution to Washington's homeless problem (November 16, 1985). The Anacostia shelter, as it happened, was in the METRO construction path and was slated for demolition the following spring. Anacostia, then, was only a short-term solution to the need for emergency shelter and HHS blamed Barry for failing to plan for a longer-term policy. Barry countered that Reagan had promised to take care of the city's homeless while HHS officials insisted that "homeless people are not a federal population." The article concluded by noting that Snyder was "careful not to say what tactics are being planned" by CCNV shelter occupants if the shelter were forced to close. Mayor Barry noted that whatever happened, the District's police force would not be on hand to take care of it (*Washington Afro-American,* November 16, 1985).

By November 19, 225 people were reported to be living at the Anacostia shelter, three-quarters of them relocated residents of the CCNV shelter (*WP,* November 19, 1985). In a press conference, Snyder called on Barry to save the CCNV shelter while HHS officials continued to reiterate that after the $3.7 million was expended by spring 1986, the federal government would no longer be involved in the city's homeless problem. Barry's office reiterated its position that the shelter was a federal problem. The timetable for the CCNV shelter closing, however, "remained in doubt" (*WP,* November 19, 1985). The next day U.S. District Court Judge Richey gave his approval for the closing of the CCNV shelter, stating that the Anacostia shelter met his requirements that alternative shelter had been found for the displaced residents. Snyder said the CCNV would appeal the decision to the U.S. District Court of Appeals (*WP,* November 20, 1985). The federal appeals court found in the CCNV shelter's favor. They were swayed by Snyder's argument that alternative sites around the city simply did not have the capacity to shelter all those requesting it in the winter months (*NYT,* November 21, 1985).

A former CCNV shelter resident, one Snyder claimed had left because of notices posted by the Justice Department on the shelter's doors stating that it was closed and those who remained risked arrest, had died of exposure a few days after vacating the shelter (*Washington Times,* December 30, 1985). The federal appeals court decision blocked federal officials from forcibly evicting residents or staff from the CCNV shelter, which would now remain open "indefinitely." On December 28, President Reagan intervened personally to overrule the HHS and halt eviction plans (*WP*, December 29, 1985). A few days later the CCNV was informed that the architectural plans developed for the renovation of the Federal City College Building had won first place for the Paul Davidoff Award of the American Planning Association (letter to Snyder from APA, November 25, 1985). A White House spokesperson said federal officials had no intention of forcibly evicting residents and would instead try to persuade them to accept alternative shelter (*Washington Times*, December 30, 1985). The CCNV held its usual Thanksgiving meal in Lafayette Park (*Baltimore Sun*, *Los Angeles Times*, November 29, 1985). In December, an Anacostia community group filed a suit to force the closing of the Anacostia shelter (*WP*, December 24, 1985). The tide was turning.

A suggestion of the resolution to the problem of the CCNV shelter and Washington's homeless came from chair of the District Council, David Clarke. In a publicized letter to Mayor Barry, Clarke suggested that Barry honor the spirit of Initiative 17 for moral reasons and start by giving the CCNV shelter $200,000 for emergency repairs. Although Clarke agreed with the mayor that the shelter was a federal responsibility, Clarke believed that this gesture "might inspire the federal government and the CCNV to settle their differences" (*Washington Times*, December 30, 1985). Even if Initiative 17 had been struck down, Clarke continued, the mayor should "take the message from 72 percent of the voters" and offer homeless people "three hots and a cot like they do in New York" (*Washington Times*, December 30, 1985). Mayor Barry conceded to this plan and offered the CCNV $250,000 after a tour of the building. He was motivated in part, he said by President Reagan's recent rejection of plans to evict hundreds of the shelter residents forcibly (*WP*, January 4, 1986). The federal government also had shown a willingness to compromise by letting the city repair the building even though it belonged to the federal government (*WP*, January 8, 1986). Repairs began on January 18, 1986 (*WP*, January 19, 1986).

District and federal officials met secretly for the next two months trying to carve out a permanent solution to the District's homeless. A committee was formed by District, HHS, and congressional officials whose goal was to start up an "ABM (Anybody But Mitch) program," according to *Post* columnist Mary McGrory (February 25, 1986). The issue, the column continued, is whether the District's homeless are a federal or local responsibility. Though a figure of $3.9 million federal dollars was talked about as start-up money for a comprehensive plan to deal with the city's homeless, the column concluded, "Nobody so far has talked about the exorbitant cost of excluding [Snyder]" (*WP*, February 25, 1986).

Meanwhile, Snyder and other CCNV members, worried that the federal government would again try to shut down the shelter, started a fast once again (CCNV press release, February 12, 1986). Twenty-three days into the fast, the *Post* noted that the Anacostia shelter was slated to close on April 30, without a plan for rehousing the five hundred men who by that time were staying there. HHS's Vieth said that the responsibility to determine where hundreds of homeless people would live when the CCNV shelter was shut down in the spring "lies with the city" (*Washington Times,* March 7, 1986). By March 8, 1986, after a frigid weekend, there were 1,014 people residing in the CCNV shelter (*WP,* March 9, 1986). On March 12, Snyder was hospitalized because of complications due to his fast (*Washington Times,* March 12, 1986).

On March 16, the Reagan administration offered to turn the CCNV shelter over to the District government and give it $5 million for repairs if Snyder would cease his fast (*WP,* March 16, 1986). Snyder was reluctant, stating that more money was needed, but the following day an agreement was reached (*WP,* March 17, 1986). The White House was said by the *Post* to be fearful that Snyder would die from his fast and that they would suffer from political embarrassment if CBS "60 Minutes" carried out its plan to do another segment on the homeless controversy. Mayor Barry was said to be upbeat about the plan and broke bread with Mitch, who had his first meal in thirty-three days (*WP,* March 17, 1986). Snyder said he would raise the rest of the funds needed from other sources (*NYT,* March 17, 1986). The *Post* took Barry to task in an editorial for his intransigence in meeting the needs of the city's homeless and did not have much good to say about Snyder either, though the paper said that he, unlike the mayor, was at least fighting for more shelter (March 19, 1986). A month later, the funds had still not been disbursed (*Washington Times,* April 15, 1986).

Meanwhile, the D.C. Coalition for the Homeless was in trouble. There were allegations of an assault on a shelter resident by a staff member at a shelter run by the group (*WP,* April 12, 1986). More ominously, the group had been accused of mishandling the $3.7 million in federal funding. There were allegations that "loans" from the funds had been made to persons connected with the group and that there were "inadequate controls and recordkeeping in the organization's handling of some of its grant monies" (*WP,* April 13, 1986). The FBI was called in to investigate. The staff member was later fired after he had been arrested for the assault and it had been revealed that he had had a lengthy criminal record (*Washington Times,* April 14, 1986).

Snyder seized the opportunity to suggest that federal officials suspend the remaining grant money the D.C. Coalition had been given (about $2 million) and stated that "the taxpayers' money is being squandered"

(*WP,* April 14, 1986). The next day, the federal government did just that (*WP,* April 15, 1986). HHS officials stated that the Coalition had "not been making regular reports" and cited the improprieties being investigated by the FBI. Snyder also appeared in the press that day stating that no federal funds had yet been released for CCNV shelter repair and that soon it would be too late to ensure that the building was remodeled in time for the following year's cold season (*Washington Times,* April 15, 1986). An investigative report in the *Post* characterized these events as consequences of "the federal government racing to extricate itself from a relationship with homeless activist Mitch Snyder" (*WP,* April 16, 1986). The next day HHS modified its suspension of the Coalition grant, stating that in the future all expenditures would need prior approval (*WP,* April 17, 1986). A "technical snag" had developed in the transfer of the CCNV shelter to the city, forestalling the release of the $5 million in renovation fund. Congress had decided to act on the measure legislatively to make sure the transfer was properly done. By May 22, Snyder threatened a new hunger strike would begin in June if the Reagan administration did not deliver on its promise (*WP,* May 22, 1986). An anonymous congressional aide said that the delay in action on the transfer of funds to the CCNV was due to several congressmen who were fearful that Snyder "was not a suitable person" to run the shelter and were reviewing his FBI file and past criminal record (*Washington Times,* May 22, 1986).[2]

While the shelter issue continued unresolved, Initiative 17 was ruled valid by a three-judge panel of the District Court of Appeals. Mayor Barry said the city would appeal the verdict but stressed that the appeal "should not be construed as opposition to assisting the homeless" (*WP,* May 21, 1986). In an editorial, the *Post* agreed with Mayor Barry and called the initiative "vague, misleading and legally loose" (*WP,* May 22, 1986).

The third fast for release of the $5 million in federal funds began with a press conference on June 1, 1986. This time, Snyder vowed to go without water because the funds were urgently needed if renovations were to be completed before winter. Most people die within ten to fourteen days if neither food nor water is ingested (CCNV press release, June 1; *NYT, USA Today, WP, Washington Times,* June 2, 1986). "Responding to Mitch Snyder's third hunger strike in two years, White House officials yesterday urged Congress to act quickly to appropriate funds to repair a shelter for the homeless," the *Washington Times* reported the following day (June 3, 1986). Snyder, however, said that Congress was working on the transfer of the property title and that "the White House has the authority to release the money, but they are sitting on it instead" (*Washington Times,* June 3, 1986). Snyder stated that twenty-six CCNV members and an additional eleven hundred supporters from around the nation would begin total fasts the following day if an agreement was not forth-coming. The next day the White House agreed to give Snyder $965,000 to begin immediate renovations. Senator Mark Hatfield (R-Oreg.) had convinced the White House to release the money from a discretionary fund of the Office of Community Services. A CCNV press conference heralding the decision was attended by Senator Hatfield and the Rev. Jesse Jackson, who compared Snyder with Gandhi and Martin Luther King (*WP*, June 5, 1986). Renovations began on June 23, 1986 (*USA Today*). The headline under the *Washington Times* photo of a demolition crew at the shelter read "Persistence Pays Off" (June 24, 1986).

In October, the *Post* reported that CCNV shelter renovations were pro-ceeding "on schedule" with a completion date of December 22 expected (*WP*, October 6, 1986). In both this story and a Thanksgiving season one, the *Post* reported that the Reagan administration was now granting "$6.5 million" toward renovating the shelter (*WP*, November 27, 1986). In fact, Congress had acted to increase the appropriation for the shelter by $1.5 million (CCNV press release, February 19, 1987). On Thanksgiving Day the CCNV held its usual dinner, this time in front of the Capitol. It was followed by a protest urging the federal government to set aside $250 million for homeless facilities and services around the nation and create a permanent office for dealing with the issue within the Department of Health and Human Services (*Washington Times*, November 28, 1986). Fi-nally, the CCNV announced that the "award winning" shelter was ren-ovated and would reopen with a ribbon-cutting ceremony and open house. The shelter's grand opening occurred on February 19, 1987, a bit over three years since the CCNV had first begun offering shelter there in January 1984 (CCNV press release, February 1987). In his typical Sny-der style, at the open house, Snyder took Mayor Barry on a tour and then announced the need for a further $5 million to complete the reno-vations (*WP*, *Washington Times*, February 20, 1987).

THE "STRANGE GLAMORIZATION" OF HOMELESSNESS AS A SOCIAL PROBLEM

CBS had taken an interest in Mitch Snyder as a result of the dramatic story he gave them to report on "60 Minutes." Not long afterward, there was talk of a movie deal to make "The Mitch Snyder Story" for televi-sion. Besides any ego gratification Snyder might have received from the film deal, the CCNV needed the money to pay the shelter's daily ex-penses. In February 1985, a deal was struck. By signing a letter of agree-ment with CBS, Snyder received an initial $50,000. If producer/script writer Clifford Campion thought he could make a credible film of Snyder's story and the film went into production, the CCNV would get an additional $100,000 (*WP*, February 21, 1985). CBS officials admitted that the upfront money was "unusually high" but was set "to help Mitch's cause and aid his financial obligations." A few days later, screenwriter Campion was visiting grates and touring the shelter with Mitch Snyder (*WP*, February 25, 1985). Snyder was not the only homeless story being produced for CBS television. In November 1985, CBS released "Stone Pillow," the story of a homeless New York woman played by Lucille Ball. It received lukewarm reviews in the *Post*, which termed it "ploddingly generic" (November 5, 1985). Nevertheless, it took homelessness straight into the living rooms of middle America.

Homelessness was also being taken on in the comic strips by none other than Gary Trudeau, creator of the Doonesbury strips. The popular Doonesbury appeared in about four hundred newspapers around the nation. Trudeau had "dropped out" for a year and spent some of it investigating homelessness in Lafayette Park. When he returned to work, his first strips had been about homelessness in the nation's capital. These eventually won him nomination for a Pulitzer Prize (*D.C. Home News*, November 15, 1985).

By year's end, CBS had made the decision to go ahead with the Snyder story. Cicely Tyson was recruited to play a homeless Black street woman and Martin Sheen had been cast to play the controversial Snyder. The actor had recently won acclaim for his role in the Vietnam War film "Apocalypse Now" (*WP*, December 24, 1985). The CCNV was given $100,000 to finance the shelter that Reagan had at that point neither funded nor closed. At the end of the year, Snyder appeared on ABC's "This Week with David Brinkley" TV show, where he engaged in a debate with Anna Kondratas from the conservative Heritage Foundation (*Washington Times*, December 30, 1985). Sheen was reported as dissatisfied with the script for the Snyder movie, which avoided criticizing anyone in the administration, particularly the president (*Des Moines Register*, January 6, 1986).

A week before shooting for the film began, the cast came to town and Mitch Snyder threw them a party at the CCNV shelter. It was paid for by the film production company. "This may be one party that Washington's social lions won't be clamoring to attend," opined the *Post* in its "Personalities" column (January 8, 1986). But Ridgewell's, the catering service for Washington's elite, catered it, complete with tuxedoed waiters. A local hotel donated cakes and hors d'oeuvres for the party and food was served on linen tablecloths replete with candelabras and flower arrangements. "It will be a real treat," remarked Carol Fennelly in one of the many preevent articles about the party, "for [the homeless residents] to be treated with such dignity and respect" (*Philadelphia Inquirer*, January 12, 1986). The strawberry cake at the affair read "Gimme Shelter" and Mayor Barry, Martin Sheen, and other political and media celebrities attended, as did numerous members of the press and about 750 homeless people (*WP*, January 13, 1986).

The party, covered by the Associated Press, was carried in a number of newspapers, complete with photos of Sheen and Snyder, who had begun to look remarkably alike (*Los Angeles Times*, January 15; *National Catholic Reporter*, January 31; *Richmond Times-Dispatch*, *USA Today*, January 13, 1986). Even the *Wall Street Journal* commented on the event (January 13, 1986). Its coverage prompted a letter from CBS president Donald Grant. After correcting a factual error in the article, Grant made the following comment about the role of the media in regards to social problems:

> You [the *Journal*] seem to imply it might be television's role to solve real problems of society. While obviously the medium cannot solve them, it can certainly help create awareness about such issues, as does your newspaper. Indeed, coverage of the homeless issue has been widely reported on national and local news and public affairs broadcasts and represented in special entertainment programming. All this has to help stimulate others who can solve these problems. That role our medium gladly shares. (*Wall Street Journal*, February 18, 1986)

The local press continued to cover the filming of the movie (*WP*, *Washington Times*, January 15, 1986) and even *USA Today* and the *New York Times* carried the story (January 17, 1986) as did *Newsweek* (January 27, 1986). The *Globe* did a feature on Cicely Tyson's transformation into a bag lady (February 11, 1986). About one hundred homeless people were hired as extras for the film (*USA Today*, January 17, 1986).

The CCNV repeated its "Alternative State of the Union" event. At the actual State of the Union address, the president had brought up homelessness by pointing out and publicly honoring Trevor Ferrell, an audience member especially invited to attend. The thirteen-year-old had been originally profiled in the *Times* at age eleven when he had started to actively help homeless people (March 12, 1984). Eventually, his family helped him open a homeless shelter in Philadelphia called "Trevor's Place" (*NYT*, September 12, 1984). Reagan now pointed him out as an example of the success of local efforts to aid the homeless. This attempt to localize the issue backfired in several media outlets. Colman McCarthy reported that Reagan was giving young Trevor a very cynical message—that he should continue to do his part while Reagan continued to ignore the plight of the poor (*WP*, February 23, 1986). More humorously, cartoonist Toles working for the *Buffalo News* had a four-frame strip on Trevor and the president. The second-to-last frame showed Reagan at his speech saying, "Trevor supplies the love, inspiration and hard work." In the last frame, the president says, "We supply the homeless." This cartoon was reprinted in the *Post* (February 15, 1986). At the end of January, *People* magazine did an extensive cover story about homeless people around the nation (January 27, 1986).

At the same time, several of Hollywood's comic notables were gearing up for *Comic Relief*, a show produced by HBO. Its proceeds would be donated to homeless people. Whoopi Goldberg, Billy Crystal, Harold Ramis, and Robin Williams all donated their time (*Washington Times*, January 15, 1986). The show aired live in Los Angeles on March 29 and was expected to raise about $2 million for the homeless, money that would be distributed through the Robert Wood Johnson Foundation (*Newsday*, March 12; *USA Today*, March 13, 1986). When the Reagan administration would not give Mitch all the funding he needed for the shelter renovation, Snyder publicized that he would "turn to Hollywood" for the remaining $2.5 million (*WP*, March 18, 1986).

In February, Hands Across America started to get organized. The idea was to raise money by convincing six million people to pay $10 each to stand with fellow Americans and link hands from one end of the nation to another for the hungry and homeless. The event's organizers hoped that "the chain will amount to more than financial success—that for one brief, stunning moment Americans will coalesce around an issue of surprising national concern," commented *Newsweek* (February 10, 1986). In April, Snyder decided he would participate in the event (*Globe*, April 15, 1986).

On May 12, the film entitled "Samaritan: The Mitch Snyder Story" was shown at a "fundraiser gala and preview" at Washington's National Theatre. Tickets ranged from $50 to $5,000 and the event was sold out. Later, celebrities and the press toured the shelter. Before the film and tour there was a dinner for the celebrities, the $5,000-level donors, and Snyder. Afterward, a reception was held and copies of the Hombs and Snyder book *Homeless in America* were sold. Many notables attended these events (*WP*, May 13, 1986). Several days later when the film was shown on CBS, Colman McCarthy (*WP*, May 18, 1986) liked it but the *Post*'s film reviewer reported "a listless and bland" Sheen as Snyder (May 19, 1986). *USA Today*, however, headlined "Sheen Makes a Good 'Samaritan'" (May 19, 1986). The *Times* lauded the production for a few "uncompromising moments" but said that the film could not completely shed television's "uplift machine" and that too many problems were resolved too completely (*NYT*, May 19, 1986). Whatever was said, the film received quite a bit of press coverage.

On Memorial Day 1986, the Hands Across America event was held. The line twisted through 4,150 miles of America and included "the rich, the poor and the homeless, movie stars and public officials" (*NYT*, May 26, 1986). There were gaps in the line but thousands joined in. Mitch Snyder, however, was not one of them. He and other members of the CCNV were in Lafayette Park forming an alternative "protest line." The reason was the last-minute decision by Ronald and Nancy Reagan to join in the event from the porch of the White House, a decision prompted by the insistence of their daughter Maureen. She had talked her parents into it after White House aides had originally rejected the idea as logistically problematic. Reagan said he had agreed to participate because "it was a uniquely American way to help our fellow man" (*Washington Times*, May 26, 1986).

Protesters shouted "What about tomorrow?" to demonstrate their concern that the one-time event would not result in a sustained commitment to help the nation's hungry and homeless, according to the *Post*. More importantly, however, they protested the president's participation in the event when at the same time he was "doing nothing to help the situation" (*WP*, May 26, 1986). Indeed, the event happened while the Reagan administration had yet to release a cent of the promised $5 million to repair the CCNV shelter. Later, it was revealed that the event collected $24.5 million, only $16 million of which went to charity. The rest went to pay expenses such as liability insurance and fund-raising costs (*Washington Times*, August 26, 1986). Many people had not sent in their promised donations; others had joined at the last minute and had not pledged anything (*NYT*, August 31, 1986). "It was a lot of publicity hype," complained the founder of Habitat for Humanity (*Washington Times*, August 26, 1986).

The CCNV staged two media events later in the year. The first was a protest held after Thanksgiving, which that year was held in front of the Capitol Building to emphasize the need for congressional action on behalf of the homeless. The protest demanded that Congress pass emergency legislation, which would provide funding for homelessness-related services (*Washington Times*, November 27, 1986, and see above). The second was a statue placed on the Capitol grounds. The life-sized sculpture depicted a homeless family in a nativity-like grouping. Below the figures it read, "And Still There Is No Room at the Inn" (*WP*, November 29, 1986). After a legal battle, the CCNV was granted permission to display the statue as part of a holiday season vigil for the homeless (*WP*, November 29, 1986). It was later removed and relocated to the Washington Project for the Arts after House leaders agreed to introduce federal homelessness legislation (*WP*, January 15, 1987).

In January 1987, Martin Sheen returned to the capital and spent a night "on the grates" with Snyder. He was in Washington to lobby congressional members to pass federal homelessness legislation and attract publicity for the issue (*Baltimore Sun, Philadelphia Inquirer,* January 15, 1987). He also lent his talents to a production of "Voices from the Street," an original play by Susan Goldman and local playwright Gary Bonasorte. Folk singer and activist Pete Seeger wrote songs and sang for the March 4 performance (*WP,* February 20, 1987). It was performed as part of the lobbying effort for the congressional bill (*WP,* January 15, 1987). Sheen and Snyder additionally organized "the Grate American Sleepout." The event was held on March 3, 1987. Marion Barry, Sheen and Snyder, actors Brian Dennehy and Terry Moore, Representative Joseph Kennedy (D-Mass.) and his wife, Representative John Conyers (D-Mich.), and House Majority Whip Tony Coelho (D-Calif.) were among those who slept out to emphasize the need for immediate congressional action on homelessness (*USA Today,* March 3, 1987). The sleepout was widely covered in the media (*Boston Globe, Evening Sun, Philadelphia Inquirer, WP, Washington Times, USA Today,* March 4; *New York Post, NYT, Philadelphia Inquirer, Wall Street Journal,* March 5, 1987). It was the last major media event before Congress passed legislation on homelessness.

NATIONAL POLICY FORMATION

There is certainly an argument to be made that policies initiated by the Reagan administration caused homelessness more than they ameliorated it.[3] Here, however, I am interested in examining what responses were elicited from the federal government as claimsmaking about homelessness continued to persist and claimsmakers continued to insist that it was a problem of national scope and importance. Several early Reagan policies to deal with homelessness were mentioned in previous chapters. First, the administration relegated homelessness to the Federal Emergency Management Agency (FEMA), which philosophically defined homelessness as something akin to a natural disaster. Its victims were believed to be temporarily dislocated in much the same way that flood or hurricane victims are. Second, the funding FEMA received to deal with homelessness was one-time emergency infusions of cash ($50 million and $70 million in budget years 1984 and 1985, respectively) (Ropers 1985). There were no plans to repeat even this one-time appropriation in 1986. This again emphasized a lack of commitment to homelessness as a social problem. Rather, homelessness was viewed as a temporary crisis. Or at least, that was what the administration was publicly willing to admit about it. Third, when pressed for federal shelter, the Reagan administration offered unused buildings on military bases. Given that bases are typically located far from urban areas, transporting homeless people there and keeping them housed and fed would present logistical nightmares to any charitable group or local government agency that undertook to do so. This invites speculation that this policy was offered cynically in full knowledge that it did not provide any viable solution to urban homelessness. By early 1987, three years after the project began, when the National Coalition for the Homeless released a study on the subject, only eight of six hundred sites identified had been converted to shelters (*USA Today*, January 15, 1987). Only $2 million of the $9 million allocated for the program had been used.

A fourth policy, the increased distribution of surplus foods, was undertaken only under pressure from activists and both Democratic and Republican members of Congress. Given the other actions of the secretary of HHS, Margaret Heckler's genuine desire to make a gesture probably supplied the motivation to collect and distribute surplus military food during this same period. But it was at best only a gesture, not a policy that would mitigate hunger. A more promising initiative was that a Task Force on Hunger and Homelessness was created within HHS at the end of 1983. According to one policy analyst, however, the task force proceeded on the assumptions that "(1) homelessness is essentially a local problem, and (2) new federal programs for the homeless are not the answer" (Ropers 1985).

I tend to take a kinder view of the efforts of Heckler, Susan Baker, Vieth, and others involved in the task force. At least at first there were indications that HHS was interested in federal policymaking around hunger and homelessness. The "model federal shelter" idea originated in the department, as did the military surplus giveaway. Directives from higher up that continued to insist on local and private solutions later apparently overrode these initiatives—except in the case of the CCNV shelter of course.

The HUD estimate of homelessness can also be considered policymaking of a sort. By documenting that homelessness affected very few Americans, the study could be used to justify the administration's desire to portray homelessness as a local problem that should rightfully be handled by local entities, preferably private charities. Indeed, "It's not a federal problem" could summarize the Reagan administration's policy position toward both hunger and homelessness through 1984. Yet the McKinney Act was passed. The remaining section explores how national-level policy evolved from a makeshift series of small emergency measures, many of them granted only under pressure to a comprehensive bill that set up a federal infrastructure for handling homelessness and allocated over $1 billion in federal revenues. I argue that "persistence" especially the efforts to fund the CCNV shelter and the "strange glamorization" of the issue played important roles in determining how federal homeless policy became possible.

FRIENDS IN HIGH PLACES

As I have detailed in previous chapters, a number of Democrats and a few Republicans in the House and Senate did express concern over hunger and homelessness. Even if some of the concern expressed by Democrats was more about embarrassing the president than it was genuine feeling for the plight of homeless people, congressional concern drove the issue forward. In 1982 Congress held its first hearings on homelessness, thus legitimating federal curiosity about the issue. A second round of hearings was held in the newly opened Federal City College Building CCNV shelter in early 1984. Other members of Congress had shown up to support CCNV activities in the early years, among them Senator Edward Kennedy (D-Mass.) and Henry Gonzalez (D-Tex.). These and other congressional figures would later help ensure that something was done about homelessness at the federal level.

In early 1985, the House Government Operations Committee declared that homelessness should be declared a "national emergency" (*WP*, April 20, 1985). This statement was based on a report prepared for the committee by a coalition of charities that received federal funding. The report concluded that the number of people seeking shelter had grown by 22 percent in the previous year and that shelters were operating at 92 percent of capacity on average. Congress had appropriated $210 million for food and service aid to charitable agencies that provided services to the homeless, but FEMA had declared it did not possess the expertise to run a permanent program. Moreover, the Reagan administration had not sought any funds for homelessness in the 1986 budget (*WP*, April 20, 1985).[4] Representative Ted Weiss (D-N.Y.), who headed the committee, called homelessness "a great unrecognized crisis" and one that required federal efforts.

Republican committee members responded that more community action was what was needed. Since the Democrats controlled the House (and therefore held the majority on the committee) the committee recommended that federal funds for food and shelter be sought for 1986 (*WP*, April 20, 1985). A week later the Heritage Foundation released its report on homelessness. The conservative think tank was called "the Reagan administration's private sector arm" by the liberal *Village Voice* (December 3, 1985) and this characterization was not without merit. The timing of the Heritage Foundation report suggests that it might have been an unofficial response to the House committee report. Unsurprisingly, the Heritage Foundation "recommended against any long-term federal spending to help the homeless, and suggested the problem could be handled better at the local level" (*WP,* April 28, 1985). Anna Kondratas, the foundation's homelessness policy analyst, blamed local city policies such as gentrification and rent control for homelessness. Rent control contributed to homelessness, the report stated, because it deterred developers from building new rental units. State deinstitutionalization policies were also to blame. Unemployment and federal budget cuts were not root causes of the problem and had just been cited by "city and state officials, in their own self-interest" (*WP,* April 28, 1985). And, of course, the report criticized the media's use of the CCNV's "two million" rather than the estimate produced by HUD.

In early 1986, the U.S. Conference of Mayors released its annual report on homelessness and hunger in large urban areas. They reported a 28 percent increase in requests for food and a 25 percent increase in requests for shelter in the twenty-five large cities included in the study. There was also an 85 percent increase in the number of homeless children reported. The report was released as the mayors gathered in Washington to lobby Congress to increase federal spending on homelessness and other urban issues (*WP,* January 22, 1986). The next month a *New York Times*/CBS nationwide poll showed that 46 percent of Americans thought that "not enough concern was being shown" for homeless people. This rose to 52 percent if the person questioned had had personal experience with seeing homeless people where he or she lived (*NYT,* February 3, 1986). The poll was limited in that it asked only if enough was being done *locally* for homeless people. No questions were posed about whether federal officials should increase their involvement in the issue. Moreover, when asked to choose from a list what they thought caused homelessness, respondents were given choices such as "unwillingness to work," "drug and alcohol abuse," and "bad economic luck," but *not* "loss of jobs" or even "lack of housing availability," according to a National Coalition for the Homeless critique of the study (National Coalition for the Homeless newsletter, March 1986). Still, even within this limited representation of the problem, a majority of respondents wanted policy toward the homeless to be improved.

Philadelphia, the city of brotherly love, was the location chosen for what was described as the "first national meeting of government leaders to specifically discuss the issue of homelessness" (*Philadelphia Inquirer,* February 15, 1986). Mayor Raymond Flynn of Boston, who had also been active in disputing the HUD figure, was the keynote speaker for the mid-February two-day event. The event did not get national press attention but did facilitate discussion among mayors about the "unfair burdens" placed on cities that provided aid for homeless people. A number of homeless people protested the event, particularly because no homeless people had been invited to testify (*Philadelphia Inquirer*, February 15, 1986).

Although the national press did not cover the event, Reagan administration officials may have been aware of it. A few days later, appearing before the House Budget Committee, Reagan's director of management and budget James C. Miller testified that the homeless were a problem for state and local governments, not for the federal government (*NYT*, February 19, 1986). He also stated that "there are a number of grants we have" to help local governments deal with the issue. When asked to name one, he cited the Community Services Block Grant program. But this program, a Democratic member of the committee stated, had once again been slated for elimination in the 1987 budget, which had been prepared under Miller's direction (see also *National Catholic Reporter*, February 28, 1986). The *Times* then went on to discuss the various statements made by top officials in the Reagan administration that, according to the paper, had "fueled criticism" of the administration. Reagan's "homeless by choice" statement and Attorney General Edwin Meese's inference that soup line attenders were just out for a free lunch were cited. The story was headlined "Homeless Are Not Duty of U.S., Reagan Aide Says" (*NYT*, February 19, 1986).

When Congress reconvened after its winter recess, the National Coalition for the Homeless was waiting with a legislative proposal entitled, "Homeless Persons' Survival Act of 1986" (National Coalition for the Homeless newsletter, March 1986). The preamble stated that homelessness could no longer be considered merely a local concern because in both size and scope it had grown beyond local governments' abilities to cope. The group was careful not to take sides on the numbers issue. It proposed first to address emergency needs for food, shelter, mental health care, and other emergencies. Second, it proposed measures to prevent homelessness by offering temporary aid to people facing an unexpected crisis. Third, it addressed what the group thought was the ultimate cause of homelessness, the lack of low-income housing. Representative Mickey Leland (D-Tex.) and Senator Albert Gore (D-Tenn.) sponsored the bill. The bill was a comprehensive statement about where the advocacy community thought homelessness legislation should be headed, stated attorney Maria Foscarinis, the head of the Washington office of the National Coalition for the Homeless. "Because the solutions cut across legislative committees and administrative departments, we expect to get it passed piece by piece rather than as a package deal," she continued (*Sojourners*, December 1986). In fact, part of the bill had passed in the last hours of the ninety-ninth Congress attached to an antidrug bill. These provisions allowed homeless people without an address to collect food stamps and also allowed homeless people to collect veterans' benefits, Social Security Disability, Supplemental Security Income, welfare, and Medicaid. An article on the provisions' implementation, however, noted that federal agencies were having trouble figuring out how to deliver these benefits to people without addresses. Foscarinis said her organization would push for "outreach programs" to hire social workers to seek out the homeless and ensure they were getting the benefits to which they were entitled (*Washington Times*, November 27, 1986).

The *Times* ran an article in March that documented the rise of "new homelessness," with special attention paid to the emergence of family homelessness as a problem. The article noted the rise in the cost of homes, the high levels at which mortgage interest rates remained (over 10 percent in late 1985), and the sharp decrease in new housing starts in the early 1980s. "The New Homelessness Has Its Roots in Economics," the paper stated flatly, and noted the Reagan administration's withdrawal of federal support for low- and moderate-income housing. Housing expert Chester Hartman was cited as arguing that without increased federal money the housing crisis would only continue to grow. Budget Director Miller's comment about homelessness not being a federal responsibility was repeated in the article (*NYT*, March 16, 1986). A few days later a Washington group announced that it would be forming a national union for the homeless (*Washington Times*, March 20, 1986). At the end of the month the Heritage Foundation's Anna Kondratas was given guest commentary space in the *Washington Times* (March 28 1986). She argued that homelessness had become a "fashionable" issue and that many myths were involved. She then detailed three "myths": that there were millions of homeless people, that homelessness was the result of Reagan budget cuts, and that the federal government was doing nothing about homelessness. She also reiterated her support for the HUD study and her views that local government policies were to blame for the rise in homelessness. As for the Reagan administration, "hundreds of millions of federal dollars were applied to the problems of the homeless every year through direct grants, federal emergency feeding programs, various block grants, and general revenue sharing" (*Washington Times*, March 28 1986). In addition "20 to 35 percent" of homeless people received direct assistance from various federal entitlement programs, Kondratas stated. She proceeded to attack Mitch Snyder and the HHS Task Force on Homelessness for supporting him. She even criticized the president for giving into Snyder's demands for $5 million to renovate the CCNV shelter, which she said would be siphoned off from other worthy HHS programs such as farm worker and other rural programs.

In April, the National Coalition for the Homeless held a joint conference with the American Planning Association to talk about "Progress to Date" (conference brochure, April 1986). The president's next contribution to the policy debate on hunger and homelessness came on the same day as actress Cicely Tyson and others testified at a Senate panel convened to consider the problem of hunger in America. Senator Kennedy (D-Mass.) and Representative Leon Panetta (D-Calif.) had recently introduced a $960 million bill to improve food and nutrition programs. Senate majority leader Bob Dole stated that he thought the $20.5 billion in U.S. food programs should be supplemented with local and state funds (*USA Today*, May 22, 1986). The president had a different opinion on hunger, however. Speaking before students from around the country gathered at the White House, the president proclaimed, "I don't believe there is anyone going hungry in America simply by reason of denial or lack of ability to feed them." Instead, he said, "Where there is hunger . . . you have to determine that that is probably because of a lack of knowledge on the part of the people as to what things are available" (*NYT*, May 22, 1986). There has been "about a three-times increase in private charity," Reagan stated. People, the president continued, are hungry because of "not knowing where or how to get this help." Also in the article, the *Times* reported that a recently released Harvard study had estimated that at least twenty million Americans were going hungry at least two days a month. Many other papers carried this story (*Daily News, Philadelphia Inquirer*, May 22, 1986).

On the same day, the *New York Times* ran a story that blamed budget cutbacks for the "wider crisis" of homelessness in the United States. An interfaith group, the Partnership for the Homeless, had released a study based on interviews with shelter providers in forty-two cities to reach this conclusion. The article also announced that the Senate Banking, Housing and Urban Affairs Committee had approved a bill that would provide for homelessness services for two years. In fiscal 1987, the bill authorized $73 million for emergency food and shelter and $50 million for demonstration shelter projects to be administered by HUD (*NYT*, May 22, 1986).

In September, the National Coalition for the Homeless held another two-day conference. This one was titled "America's Homeless: Strategies for National Solutions" (National Coalition for the Homeless brochure, September 26–28 1986). One of the many workshops was on "national legislation." Tireless attorney and advocate for the homeless Maria Foscarinis was the workshop coordinator. She stated that the Coalition was especially targeting for passage provisions of the previously introduced legislation that would prevent family homelessness. More than five hundred people from all over the nation attended the conference. In an echo of President Franklin Roosevelt's famous words, keynote speaker Mayor Flynn of Boston stated, "In the end governments will not be judged by their tax bills or balanced budget but by how they helped the least among us" (*Sojourners*, December 1986).

The CCNV wrote every member of Congress after the conference to urge them to act immediately on homelessness. "It is unconscionable that FEMA . . . has spent less money on homelessness in America in the past three years than the city of New York has spent on its homeless in just the past year," the letter read in part (CCNV letter to Congress members, September 29, 1986). The group continued its attack on the HUD study all through this period (*Washington Times*, October 15, 1986; and see Chapter 5). After Thanksgiving at the Capitol, Snyder organized a protest to demand federal legislation and stated that he would remain on Capitol Hill until Congress, which would convene again in January, passed emergency legislation providing more money to shelter and treat homeless people (*Washington Times*, November 27, 1986).

On December 13, a conference aimed at "social policy makers, social scientists and activists" took place at George Washington University in the District (brochure issued by the chair of the university's sociology department, December 1986). Participants included Snyder, Foscarinis, Hayes, and social scientists Richard Appelbaum, Elliot Liebow, Richard Ropers, and Peter Rossi, among others.

When House leaders came back to town in January they rapidly proposed a $500 million emergency package of aid which they hoped would reach homeless people by early spring. The CCNV and its homeless nativity statue were also at the Capitol. Though the original display and protest permit had expired December 30, the group had been granted reprieves by House leaders every day since. On January 9, 1987, the same day the legislation was announced, House Speaker Jim Wright (D-Tex.) also called Mitch Snyder to meet with him to let him know that the group could end its vigil and move its statue because Congress had acted. The bipartisan proposal included $170 million for emergency shelter, $100 million for family housing under the Section 8 rent subsidy program, $30 million for transitional housing, and $100 million for new health care programs for homeless people. It also contained funding to renovate federal buildings for shelters (*WP*, January 9, February 8, 1987). House Speaker Wright also made a publicized visit to the CCNV shelter, where he condemned Reagan administration inaction on the issue. Wright did acknowledge that the administration had proposed that $100 million be allocated to homelessness in the 1988 budget but argued that the House figure was "more realistic." The speaker said he was heartened that the president "at least recognized the reality and the importance of the problem" (*WP*, January 11, 1987). Wright, who had only been elected speaker a few days before, said that he was confident that the House bill, rather than the administration's budget proposal, would prevail. Sixty House members had signed on to become cosponsors of the bill and Speaker Wright made a commitment to "fast-track" the bill (CCNV letter urging supporters to call their legislators, January 21, 1987). When the bill was originally introduced by Representative Tom Foley (D-Wash.) it was termed the "Foley-McKinney Urgent Relief for the Homeless Act" (H.R. 558). Representative McKinney (R-Conn.) was one of six Republicans who originally signed on as a sponsor. Besides Foley and McKinney, Representative Mick Lowry (D-Wash.) also worked on the draft of the bill (*WP,* February 8, 1987). By the end of January, the bill had eighty-two cosponsors in the House, among them seven Republicans. The House passed a small bill ($50 million) granting the homeless immediate aid on January 27 (296–79) and the Senate followed shortly, with a margin of 77–6 (*National Catholic Reporter,* February 6, 1987), using funds transferred from FEMA's disaster relief allocation.

The *Times* announced, "A new issue has captured the attention of Congress" in an article describing the immediate homelessness aid bill and the larger one (February 7, 1987). Several factors were responsible for this new focus of attention on the issue, according to the paper. First, was Speaker Wright's "strong personal commitment" to the issue. Second, was "a heightened concern on the part of many Americans for the homeless." This concern seemed to extend right to the offices of Congress. A new group, "Hill Staffers for the Hungry and Homeless," had formed with the goal of collecting and distributing aid to the needy and organizing to volunteer to work in local shelters. Third were the efforts of lobbyists, such as Maria Foscarinis, who was quoted in the article. The CCNV was reported to have met with seventy-five legislators over the holiday break. Fourth was the combination of new leadership in the House combined with a return to Democratic control in the Senate. Even the reluctant president seemed to be coming around. The administration was said to have a "new willingness" to deal with the issue on the federal level and Mitch Snyder was quoted as saying, "We don't expect a veto of the homeless legislation now, although we would have a year ago" (*NYT,* February 7, 1987).

The following day Colman McCarthy discussed the new momentum in his *Post* column (February 8, 1987). He reported that Wright's strong commitment to the issue came in the wake of a visit to the CCNV shelter, one urged on him by Snyder. "The Speaker of the House didn't speak much in the poorhouse. Most first-time visitors don't. They gape, listen and wonder privately what kind of government and economy allow human beings to sink this low," said McCarthy (*WP,* February 8, 1987). At the shelter Wright did say that the proposed legislation amounted to $2 per American. "I just don't believe that the American people would turn their backs upon the needs of their fellow Americans for a clean and warm and safe place to spend the night for $2," said Wright. McCarthy concluded with the comment that if Wright were able pull this off, congressional members who had been elected during the Reagan era would be "in for a political first: voting for the poor and being on the winning side" (*WP*, February 8, 1987). The CCNV shelter held its grand reopening just two weeks later and on the eve of the House vote, the "Grate American Sleep Out" was held.

The bill, which had grown to $725 million to be spent over two years, was approved by the House on March 6, 1987, by a margin of 264–121. The *Times* stated that the Reagan administration "opposes the legislation but has not yet threatened a veto" (March 6, 1987). The Republican leader, Bob Michel (Ill.), had tried to force Democrats to require that the funds for the bill be offset by reductions in spending elsewhere. His proposal was narrowly defeated by a vote of 207–203. "This is a national problem that needs immediate local action," said the House minority leader (*Wall Street Journal*, March 6, 1987). Representative McKinney (R-Conn.) came to the rhetorical aid of the Democrats. " 'What are your priorities?' he asked his colleagues. 'Are you for the people or are you for the budget?' " (*NYT*, March 6, 1987). Many other amendments to the bill were attempted. Among those rejected was one sponsored by Representative Tom DeLay (R-Tex.) that would have mandated an audit of the CCNV shelter (*Wall Street Journal*, *WP*, March 6, 1987). "The Senate is likely to propose a smaller spending package, which would also be easier to sell the Reagan administration," stated the *Christian Science Monitor* (March 9, 1987).

Representative Mickey Leland (D-Tex.), the original sponsor of the National Coalition bill, wrote of his night on the grates, which he and other Congress members agreed to do "because Mitch Snyder invited us." The Congress member noted that Snyder had been sleeping on a grate since Thanksgiving to get Congress to act and indicated that he had respect for his "nonviolent methods." But the explosion of homelessness is not, the representative opined, "an artifact of the media or Mitch Snyder." Instead, he said it had been documented by countless studies, most importantly that of the U.S. Conference of Mayors, which had reported marked increases in homelessness every year since 1983. He concluded with noting that the nation's poor had been suffering from "draconian cuts in programs that formerly carried them through bad times." It is better, the House member stated, "to ameliorate their situation bit by bit than not at all: $500 million is more than symbolism" (*WP*, March 9, 1987).

The Senate introduced the bill on March 24, 1987. Senate Majority

Leader Robert Byrd (D-W.Va.) promised to make the bill's passage a legislative priority. The bill was cosponsored by Minority Leader Bob Dole (R-Kans.) and would authorize only $500 million for fiscal 1987. The bill would also create the "Interagency Council on the Homeless," Byrd reported, which would be charged with coordinating federal assistance to state and local programs and with compiling an annual report to the president about the problem. Byrd promised to get the full Senate to take up the legislation before its Easter recess began on April 11. The Senate's version of the bill expanded HUD programs for the poor, required states to submit plans for how they would deal with homelessness, and authorized additional funding for emergency food and shelter programs under FEMA. It also would improve access to food stamps, expand grants for health-care delivery for homeless people, require states to provide public education for homeless children, expand mental-health services, and establish a demonstration job-training program for homeless people (*WP*, March 24, 1987). The Senate bill was almost waylaid by a last-minute attempt on the part of Senator Gordon Humphrey (R-N.H.) to force the Senate to repeal its recent $12,100 pay raise to itself. Senator Byrd accused Humphrey of pointing "a killer-amendment gun" at badly needed legislation (*WP*, April 9, 1987). After two days of wrangling, this amendment was brushed aside and the Senate passed a $423 million aid package by 85–12. The bill then went to conference with the House (*WP*, *USA Today*, April 10, 1987). The bill would provide $37 million for New York, the city with the nation's largest emergency shelter program (*Newsday*, April 10, 1987).

On July 24, 1987, President Ronald Reagan signed the new law. It was the first comprehensive effort by Congress to address the problem of homelessness, the *Times* reported (July 24, 1987). The bill authorized slightly more than $1 billion in federal aid for homelessness-related programs and services. The president signed the legislation in the evening with no fanfare, which an anonymous White House official stated was to demonstrate the president's "lack of enthusiasm" for the bill (*NYT*, July 24, 1987). The bill was named for Representative Stewart B. McKinney (R-Conn.) who had died from an AIDs-related illness a few months before the bill was signed. The bill authorized $430 million in aid for fiscal year 1987 and an additional $616 million for 1988. Provisions included the formation of the Interagency Council made up of fifteen heads of federal agencies, $220 million over two years for emergency shelter programs to be distributed by HUD, funds for job training and education of homeless adults, and money for insuring that homeless children receive an adequate education. Services for chronically mentally ill homeless people were also funded by the legislation, as were drug and alcohol treatment programs and health care. The new law also required HUD to assess federal buildings for their usefulness for homeless shelters.

The advocates, represented in the *Times* by Maria Foscarinis, had this to say about the bill: "The new law will provide material aid that is badly needed. It also represents an important recognition of the federal responsibility to deal with homelessness. But it is only a first step. There must be longer-term efforts to address the causes of the problem, as well as the symptoms" (July 24, 1987).

SOCIAL PROBLEMS OUTCOMES

When has social problems claimsmaking achieved success? A problem can be said to be successfully constructed if there is widespread recognition of the problem as a serious concern. This might be evidenced by notable amounts of reporting on the topic in the news media and by direct public indications such as polls and the results of referendums. An added indication is that a number of public officials speak out frequently about the issue, thus further legitimating the problem as a public concern. Acceptance by the public, by important purveyors of public information, and by the political authority structure that something is indeed a serious social ill marks the successful construction of the problem.

Claimsmakers, however, construct social problems in order that something might be done about them. If we follow claimsmakers' purposes for their activities to their conclusion, we need to examine what constitutes a social problems outcome. In their landmark work, *Constructing Social Problems* (1977), Spector and Kitsuse discuss several "natural histories" or patterns that social problems go through over time. Blumer (1971), for example, cites five stages that a social problem goes through: (1) emergence, (2) legitimation, (3) mobilization, (4) formation of an official plan, and (5) implementation of the plan. Other authors have suggested more or less complicated versions of these same basic steps in the career of a social problem. I believe all these descriptions of social problems histories tend to presume too much rational behavior. Social life is too complex and is shaped too much by emotion, coincidence, impulse, interests, power struggles, and other nonrational behavior for social problems histories to unfold so straightforwardly. Nevertheless, claimsmakers do have outcomes in mind when they undertake construction activities and often these are framed as ameliorative actions taken by "officials." In other words, though the road to social problems outcomes is perhaps quite a bit more rocky and winding than Blumer would have us believe, claimsmakers very often define the formation and implementation of an official plan as what they are after when they undertake to construct a social problem. In general, the outcome desired for most social problems by most claimsmakers is "ameliorative action." What actions constitute satisfying this claimsmaker demand depends on the nature of the problem, the perception of the remedy, and at what level the remedy must take place in order for claimsmakers to feel satisfied that their problem has been recognized, legitimated, and dealt with.

In this case, claimsmakers from all quarters of the iron quadrangle eventually settled on the idea that only consistent government recognition and action at the national level would suffice to deal with homelessness. The provisions of the McKinney Act perhaps satisfied none of the claimsmakers completely, and to many the legislation could only be viewed, as Foscarinis noted, "as a first step." Still, it was an impressive achievement by any measure. First, it was an undeniable victory on symbolic grounds. The U.S. Congress had agreed, by large majorities in both houses, that homelessness was a serious social problem, one worthy of investing more than a $1 billion in. Second, despite Reagan's obvious "lack of enthusiasm" and reluctance to sign the bill, he nevertheless did sign it. Claimsmakers could rightfully state that they had marshaled enough other Americans and power brokers to their cause to force the president to recognize a social problem against his will. Furthermore, at least some of the provisions of the bill gave official recognition to homelessness as a *housing* problem and one that could be prevented through federal rent subsidies. This was a symbolic victory indeed over an administration that had vowed to get the federal government out of the housing business.

The material victory was less impressive. By the time the bill was signed, New York City alone was spending $200 million a year to shelter its homeless population. One billion to cover the entire nation would not by any means ameliorate homelessness. Nevertheless, claimsmakers did win one substantial concession—the Interagency Council demanded by the Senate meant that a federal bureaucratic structure would be put in place to deal with the issue in the future. No longer would homelessness be treated as a "natural" and temporary disaster under the purview of FEMA. The McKinney Act acknowledged homelessness as a "permanent" social problem, one in need of ongoing federal attention. Though surely advocates had desired a "cure" for homelessness rather than mere palliative treatment, the act did recognize homelessness as a serious and ongoing social ill. If the government lacked the will to end homelessness, at least in the aftermath of the McKinney Act it was permanently on the social problems agenda of the federal government. This portended ongoing funding to deal with the problem.

If the McKinney Act was both a symbolic and material victory for claimsmakers, how did the actions of claimsmakers manage to produce such an outcome? In the remainder of this chapter I consider claims-makers actions within the contexts they confronted, shaped, and were shaped by as they proceeded from the problem acceptance stage to "doing something" about homelessness.

THE ENVIRONMENTAL CONTEXT

There were many environmental aspects of context, from local political-authority structures and the economy to the weather that had mattered in shaping homelessness as a national-level social problem. Since policy-making is a political activity, perhaps the political-authority aspects of context were the most pertinent in the outcome phase of homelessness as a social problem. Other aspects were pertinent, however, and deserve comment. The weather, for example, continued to act in its role as terrible resource. Winter brought exposure deaths and these always served to remind all concerned of the ultimate cost of doing nothing.

The generally weak economy in the first years of the Reagan admin-istration and continued high rates of unemployment also were resources in helping to ensure that homeless policy would be forthcoming. Many of the nation's large cities suffered high rates of unemployment resulting in an upsurge in demand for antipoverty measures and the funds with which to finance them. The *Times* often called for increased federal aid to deal with the results of economic downturn in the city, while the *Post* took up this position for the nation at large. Individuals, too, of course noticed the weak economy and often were affected by it. In the context of homelessness this produced (as is further discussed below) fear that perhaps homelessness was not an abstract phenomenon but a looming possibility. The economy then continued to provide a backdrop of vul-nerability against which homelessness played itself out as "worst case scenario." This helped to generate sustained interest in the issue and a desire for something to be done for those most vulnerable to destitution.

Political Contexts

The District of Columbia

One feature that became quite important in the outcome stage of the construction process is the political structure of the District and its unique relationship to the federal government. At this point, the District of Columbia had only been operating under "home rule" for a bit over a decade. This arrangement gave District representatives the authority, function, and powers of state officials without control over revenue and its distribution, which remained controlled by Congress. In the early 1980s District voters had approved statehood for "New Columbia" as it was to be called and a bill had been introduced in Congress to grant statehood to the District (http://www.narpac.org). Because of the flux in Washington's political arrangements, the extent of the District's autonomy was still in the process of being delineated. The House Committee on the District still had influence over how the city was run and control of its budget. This made for productive confusion in the case of homelessness.

Since the District was of uncertain legal status, so too, it could be argued, were its citizens. The status of the District in relationship to the federal government made it possible for Mayor Barry to argue that homeless people in the District were a "federal" population and should be cared for with federal funds. This argument was largely symbolic and was meant to remind the Reagan administration of the promised $5 million for the CCNV shelter. Still, because of the District's special status as a federal protectorate of sorts, it was an argument that could be made about Washington and nowhere else. Since the federal government held the District's purse strings, when Mayor Barry pleaded poverty, it was the federal government that had to take the blame for a budget that did not allow for the adequate care of all the city's homeless. The District's close relationship with the federal government also made all of Washington's problems de facto national problems because of congressional oversight. This gave District citizens and their leaders accessibility to several members of Congress on a regular basis. Mitch Snyder, for example, used the fact of congressional oversight of District matters to plead the case for the CCNV shelter remaining open in front of the Committee on the District. All in all, the District's special status helped to highlight homeless people as a potential federal responsibility.

Divisions in the Federal Government

During the Reagan administration Democrats always remained in the majority of at least one of the houses of Congress. This made the Reagan administration unable to pursue its policies with the carte blanche approach that is possible when the legislative and executive branches are of the same party. Homelessness was an issue made for the Democratic party. Despite the push to balance the budget by cutting federal spending as the Reaganauts sought to do, it could be easily argued that doing it on the backs of the truly destitute was going too far. There was a solid Democratic constituency for welfare state policies, enlarged in this case by how extreme homelessness was as a social condition.

From early on in the problem construction process, homelessness and hunger were appealing to some, especially liberal Democrats such as Ted and Joseph Kennedy, Henry Gonzales, and Pete Stark. As the issue became more prominent such Democratic luminaries as Tip O'Neil, Jim Wright, and Robert Byrd also saw fit to lend their support to the issue. As Reagan successfully turned poor mothers into "welfare queens" the Democratic party sought a way to retain poverty policy as "its" issue. Homelessness and hunger presented good opportunities to retake some of the turf lost through Reagan's incessant and increasingly persuasive arguments to the public that only those who worked deserved a slice of the American pie. The denouement of homelessness as a social problem—the McKinney Act—became overwhelmingly popular with Democratic members of both houses of Congress and was actively pushed by the leadership in both houses as well. Though the Democrats had seen retrenchment on most poverty-related programs through the 1980s, this new area, at least, could be one of expansion.

The Republican party was far from united behind Reagan's ideas about the poor. Many congressional Republicans were moderates, used to voting for the types of bipartisan antipoverty legislation that had marked the 1960s and 1970s when their party had often been in the minority in Congress (Katz 1989). Though they would become more so as the decade progressed, Republicans during the first half of the 1980's were not uniformly dedicated to erasing the Democratic approach to poverty policy that had been ascendant since FDR's creation of the American welfare state. This allowed for some Republican-initiated bills (such as Dole's to distribute surplus food) and for cosponsorship and small amounts of Republican support on the McKinney Act and other homelessness-related legislation. It was clear that some Republican members of Congress had personal sympathies for the issue during this period. These sentiments aided in preserving the remnants of bipartisanship over this element of poverty policy.

Moreover, there was dissension within the Reagan administration itself. As is often the case, the social welfare divisions (such as HHS) of the administration were filled with people a good deal more liberal in their thinking about poverty policy than the president. Beyond any personal sentiments about the efficacy of retaining or expanding certain portions of the previous decades' poverty policies, from an institutional standpoint HHS would only see its purview and its power shrink if the programs it administered did not expand. And during the Reagan years most programs administered by HHS experienced substantial funding cuts. For that reason alone, HHS could be expected to be in favor of a federal role in dealing with homelessness. Beyond this, however, were the personalities of Margaret Heckler, Harvey Vieth, and Susan Baker. All of these people, for different reasons, had backgrounds of concern for those less fortunate. To the extent these people took initiative on the issue, and they often did during these years, their approaches could be viewed as profoundly different from the president's. Together these motivations inclined HHS to call for an expanded federal involvement in the issue. This can be seen in the formation of a policy task force in the agency, the idea of federal shelters, the intervention with the GSA to secure the Federal City College Building for CCNV use, and the reallocation of military surplus foods to food banks. Although these were modest and limited policy initiatives, even they went further then the Reagan White House desired.[5] The uneven tempo of the Reagan approach to homelessness during most of his administration can be attributed to dissension within the ranks that was eventually "corrected" when the upper echelons of the administration attended to homelessness as an issue. The president's policies toward homelessness only seemed to align with the sentiments of HHS when they were made under duress (such as from Mitch Snyder's fasts).

The Failure of the "Anybody But Mitch" Policy

Another interesting twist in the Reagan administration's approach to homelessness was the decision to attempt to retreat from federal involvement in homelessness through the "ABM" (Anybody But Mitch) approach. It had been hoped that the D.C. Coalition for the Homeless could have acted as a transitional group while the federal government extricated itself from direct federal involvement with homelessness and from any continuing relationship at all with the CCNV. Where once the administration had been so stingy, first promising and then withholding funds to repair the CCNV shelter, the administration was very quick to offer the D.C. Coalition for the Homeless $3.7 million even though the group had little experience with managing a project of the size envisioned. This planned retreat from federal policy involvement failed, however, for several reasons.

First, there was Mayor Barry's refusal to cooperate in the plan. The plan had been hastily put together and Barry no doubt realized that if the federal government were successful in withdrawing from the issue, the mayor's office would be left to manage whatever remained of the ABM plan with insufficient funds. Supporting the original bargain made between the Reagan administration and the CCNV was one technique for wresting more federal funds while delaying the need for building an extensive infrastructure to manage the problem at the city level. Second, there was the CCNV's persistence, an attitude easy for the group to maintain because of its thorough knowledge of the service-providing community, the costs of providing services, local politics, and the numbers of those in need of assistance. At this time, Mitch Snyder and his compatriots were the only experienced service providers around and they had an operational shelter. The CCNV well knew the inadequacies of the plan to open and close many temporary shelters and the mayor could be counted on to have problems with this federal attempt to disown the problem. The group's long and active involvement with the issue should have signaled to the administration that it would not give up the issue easily. Nor did it. Finally, the administrative limitations of the D.C. Coalition for the Homeless helped bring down the federal withdrawal plan. The rapid timeframe the plan demanded and the inexperience of the Coalition did not make for a happy combination. Failure would have been likely for any group charged with carrying out such a hastily contrived policy. Between the failings of HHS's preferred shelter providers, the intransigence of the mayor, and the persistence of the CCNV, the HHS plan was derailed. And indeed it was quite unrealistic for the federal government to think it could wash itself clean of what had become a prominent social issue.

An Alliance of Concerned Officials

In a certain sense the drama played out between the CCNV and Mayor Barry on the one side and the federal government on the other was a microcosm of how homelessness had taken shape around the nation for several years. The country was in an economic slump during the formative years of homelessness as a social problem. This meant local tax bases in larger cities across the nation had shrunk. Many mayors were facing nearly unprecedented rates of poverty, unemployment, and homelessness with a shrinking budget with which to deal with these ills. It is not surprising under these circumstances that the U. S. Conference of Mayors was one of the groups most concerned that the federal government take some role in easing the problem of homelessness. Like Mayor Barry, mayors all over the nation wanted federal funds to help them manage whatever emergency programs they had cobbled together to stem the rising tide of homelessness. Mayor Barry may have had some unusual cards to play because of his unique relationship (both geographically and politically) with the federal government. But like with other mayors, the bottom line was cities needed federal funding assistance if they were to deal with homelessness during a time of economic uncertainty. This made mayors the natural allies of advocates for the homeless, who wanted federal action on this issue for moral reasons (which of course some mayors may have shared). Governors were not far behind in desiring federal aid for homelessness. Thus, local and state officials and issue advocates could unite with federal lawmakers who saw homelessness as an issue that would further their interests. This proved a formidable coalition, especially when it was aided by celebrities and the media.

THE INTERPRETIVE CONTEXT

As the *Post* pointed out in the editorial cited at the beginning of this chapter, homelessness as a social problem had undergone a "strange glamorization" on its way to becoming an important national social problem. Had homelessness had somehow become romanticized, alluring, fascinating, and exciting as a social problem? Although the *Post* grumbled about this fact, their record of coverage of the issue suggests that they did not escape the issue's allure nor did the many other national and local media outlets that continued to give the issue regular and often prominent coverage. In this section I discuss in what sense can we conceive of homelessness as "glamorous" and how this shaped the outcome of the issue in the McKinney Act.

Homeless People and Their Stories

Homelessness, of course, has a long history of being linked with romanticized visions of rail-riding hobos, tramps, and mysterious travelers. Many of the profiles of "bag ladies" and "bums" in the media during the early 1980s stressed their unique attributes and modes of making ends meet. Homeless people were often portrayed as "characters" living interesting lives, often lives touched by mystery or tragedy.[6] Another early motif was of the "wino," "crazy," or "odd bird." These were pitiful, and at times perhaps contemptible people but people not much like the rest of us. As the decade progressed these earlier images gave way first to "street people," who, as Spencer (1996) notes, often were associated with mental illness and looked upon with fear, and later to "homeless people." Homeless people were at times portrayed as "normal" Americans who had somehow "lost everything." Young men were roaming the nation in their cars looking for work, entire families were ensconced in "tent cities." This latter group, especially when children were included, was often portrayed as homeless through no fault of its own.

All of these images have their allure. The early images of "bums" and "bag ladies" interest us because these people have lived their lives so differently from the norm. "Crazies" and "winos" are compelling in their pitiable, despicable, and strange behavior. Street people sometimes instill fear—another type of allure. And as the image of a homeless person became normalized as someone who had just lost a job or had had a bit of bad luck, homelessness incited the kind of awful fascination that occurs when this person could be your relative, your neighbor, or yourself. The diverse group of people who were clumped together under the rubric of "homeless" for a wide variety of reasons had their own kind of "strange glamour." This helped draw claimsmakers and supporters to the issue.

The Hero of Homelessness

A second aspect of the glamorization of homelessness was, of course, Mitch Snyder himself. Whatever else Snyder added to the issue, it is indisputable that he added the allure of total dedication. Some people interpreted Snyder's unwavering interest in the issue and his willingness to go the distance to get what he wanted as some sort of power or ego trip. Others saw him as Gandhi-like. In either case, Snyder was a singular individual, one driven to take extreme actions such as being arrested, living on the grates, or starving himself in order to achieve his goals. This attitude proved quite alluring to the media. Snyder was a hero for the homeless or a self-serving obnoxious attention seeker. But in either construction, his intensity and his actions created glamour. Snyder could fascinate even such hardened reporters as Mike Wallace of "60 Minutes." Snyder, his group, and their actions added much appeal to the issue.

The Glamor of Drama

The press as has been discussed thrives on drama. Drama in itself is glamorous because it evokes strong emotions and creates interest through being different from everyday life. Thanks mostly to the CCNV, homelessness as an issue produced many dramatic moments. Several times a year, the group would embark on a media-friendly campaign that was both photogenic and dramatic. Though it is important not to overstate this attribute for a poverty-related social problem, homelessness had more than its share of drama attached to it. Social problems concerning poverty must be covered in the media, particularly in cities with large Democratic majorities such as New York and Washington. A major paper's obligation's to provide balanced coverage and satisfy constituency demands requires that some attention be paid to these issues. But dramatic accounts are not often available and press accounts of poverty mostly consist of policy discussions and occasional profiles of afflicted people. Dramatic activities such as the sit-ins, arrests, prayer vigils, and fasts provided local papers from around the nation with photos of drama and a relatively attractive way to cover a typically unexciting topic. The drama surrounding homelessness helped to make it unusually alluring for a poverty-related issue, thereby providing an added incentive to press coverage.

Confrontation is one particularly alluring form of drama to the press. Again, homelessness provided plenty of overt confrontations. In New York in the early years, Mayor Koch was confronted by homeless advocates and he traded accusations with state officials over who was responsible for the city's homeless. The CCNV at first confronted local religious and District government officials. Later the group kept up a nearly constant confrontation with the president, by publicly fasting to get him to change his mind, by sitting outside the White House waiting to meet with him, by holding Thanksgiving soup lines in front of his mansion. At various other times the CCNV confronted the District police, the Park Police, the courts, the GSA, HHS, and Mayor Barry among others. These acts of nonviolent confrontation, as they always were, added glamor to the issue because they increased excitement with the potential that something interesting or important was or would be happening. Moreover, these confrontations always had an element of David and Goliath embedded in them, and as this biblical story suggests, it has long been appealing to people to watch to see if a "little person" can use pluck, courage, and wit to overcome a superior force. Such were the glamorous motifs of the drama of homelessness.

Celebrity Glamor

From the early days of problem construction, the CCNV sought to involve political celebrities in the issue. Members of Congress and other highly placed officials dived into dumpsters, ate salvaged food, toured caves of surplus food, and attended hearings, soup lines, tours, and parties at the CCNV shelter. The involvement of these political celebrities helped to increase press coverage and therefore the public profile of homelessness. And gradually, Snyder himself became a celebrity and one of a very unusual kind. Over the years he was profiled in many of the nation's newspapers and magazines. It was not until he became a subject of "60 Minutes" in 1984, however, that Snyder garnered the attention of

Hollywood. The "60 Minutes" profile had led directly to talking about making a film for television. This project in turn made Snyder and his issue more visible to Hollywood. Martin Sheen and Cicely Tyson, of course, became intimately familiar with the issue during their work on the film. Both went on to be volunteer lobbyists for homelessness and hunger (*USA Today*, May 22, 1986). Dick Gregory and other liberal film and television stars also became involved, some as a direct consequence of Sheen's urging. Valerie Harper (a costar on the "Mary Tyler Moore Show") was photographed talking with Mitch Snyder (*National Catholic Reporter*, May 23, 1986). Brian Dennehy (soon to become ubiquitous on television and in film) spent a night on the streets with Snyder. Other actors such as comedians Robin Williams and Whoopi Goldberg added their cachet to the issue by donating the proceeds from a special television show to the cause ("Comic Relief"). Still other celebrities attended the Hands Across America event. Celebrities added their special glamour to the issue, making homelessness even more media worthy and making the issue known to a wide general audience usually concerned with the goings-on of the stars.

An Issue of Broad Appeal

Although homelessness was not and could never become a depoliticized issue that everyone could get behind (such as childhood cancer or birth defect prevention), homelessness did become an issue imbued with a certain "strange glamour." For some, allowing destitution to become so absolute and visible was an extreme step that civil society could not permit. For others, religious or humanitarian impulses prompted involvement in the issue. For still others, homelessness fueled fears and imaginings about daily life undone and this provided a motivation to intercede. A few saw ways to press political agendas through taking up the issue. And some were attracted to others' dramatization of the issue. However, homelessness because it was an issue that could serve a variety of symbolic and political purposes, was a social problem that was attractive to surprisingly many Americans.

A CASUALTY OF THE GLAMOUR OFFENSIVE

The president, a creature of Hollywood himself, was perhaps especially vulnerable to a "glamour offensive." Though I do not mean to suggest that the glamour that had attached itself to the issue was the only reason that Reagan conceded defeat and signed the McKinney Act, he surely knew successful marketing when he saw it. He also knew what damage the media could do and at what levels the average American was paying attention. The threatened "60 Minutes" update, showing a dying or even dead Mitch Snyder and a president who refused to appropriate money for a homeless shelter in the nation's capital would have reverberated through the media for many news cycles, especially so close to the presidential election. Reagan was a master at making himself look kindly and affable, even when delivering his harshest criticisms of the welfare state. But perhaps because this was a persona beneath which beat a social Darwinist's heart, it was difficult for Reagan to avoid looking callous and indifferent when confronted with the straightforward motivations of the CCNV and Snyder. Besides, he and his top aides had made insensitive comments about hunger, homelessness, and the people who suffered these just often enough to reinforce the impression that the administration was at best apathetic about the issue. Right up through his reluctant signing of the McKinney Act, the Great Communicator had failed to communicate concern for the issue except for the brief moment he had been part of Hands Across America. Ironically, this activity turned out to be a demonstration of the inadequacy of the private measures to combat homelessness the president was always touting. The symbolic resource of sincerity, which Snyder and the CCNV had in great quantities, coupled with the glamour offensive, wherein politicians, stars, and the media all colluded to make homelessness an attractive issue, simply were too much for the president, despite his purported "Teflon coating." This issue was going to stick.

PERSISTENCE AS A RESOURCE

It took persistent claimsmaking for nearly three years for the CCNV to finally succeed in its efforts to secure, run, and fund a shelter near the nation's Capitol Building. The choice of site for the shelter was far from accidental. The group wanted a shelter near the head of government so that homelessness would never be far from sight of the nation's lawmakers. Since the Federal City College Building is close both to Union Station and the Capitol Building, siting the shelter there enabled homeless people to use the station's many useful resources while at the same time ensuring that homeless people would be a daily presence in the lives of government officials. Strategically speaking, it is difficult to imagine a shelter better situated for reminding federal lawmakers of their duty toward the most destitute Americans. Indeed, it was often after a visit to the nearby CCNV shelter that lawmakers such as Speaker Wright became convinced to do something about homelessness.

The struggle for this particular shelter was recounted in some detail here for a number of reasons. First was to demonstrate how much persistence was required to get the recalcitrant Reagan administration to agree to the shelter and then make good on the agreement. Second was to demonstrate the efficacy of persistence in forging the outcome of a social problem. In the end it was easier to accede to the CCNV's demands (or at least some of them) than it was to derail or ignore the group. A third reason this struggle was detailed here is metaphorical. Claimsmaking activities are attempts to "change the world" in some sense, a push to get social actors to think and act differently about an aspect of the social context. But "the world" can often be quite obdurate and resistant to change even while society continues to be elaborated over time through social interaction. In this case, however, persistence paid off with the dividend of a "model" shelter. This in turn emboldened the CCNV to continue to make the case for further national involvement in ameliorating homelessness. And the CCNV's persistent attention to homelessness in general was one central reason why this problem was successfully constructed in the first place.

Creative persistence is often a feature of successful social problem construction. It is especially important in the amelioration phase of claimsmaking activities, especially when, as in this case, there are clear adversaries to a particular construction of the problem. Claimsmakers do not merely have to stick with their claims. They must constantly fine-tune them in reaction to constantly evolving conditions of context and reactions to their claims. Homelessness eventually had many claimsmakers involved in different types of persistent behavior. The CCNV made highly public "trouble" over the issue and celebrities enhanced its status. The media continued to underline its importance both locally and nationally by continuing to cover it regularly. Lawmakers at all levels clamored for something to be done. And behind the scenes the courts considered the issue and advocates prepared their legislation and lobbied lawmakers repeatedly, urging them to take the matter seriously.

Persistence on a wide variety of fronts constructed "doing something" about homelessness as necessary, desirable, and imminent. It is the impression of inevitability that makes persistence a valuable symbolic resource in "solving" a social problem, especially when amelioration presumably requires government intervention, as was the case here. Creative persistence can both build momentum for an issue and make continuing inaction seem pointless. The persistently squeaky wheel does eventually get greased because the alternative is to be driven crazy by the continued noise. This is a lesson that the CCNV learned early on in its efforts to fight for recognition and resources for homelessness and one it used to good effect.

BACK TO BASICS

One reason the McKinney Act was enacted was simply because the Reagan administration's position on homelessness was unpersuasive as politics. The Reagan era ushered in a turn in politics toward "market-based" solutions to all human problems. But in attempting to dismantle the alternative approach—the idea that some human problems are best dealt with collectively, which in a democracy means via the elected government—Reagan overreached his grasp a bit. The creation of the welfare state and its effect on the Great Depression were well remembered by many older Americans. For many the War on Poverty was still remembered as a moment when the nation had come together to provide for all. In particular, African-Americans had seen their prospects brighten when they were finally included as recipients of welfare and other government antipoverty programs. Decades of welfare state expansion were not to be dismantled so easily. And homelessness represented very well the specter of a nation with no recourse but the market. As Speaker Wright had noted when he decided to push for the McKinney Act, Americans were willing to spend federal tax dollars on the basic protections from the elements and from starvation that the nation could offer homeless people.

Reagan, of course, had not argued that the market should be the sole caretaker of the homeless. His reluctance to deal nationally with homelessness also had its origins in a political philosophy that stressed a limited role for the federal government. He had suggested two other ways to deal with homelessness: local government and charitable organizations. This was in keeping with his conservative philosophy, which often seemed combined with a romanticized view of America as it was imagined to be in the Colonial era. In this happy time, small towns dealt with their problem populations locally and, when necessary, citizens established charities to take care of local unfortunates. Modern urban America, with its huge populations, entrenched problems, and declining tax revenues, however, bore little resemblance to this image of local self-sufficiency, and modern local officials were not convinced that local resources were sufficient to deal with this problem as well as with other big-city woes. Those who worked in charitable organizations were likewise not persuaded that their mostly underfinanced groups could continue to manage what to all appearances seemed like a burgeoning new group in desperate need of assistance.

Moreover, the United States is a highly religious country. Several religions practiced widely in this country, particularly Catholicism, have compassion for the poor as a central tenet. Even Americans who had basically agreed with Reagan's call for a minimalist approach to federal government might disagree that this issue should be dealt with under that general principle. Though they might have conservative politics, many Americans' religious beliefs forbade them to ignore the poor. Surely Susan Baker, a devout Catholic, who was married to Reagan's chief of staff, was representative of this very American division between religious and political impulse. Those of religious faith and those who dealt with the issue at the street level were additional "silent constituencies" for federal intervention in the issue.

For all its radicalism, it was the CCNV rather than the Reagan administration that held mainstream views on homelessness. Americans, like the CCNV, thought that homelessness was a blight on society. Americans, like the CCNV, agreed that something should be done about it. The religious bases for these sentiments were also in keeping with mainstream sentiments about the poor, at least in an abstract moral sense. The federal government seemed an obvious entity to turn to in order that something might be done. As I have argued elsewhere, advocate claimsmakers had several interpretive resources that they were able to use to good advantage in constructing homelessness and marshaling support for ameliorative action. These included evoking moral frames of Christian charity and humanitarian aid. Both these frames proved to be resonant, not just with the general public but also with other members of the iron quadrangle of claimsmakers. Beyond these moral and emotional frames, claimsmakers argued that viewing homelessness as a national problem and doing something about it was necessary on more rational grounds of duty to nation and fair play. Together these made a persuasive case for aiding homeless people.

In the end, advocates got both more and less than they had asked for when they raised homelessness as an issue some years before. When homelessness was a "new" social problem, advocates both in Washington and New York had advocated for a simple remedy—housing. When faced with the political realities of the day, these demands were quickly downsized to a plea for "shelter," and this advocates in both cities accomplished through quite different means. Later, when the Coalition for the Homeless had become a large and well-organized advocacy group, a complex piece of legislation was constructed with hopes that pieces of it would be taken up by various congressional committees and gradually, some portions of the proposal would be passed. Instead, this initiative led, in a very short period of time to a comprehensive bill with provisions ranging from subsidized housing and job training to the education of homeless children. Though it may have been, as the Coalition's Maria Foscarinis put it, "a first step," the Stewart B. McKinney Homeless Assistance Act of 1987 did set up an infrastructure for providing a range of services to a population barely recognized as existing just six short years before. Many people came to have no homes during the Reagan era. Homelessness was surely not a problem constructed out of "thin air." But for homelessness to become the kind of problem it did become and for homelessness to be resolved with federal legislation, it took the social problems work of a variety of social actors. Though the many claimsmakers who participated in constructing this social problem may not have gotten the resolution they were seeking, homelessness remains on the nation's social problem agenda and homeless people remain of concern to a great number of Americans. Such are the unintended outcomes of social problems work, a topic I consider in the final chapter.

NOTES

1. Sometimes problem recognition is also a difficult claimsmaking achievement because the very existence of a problem challenges powerful others and their resources. That smoking is dangerous to health, that priests abuse children, and that major corporations "cook their books" are all examples of problems that were difficult to construct in the first place because the interests of powerful others (such as Phillip Morris Corporation, the Roman Catholic church, and the Enron and Anderson firms) were challenged.

2. In 1970, Snyder had been arrested for auto theft and sentenced to three years in prison. The following year, after being transferred to a federal prison in Danbury, Connecticut, Snyder met Phillip and Daniel Berrigan, priests serving time for destroying draft board records. These men instructed Snyder on radical Christianity, nonviolent protest, and anarchist political theory, and in so doing changed his life (Blair, *Esquire,* December 1986). Subsequently, of course, Snyder was arrested and jailed numerous times in conjunction with his protest activities.

3. See Burt (1992), especially Chapters 4 and 5 for evidence of Reagan policies as causing homelessness. Housing expert Chester Hartman, writing in the *Progressive* (March 1985), also has a good summary of this causal argument.

4. This did not come to pass and Congress appropriated $306 million for community block grants in 1986. The administration pursued the same tactics in the 1987 budget (*National Catholic Reporter,* February 28; *NYT,* February 19, 1986).

5. The Center on Budget and Policy Priorities, a nonprofit federal policy analysis group headed by a former Carter administration official, noted that the Reagan administration planned to cut federal programs for the poor by an average of 10.7 percent in the proposed 1988 budget. The programs slated for cuts included

subsidized housing for the poor and community development block grants—two programs that directly impacted homelessness. The Reagan administration had proposed to cut community development block grants—up until the McKinney Act the source of most federal funding to run shelters and feeding programs— by 19.4 percent for 1988 (*WP,* January 14, 1987).

6. See J. William Spencer (1996) for a detailed investigation of the transformation of "bums and bag ladies" to "homeless people" as represented in the *Chicago Tribune.*

8

Fifteen Years Later
The Unintended Consequences
of Social Problem Construction

INTRODUCTION

Claimsmakers were indisputably successful at gaining recognition for homelessness as a social problem during the Reagan era. All sorts of social actors, from politicians to the press, from celebrities to common citizens, came to believe that homelessness was an important, even pressing problem. It is also clear that "something was done" about this problem. The McKinney Act was passed along with various other federal initiatives, such as releasing surplus food, reallocating federal buildings, and providing FEMA funds for local service provision. Locally, advocates and social welfare organizations opened shelters, organized feeding programs, and offered other services for homeless people. On both the criteria of recognition and ameliorative action, claimsmakers for homelessness as a social problem accomplished much in a short period of time.

Constructing a social problem and solution, however, is quite a bit more complex than these simple criteria suggest. First, social problems, including homelessness, can be constructed in a variety of ways. Second, solutions to social problems do not follow logically and rationally from whatever construction may have become dominant. Instead, as I have documented, there is a complex series of interactions between claimsmakers and other actors, and both of these types of actors are constrained and enabled by various elements of context. Thus does social life become elaborated as time proceeds. This complex and ever-changing pattern of context-embedded interaction is always a bit, and sometimes quite unpredictable. Any concerted action by claimsmakers is therefore likely to

produce unintended consequences. At times these include ironic outcomes, which are defined here as outcomes having the opposite effects
of the stated intentions of claimsmakers. And because claimsmaking is
context dependent and evolving, some problem elements that, in a more
rational world, should have become part of the problem's construction
do not become part of the claimsmaking terrain. These silences are also
important to consider when evaluating social problems outcomes. Social
problems outcomes, then, can be defined by their ironies and silences—
their unintended consequences—as well as by their ameliorative
accomplishments.

It is also the case that as they set out to construct a social problem,
claimsmakers rarely have a well-developed plan for problem amelioration that includes a specific solution. Claimsmakers' plans for the resolution of a social problem evolve as the construction process proceeds
and as social life is elaborated as a result of their claimsmaking efforts.
These complexities make it difficult to assess if claimsmakers achieved
what they wanted from the claimsmaking activities in which they engaged. Here I explicate some of the consequences of claimsmaking about
homelessness in the 1980s, many of them quite unintentional.

IRONIC CONSEQUENCES OF THE SOCIAL
CONSTRUCTION OF HOMELESSNESS

Homelessness as a Permanent Social Problem

Homelessness obviously has not been "solved" in the sense that it has
disappeared from the social landscape. Instead, it has become an institutionalized social problem, not a temporary blight. In 1979, Robert
Hayes and other early advocates in New York had argued for housing,
not merely shelter for the small population of homeless men, then
thought to number in the hundreds. Although the *Callahan* decree confirmed that it was the responsibility of the state to provide New York
residents with shelter, negotiation over implementation of the lawsuit's
finding reduced the conception of "shelter" to one of barely adequate
emergency shelter. In order to get the city to implement the decree at all,
advocates had to sacrifice their larger goal for one that was much more
modest. In Washington, activists took a different approach, believing that
emergency shelter was the first and most necessary step because it saved
lives. More permanent housing, although necessary, took a back seat to
ensuring survival through the provision of emergency shelter.

This focus on shelter, rather than housing, enabled homelessness to become constructed as a prevalent social problem. Many in the market-based American culture might disagree that permanent housing is a public responsibility. Preventing people from freezing to death by offering them some kind of shelter, however, is something more easily seen as part of the country's "social safety net." Beyond being a viable public policy idea because it calls for only a modest response to the problem, providing shelter satisfies a basic moral impulse of a civilized society, one that calls for assisting "neighbors in need." Early positive responses, especially by the local governments in Washington and New York, to a "downsizing" of the problem of homelessness from one of lacking a home to one of lacking shelter, encouraged claimsmakers of all sorts to focus on what they could reasonable achieve (shelter). Housing for poor and sometimes unconventional people was a much more difficult goal, one requiring much more financing and a long-term policy commitment. Had claimsmakers stuck to this as their main construction of the problem's solution, it is unlikely they would have been able to achieve success in either the areas of problem recognition or amelioration.

The construction of homelessness as a problem of not having shelter instead of one of not having housing shaped this social problem's outcomes in major ways. Shelter provision became the common response to homelessness and one that has become institutionalized. Most cities of any size now have an array of public and private shelter programs with intake facilities, assessment protocols, and placement offices. Preventing homelessness in the first place and providing permanent housing are not the primary policy "solutions" in practice, though some federal and local funding continues to be allocated for both these activities.

Indeed, according to the Urban Institute, homelessness has continued to grow since the early 1980s, even during the economic boom period of the late 1990s (www.urban.org).[1] A 1995 telephone survey found that 3 percent of Americans with telephones admitted they had been homeless sometime between 1985 and 1990 (Link et al. 1995a). When these findings are corrected to include children, a midpoint estimate of seven million Americans said they were homeless during this time period.[2] During the first two years of the new millennium, The National Coalition for the Homeless reported that shelter use reached an all-time high in large urban areas, including New York (*Safety Net*, Autumn 2002). The 1996 Urban Institute study found that there were 40,000 homeless assistance programs of one type or another offered at 21,000 different locations. These included 5,700 emergency shelter programs around the nation, 4,400 transitional housing programs, 3,500 soup kitchens, 3,300 outreach programs, 3,100 voucher distribution programs, and 9,000 food pantries.

These figures suggest that far from being ameliorated, homelessness has instead become a social welfare growth industry (http://www.huduser .org/publications/homelessness/ch_2h.html).

Homelessness as a Social Welfare Growth Industry

In the years since the events recounted in this volume, homeless people have become a new category of welfare client for which complex treatment protocols have been developed. An entire social welfare bureaucracy has grown up around the assessment and treatment of the homeless population for putative individual deficits such as drug and alcohol addiction, mental health problems, lack of education and job skills, lack of parenting acumen, and a paucity of "life skills."[3] Many homeless programs, especially those for families, have come to resemble inpatient addiction facilities, or, as my colleagues and I have termed it elsewhere, institutions of "therapeutic incarceration" (Gerstel et al. 1996). Often, homeless people are required to successfully complete lengthy treatment protocols before they are deemed ready for "transitional" housing. Homelessness has become a "problematic lifestyle choice problem"—a personal failing akin to addiction or criminal offense.

This construction of homelessness has in turn spawned the growth of a new sector of the welfare bureaucracy, one with a growing client load. The construction of homeless people as failed individuals enabled the development of this new bureaucracy. Most of the funds earmarked for homelessness go to pay for the running of temporary facilities and services and to pay the salaries of the many people who work in the homelessness industry. This conception of homelessness provides middle-class jobs, which in turn, creates a constituency that finds it in its interests to keep homelessness constructed as a problem of failed individuals. The counterconstruction, one of a society that failed and continues to fail at providing affordable housing or wages that are sufficient to pay housing costs, never took hold during the Reagan era, the problem's initial construction phase. Fifteen years later, a number of sectors of social welfare service providers, including mental health counselors, job placement experts, health care providers, early childhood education providers, substance abuse counselors, lifestyle management professionals, and education and job training experts, all have a stake in keeping homelessness constructed as a problem of individual-level deficiencies. Despite rhetoric and some federal policymaking (see below) to the contrary, it is unlikely at this juncture that homelessness will be (re)constructed as a problem of available, affordable, and appropriate housing. Such a reconstruction simply is not in the services-providing community's best interest. Thus a focus back in the 1980s on the short-term solution of emergency shelter has led to the ironic development of a new social welfare bureaucracy that is inevitably concerned with maintaining homelessness as a problem necessitating personality-restructuring therapies delivered in a short-term shelter environment.

Homelessness as a Normal Part of the Social Fabric

Another unintended consequence of the way homelessness was constructed in the 1980s is that it has now become, not an anathema, but a normal feature of American life, as inevitable as winter. Homelessness is no longer viewed as a temporary feature of an economic downturn, as many types of claimsmakers tried to portray it during the Reagan era recession. It has become a feature of every economic cycle, including times of economic expansion, such as that which characterized the late 1990s. Seeing ill-clothed people pick through the trash and shuffle through the streets of our cities with all their worldly possessions has become normalized. Our shock at homelessness, once a resource that claimsmakers drew on to provoke outrage and sympathy and a public will to "do something," has given way to feelings that nothing can be done to end homelessness and that we are doing the best we can to manage the problem. The 1980s construction of homelessness, one that often emphasized nonnormative individuals and their unconventional choices has returned to reinforce a sense of policy helplessness a decade and a half later. In the end, homeless people remain typified as "people with personal problems" instead of "people with poverty-related housing problems." Both characterizations of homeless people were prevalent (and often intertwined) in the 1980s. But it was the individual deficit construction of homeless people, best exemplified by the deinstitutionalized psychiatric patient typification that was the dominant construction early on in New York that proved most durable. That this construction of homelessness prevailed should not be blamed on the efforts, or lack thereof, of claimsmakers. Instead, an obdurate American context, which hastens to attribute causality for any problem to individual rather than social features was surely most culpable. But when advocate claimsmakers acceded to pursuing the short-term goal of emergency shelter provision rather than sticking to the larger demand of housing, they inadvertently set the stage for both normalizing homelessness and ensuring that it is primarily viewed as a problem of individual failings.

Institutionalized Republican Policy

One final irony that demonstrates just how much homelessness has become normalized is George W. Bush's policy approach to the issue. Though, as early observers have pointed out, his administration is steeped with former Reagan appointees and their policies, this is most definitely not the case when it comes to homelessness policy. Indeed, a policy briefing sheet on the HUD website (dated December 5, 2002) boasts that, under Bush, the Interagency Council on Homelessness has been reactivated and expanded to include eighteen federal agencies involved with homelessness. The briefing also reported that in late 2002 FEMA released $140 million to the United Way for distribution to its member groups to provide food, shelter, and utility assistance for homeless and nearly destitute people. The coordinator of the interagency council was quoted as saying that prevention of the loss of housing is as important as intervention with food and shelter. "Faith-based organizations," a favored group of service providers under the Bush administration, were reported to be managing a third of the 1,400 units of transitional housing funded by the Veterans Administration. Another favorite method for carrying out poverty policy, "public-private partnerships," could be noted in the announcement that the Corporation for Supportive Housing was sponsoring an initiative among housing developers to provide 150,000 units of supportive permanent housing. The briefing ended with an invitation to visit other government websites to find out more about the Bush strategy to end homelessness (http://www.ich.gov/about/index.html).

Legislation that was passed in 2002, the Community Partnership to End Homelessness Act (S. 2573, H.R. 2620), reauthorized and amended the housing sections of the McKinney Act. It was designed, according to the National Alliance to End Homelessness, "to realign the incentives behind HUD's homelessness assistance programs to achieve the goals of preventing and ending homelessness within ten years" (http://www.naeh.org/pol/congress/CPEHAhighlights.htm). The act requires 30 percent of total funding for homelessness to go into "permanent housing development activities" and mandates that 10 percent be spent on permanent housing development for nondisabled families. The conference committee report on the bill emphasized the need to find permanent housing for those who are "chronically homeless" (http://www.naeh.org/pol/papers/2002VAHUDBill.htm). Even under a Republican administration that hearkens directly back to the Reagan era in many other respects, homelessness has become a part of uncontested poverty policy. And, at least according to pro–Bush administration rhetoric, there is a commitment on the part of the administration to solve homelessness through prevention of eviction and through providing housing. It would seem that this Republican administration at least, has concurred with the Reagan-era advocates such as Robert Hayes, who claimed that housing was the best solution to homelessness.

SILENCES

Race as a Nonsalient Feature of the Construction of Homelessness

As mentioned in the introduction, the population of "new" homeless that arose during the 1980s had a markedly different racial composition than the skid row populations of decades prior to the 1980s. Increasingly, homelessness was a problem that disproportionately affected men, women, and children of color, and in many large cities, including Washington and New York, particularly African-Americans. The CCNV was well aware of this fact and from time to time the group emphasized the racial composition of the new homeless populations, as did other advocate claimsmakers such as Hopper and Baxter in New York. The overrepresentation of Black Americans in 1980s homeless populations might have led some claimsmakers to argue that homelessness was, at least in part, a manifestation of racism. It was demonstrable, after all, that the nation's people of color were paid markedly lower wages and, because of housing discrimination, had less access to the available housing stock than did white Americans (Massey and Denton 1993). Yet homelessness during the 1980s did not became a problem linked to racism. It is not possible to say with any certainty how a racialized construction of homelessness would have changed the claimsmaking narrative and elaborated social context. But it is quite likely the story would have turned out differently had homelessness become an issue of race discrimination.

There were several factors that colluded to prevent this construction of the problem. First, no consistent claimsmakers emerged during this period who took a specifically racial perspective on homelessness. Among the advocates, the CCNV was perhaps best equipped to undertake such a role. From the group's inception, membership had been concertedly interracial. But during the 1980s, the group's most visible leaders, those most likely to be mentioned and photographed by the press, were Mitch Snyder, Carol Fennelly, and Mary Ellen Hombs, all of whom were white. While African-American mayors spoke out on the issue, none of them emphasized homelessness as a form of racism. And Black civil rights groups were slow to pick up on the issue.

Second, Washington and New York are both home to Black newspapers, another possible source of racialized claimsmaking around the issue. New York's *Amsterdam News* did occasionally treat the topic as one pertinent to race (for example, "Homelessness among Blacks Now Epidemic," December 26, 1981). A review of the *Washington Afro-American*, a paper to which many of the country's Black political notables regularly contributed columns, revealed that the paper occasionally covered the topic, though seldom on page one (but see, for example, November 2, 1982; January 20, 1987). The paper occasionally covered the CCNV and its activities (for example, November 6, 1984; December 17, 1985), and other local shelter issues (November 20, 1984; November 26, 1985). It rarely, however, specifically discussed homelessness as an African-American issue (but see February 8, 1986; June 9, 1987) or devoted column or editorial space to the issue (but see November 2, 1982; February 7, 1984). The paper instead focused on civil and legal rights for African-Americans, and while economic rights (or the lack thereof) received some coverage (November 20, 1984; November 5, 1985), these were infrequently discussed as a form of discrimination. Homelessness in both papers was most often featured as a local issue, at times in relationship to shelter placement against the wishes of Black neighborhood residents, who felt their (often already impoverished neighborhoods) were bearing a disproportionate share of the consequences of the economic downturn (*Amsterdam News*, January 2, 1982). Although later, homelessness would be taken up at least sporadically as an example of racial discrimination, during the Reagan era, this suggestion was muted at best.

There is also evidence that suggests that white homeless people were disproportionately emphasized in the majority press and by some claimsmakers in an effort to broaden the appeal of homelessness in white majority racist America (see *Newsweek*, January 2, 1984). The idea that "homelessness could happen to anyone" was made more believable if that "anyone" were white unemployed parents in a two-parent family.

These factors combined to silence race discrimination as a main ingredient in the construction of homelessness.

Gender and Homelessness: Another Kind of Silence

After 1987, homelessness did become a gender issue, fueled by New York's homeless family explosion and the popular expose of homeless family shelter life *Rachel and Her Children*, by Jonathan Kozol (1988). During the early 1980s, homeless mothers were sometimes the featured characters in sympathetic treatments of homelessness by the press. In another way, however, family homelessness was not successfully politicized as a gender issue. For example, family homelessness was not expressly linked to inadequate welfare payments or the practice of "churning"—cutting families off welfare for bureaucratic infractions such as failure to keep an appointment with the welfare office. The social problem of homelessness, while linked to hunger, was infrequently posed as a problem resulting from inadequate public assistance payments (either the general assistance payments that went to single impoverished people or the more widely known program for poor families, AFDC).

Instead, family homelessness became part of the "solution" to the AFDC cuts and churning that characterized the policy of the Reagan administration and it remained so when AFDC was ended during the Clinton administration. During the Reagan era, family homelessness was a substantively small problem that perhaps could have been contained but it exploded soon afterward as housing prices continued to skyrocket while public assistance's purchasing power continued to plummet. In twenty-first-century America, homelessness has become a substantial part of the poverty policy aimed at families, one requiring an impoverished mother to lose everything in order to have a chance to eventually gain a stable situation for her children. It is perhaps unrealistic to imagine that had family homelessness been raised as a central issue by claimsmakers and its link to cuts in public assistance emphasized, Reagan's "welfare queen" trope might have been undermined, and with it, the push for AFDC's curtailment and eventual demise. But not linking the two during the Reagan era helped to enable "ending welfare as we know it," thereby ensuring a steady stream of homeless families.

I have argued here that the early turn in claimsmaking toward making homelessness a problem of inadequate shelter rather than one of inadequate housing had many consequences for later rounds of claimsmaking and for the shape that outcomes would take. Surely the central one remains the extent to which homelessness as a social problem remains insecurely linked to housing policy. Although lip service and some funding has been given to the provision of housing, the structure of the McKinney Act, the composition of the Interagency Council and subsequent funding rounds remain geared to shelter and services provision, not housing, despite rhetoric to the contrary. Fifteen years of providing shelter and personal rehabilitation services along with ever-growing rates of homelessness suggests that homelessness remains primarily a problem of unaffordable, unavailable, and inappropriate housing. Yet for the past decade and a half, national social policy has failed to respond to the need for "supportive housing" for those who are impoverished, mentally ill, or merely unconventional. An emergency shelter continues to be the only home offered to many people in need.

The claimsmaking activities of the decade between 1977 and 1987 brought to the fore the social problem of homelessness in a dramatic and compelling way. In the end, it must be said that claimsmakers were much more successful in raising the issue than in "solving" it. Yet a tremendous amount of social policy change has taken place around this issue in the past fifteen years; indeed an entire social welfare bureaucracy has been created to deal with the issue. These are not trivial accomplishments, even if they are at times unintended or even ironic ones. Claimsmakers around the issue of homelessness did "change the world." The continued elaboration of the social world is left to the would-be claimsmakers of the future.

NOTES

1. The Urban Institute conducted a study in 1987 in which it estimated that there were 500,000 to 600,000 homeless people nationwide during an average week in February. When they replicated this study in 1996, they estimated that the figure had grown to 842,000 adults and children. The estimated number of people likely to experience homelessness at least once during 1996 was between 2.3 and 3.5 million, or between 0.9 and 1.3 percent of the U.S. population (www.urban.org).
2. In stark contrast to the previous decade's controversies over the estimated number of homeless people, the Link et al. (1994) data were used by the Clinton administration in *Priority Home!* a 1994 publication of the Interagency Council on Homelessness.
3. Life skills typically include housecleaning, managing a monthly budget, balancing a checkbook, and other family-keeping activities. (For a further description, see Gerstel et al. 1996.)

Postscript

The Community for Creative Non-Violence (CCNV) still exists thirty some years after its founding in 1970. Many group members now live in the Federal City College Building, the shelter the CCNV fought so hard for in the mid-1980s. The building has a new address, however. The District of Columbia renamed the street it is located on Mitch Snyder Place. The Federal City Shelter, as the CCNV refers to it, has truly become a model homeless shelter. It houses over a thousand homeless people on a typical night, divided into sections for older and physically challenged guests, single mothers with their children and single women, and homeless men. Another half floor of the huge building is home to staff and guests of the shelter. The staff lives onsite and receives no salary for their efforts. In addition, many other volunteers help run the shelter, either on a regular or sporadic basis. College community service groups and interns from around the country and from Europe have come to live and learn at the shelter. The shelter has a free clothing store, a mailroom with daily mail service, a room for meeting with legal advisors, a large maintenance facility, a library, and a well-staffed administrative office. There is also an infirmary that provides posthospital care for thirty homeless people. The Mitch Snyder Arts and Education Building adjacent to the main shelter provides job training, GED classes, literacy programs, and other specific interest classes such as poetry, sign language, drawing, and African-American history. There are computers for job training purposes, a photographic darkroom, and, when I was last there, two talented artists-in-residence who provided paintings and murals for the building and training for those interested. There is a separate residential drug and alcohol rehabilitation program, "Clean & Sober Streets," housed in the building. Most impressive is what has become of the CCNV's food scavenging efforts. The D.C. Central Kitchen is located on the ground floor of the building. Founded in 1989, it carries on the CCNV tradition of retrieving surplus food from area restaurants and grocery stores. Food is then prepared in a huge, well-equipped kitchen and meals are sent around the city to serve three thousand people every day. The kitchen provides initial job training for homeless people, and runs a catering company (using purchased foods) that provides additional job training.

The CCNV continues to be a racially diverse, racially integrated group drawing people from a variety of religious commitments. Many members first experienced the community as guests at the soup kitchen or shelter.

The CCNV brochure states:

> We push and pull one another along paths of greater responsibility and commitment, personal non-violence, and lessons in love. Together we serve directly, and through acts of resistance, we stretch the meaning of our faith. We try to turn beliefs into daily acts.

Mitch Snyder died in 1990.

APPENDIX

Considering the Constructionist Approach

This appendix articulates the theoretical and methodological framework within which *Seasons Such As These* is set. It is meant to be read by students of social problems who want to know a bit about some of the issues underlying social problems constructionist research and my decisions about how to resolve these issues. In thinking about how to conceive this research and how to represent it to others, it seemed necessary not only to design a methodology but also to reflect on ontological and epistemological matters underlying the method. Constructionism's positions on what exists and how we know what we know are quite different from how those matters are conceived in most other forms of sociology and from how most people operate in their everyday lives. In what follows I briefly outline constructionist ontology and epistemology and demonstrate how these presuppositions guided my methodological choices.

CONSTRUCTIONIST ONTOLOGY

All sociological inquiry presupposes some sort of ontology, a vision of what kinds of entities are held to exist and under what conditions and relationships.[1] As Gubrium and Holstein point out, "Conceptualizing a method is, first and foremost, a matter of formulating a way of thinking about a phenomenon," a process of reflecting on "how to orient to the subject matter in the first place" (2000:81). Often the ontology implied or endorsed by a brand of sociological practice, such as constructionism, receives inadequate reflective attention. Yet as social realist Margaret Archer notes, ontology plays a "powerful regulatory role" (1995:16) in determining explanatory methodology. Ontology acts, as she says, "as both

207

gatekeeper and bouncer for methodology" (ibid.:21). A social ontology identifies "what there is to be explained" (ibid.:17) and rules out that which is deemed nonexistent.[2] It also directs our gaze toward certain analytical subject matters and away from others. One's presuppositions determine how one proceeds empirically and analytically, whether they are overtly articulated or not. If explicated consciously, a set of presuppositions can be used as a tool, a map guiding the choice of subject matter and the analytical process one employs as one proceeds toward an empirical goal. That is how I have used my reflections on constructionist ontology in this work.

Presuppositions

The Status of the Natural World

Constructionists have often been accused (sometimes with justification) of being antirealists because of our commitment to the presupposition that social realities are constructed. The most common charge is that constructionism rests on the presumption that "the real world" is *nothing but* objects constructed by groups of people, a stance that non-constructionist social scientists find absurd. A related antirealist position that is derived from phenomenological sources is that reality is dependent on our perception of it, on human consciousness (Searle 1995). Another version of these positions is that reality might exist independently of human consciousness but that "fact" is irrelevant because reality only exists for human beings because of our consciousness and interpretive abilities.

My own position is that antirealism conflates how we interpret the world and that we do interpret it (which could be called our social activities), with what belongs to the natural world. Many constructionists who do not subscribe to the antirealist position have been accused of doing so, including myself. So first I want to make my position on the "real" (that is, natural) world clear and define my position on its relation to the social world. I find persuasive the realist (and mundane) idea that that there is a natural world (of earthly ecosystems, star systems, galaxies, etc.) that exists independently of our awareness of it and would continue doing so if all human consciousness were erased from our little planet.[3] Philosopher John Searle terms this ontological position "external realism" and defines it as the position that "the world (or alternatively, reality or the universe) exists independently of our representations of it" (1995:150). To believe otherwise I find to be at once arrogant and premodern, in the sense that antirealism can be said to be a prescientific, indeed, pre-Copernican type of belief. With its roots in Western philosophical and theological traditions, it presumes humans have some elevated and central teleological status in relationship to "the real world" and that human consciousness is central to the workings of the universe. My version of constructionism instead presupposes an externally real world.[4] I view the external realist ontological position as being derived from the humility that science has taught us about our place on earth and in the cosmos.

The Status of Human Action

We human beings, however, do build and rebuild, interpret and reinterpret, our world and we engage in this social "worlding" (Pollner 1987) continuously and in extremely complex ways. All of our "worlding" activities involve the natural world in some form or other, if only that our "constructions" happen within our brains and among separate biological entities (other people). Though "worlding" is a powerful process, it does not follow that the natural world is dependent on it. Again, here I concur with realists that it is quite the opposite: the existence of the social presupposes the existence of the natural world. This ontological position—a squarely scientific one that we are but one of the universe's types of entities and in no way causative of the universe's existence—has epistemological consequences for the analyst of social problems as I demonstrate below.

When I say, as a constructionist, I am committed to the idea that the world is "socially constructed" what I mean is that we are forever interpreting and defining the natural world, transforming it into social concepts, patterns, and objects. Much of our social world ("structure" and "culture") is made of more or less invisible and abstract concepts that, though they are often symbolized concretely (for example, the physical document of our Constitution), are mostly wholly "constructions." *What* we make of the world, however complex our constructions, should not be confused with the idea *that* we make it or that what we make of it is all that matters. Instead, we are constrained by the material world. We cannot reconstruct or deconstruct gravity and transform it to "levity" (Best 2000) and "the real world" will go on (or not) regardless of all our constructions. This presupposition holds even though our only access to the world (the universe, reality) is through our perceptions and interpretations of it within our human consciousness.

In the ontology that guides my kind of constructionism, we are complicated social creatures who continuously construct complex social edifices "on top of" the world but we are not gods creating the universe nor is the universe dependent on our acknowledgment of it. Nor, importantly, does the natural world "matter" only because we perceive and interpret it. This moral valuation of the world as mattering only because of our interpretations is also an unsupportable human-centric stance. Regardless of humanity and our actions, the world *is*. What the ultimate state of its "mattering" is cannot be known.

The Status of the Social World

Because we are both social and sentient, humans do create concepts to define and interpret the world and their relationships with one another and to communicate these interpretive processes to one another. This is what Pollner intends when he employs the term "worlding" (1987). We cannot, given our sentience, live in "the state of nature," an uninterpreted natural world. Instead, we constantly, though within constraints, "make something" of the world we confront. And because we are social, we make something of our world in interaction with each other, and in so doing, we also continuously define and redefine our relationships with one another. Our social world, and what we make of external reality, is comprised of *activity*, that of social interaction and interpretation. Schutz (1962) terms this interpretive activity, its communication to others, and its consequences "typification." Broadly speaking, typification, the act of interpreting what we confront, is the basic human social activity.

My ontological position on the social world is that all that is social is comprised of interpretations by human beings in interaction with one another. In other words, all that is social is *constructed* through human interaction. This goes for the human-interpreted natural world (a tree as shade or lumber) as well as the most abstract social concepts (money, democracy, religion, race, etc.). Basically, this is the interactionist position on the nature of the social world. Interactionists do not subscribe to the idea of a separate kind of ontological entity called "social structure." We believe those who do see "structure" as somehow apart from human activity are engaging in "reification"—giving an abstraction such as "religion" or "government" or "gender" the ability to engage in causal actions. Interactionists are committed to the idea that only people engage in causal social actions. In general, I concur with this commitment to locating causality only within human action. Social structure, as sociologists commonly talk about it, should be viewed as purely metaphorical—a shorthand and extremely useful way of talking about complex social interaction processes and patterns. That is what I mean when I talk of social institutions and other social "structural" elements in this investigation.

In one sense I differ with some interactionists, particularly perhaps ethnomethodologists, in that I emphasize the relevance and importance of the passage of time as it affects human social life. In this I again invoke phenomenological sociologist Alfred Schutz (1962). He argues for the importance of what he terms "sedimentation." By this he means that though all things social are activities (the activity of worlding or in Schutz's vocabulary "typification"), building and maintaining the social world has been going on long before any current social actor comes on the scene. The current actor is presented with the results of previous rounds of social interaction *as if* they are objective. So money, the Catholic church, or the legal system seem to have the same ontological status, the same level of reality, as mountains, molecules, or the moon to everyday actors.

This is compounded by the inevitability that the natural world also has been previously interpreted by earlier actors and because in the socialization process we do not distinguish between external realities and social constructions. In fact, we cannot since it is impossible for us to talk about the world without representing (interpreting) it. Though both molecules and money are typifications and as such are subject to revision through (re)typification, of the two only money as a concept depends on our continuing social and interactive belief in it. As Searle points out (1995), if we all quit believing in "money" as a social concept, it could and would disappear. This is not the case for what we have designated "molecules" or "the moon" though presumably both could disappear from human relevance if we tried hard enough (this would be difficult in the case of the moon but most of human history has been lived without "molecules"). The status of the social world (and by this I mean all things that have been perceived and interpreted by sentient human beings) in my version of constructionism is that in everyday life most of it appears objective and obdurate, as given, to social actors. Husserl, a phenomenologist who influenced Schutz, calls taking the sedimented, preinterpreted world as given "the natural attitude." Indeed, it is essential that most of the time we take most of the world as given because, as Randall Collins notes, comprehensible "social interaction depends upon tacit understandings and agreements not to attempt to explicate what is taken for granted" (1981:985).

Schutz would add that everyday actors' acts of suspending belief in the constructedness of the social world is also convenient and probably necessary while they are attempting to (re)typify some aspect of it (Schutz 1962). Actors' practical projects structure which elements of the life world have more "relevance" to them and which have less (ibid.: 227). Actors see those elements that are foregrounded as crucial to their current projects (such as the social problem they are attempting to retypify) as social constructions that can be changed. The constructedness of other features of the life-world, not as crucial to their project, is left unacknowledged. Instead, they tend to be tacitly accepted as given in a mundane sense (Pollner 1987; Schultz 1962).

To sum, typifications of norms, values, social institutions, the inter-preted natural world, and all else social have a tendency to be taken for granted or "given" by current social actors for three reasons. First, typ-ifications (for instance, money, democracy, the Catholic church) carry the authority of history; they are representations constructed long before our birth. Second, typifications are presented to us in interaction with others mostly as given, as social facts and collective representations in the Dur-kheimian sense, imbued with the authority of the collectivity. Third, in order to act effectively in the world we must pay only selective attention to its constructedness; to do otherwise is too overwhelming. I emphasize that the reason most elements of the social world appear to us as "given" at any particular time is because they are being maintained as more or less stable constructions by the actions of current actors. Thus money, for example, retains its exchange value through people's everyday continued use of it coupled with their continued belief that certain bits of paper, metal, and, now plastic and computerized data transfer, *have* exchange value.

This history of human action, reinvigorated and given import by ac-tors in the present, forms the *conditions of action* in which current actors are embedded and with which they must contend (Schwalbe et al. 2000: 420). Here this sense of the world-as-it-is is termed *context* following constructionist tradition. This is not to say that social actors are com-pletely dominated by the context into which they are born and in which they must live. Rather, Schutz says,

> We have to dominate it and we have to change it in order to realize the purposes which we pursue within it among our fellow-men. . . . These ob-jects offer resistance to our acts which we have either to overcome or to which we have to yield. . . . World, in this sense, is something that we have to modify by our actions or that modifies our actions. (1973:209)

The causal properties of context, however, are derived only from social actors who are engaged in maintaining typifications, and not from any separate entity termed "structure." Discussion of structural elements such as "class" or "government" in a constructionist framework must be looked at as merely linguistic conveniences for representing all the social interactions necessary to uphold the idea of "class" or of "govern-ment." Constructionists subscribe to the idea (as do interactionists in general) that these elements are complex patterns of social interaction, nothing more.

As defined above, typification is what all people everywhere engage in as they confront the world. In their interaction with others, people often make a concerted effort to persuade others of their typification of something. When they do, they are engaging in *claimsmaking activities.* While claimsmaking can be broadly interpreted as assertions about the nature of "reality," in constructionism claimsmaking can be more narrowly defined as the activities people engage in when they overtly attempt to persuade others of their views in order to create, change, or maintain a certain typification. Since the subject here is social problems, this can be further defined as an effort to persuade others of a certain typification of a social problem. Usually the desired typification not only defines the problem but also implies or articulates a "solution" to the problem.

The ontology of my version of constructionism, then, is based on three presuppositions. First is an acceptance of external realism and a rejection of the antirealist presumption that the world is *nothing but* our constructions. While our constructions are what is relevant for us, the world *is,* regardless of us. Our social world is constructed "on top of" this external reality. Second, a basic premise of symbolic interactionism is that the social world, including both claimsmaking and context, is comprised of the activity of social interaction and interpretation. Third, inspired by Schutz's application of phenomenology to sociological methods, the social world achieves its order and meaning, its changes and continuity within, and in reference to, the passage of human life through time, through history.

TWO EPISTEMOLOGICAL ISSUES

Another charge made against constructionists is that we are "cultural relativists" who are committed to believing that all typifications are equal. In a certain technical sense, this is a valid charge, if by "equal" we mean "equally valid as objects of investigation." If some people are persuaded by a typification it is valid *as a typification* by definition.[5] This is not to say all typifications are equally reasonable (equal on logical or empirical grounds) or have equal moral status. As Best (among others) has wonderfully demonstrated, outside the scientific community reasonableness is not a necessary criterion for a claim to become a typification. This is as much the case for cultural subgroups [some people believe in satanic ritual murder (1993)] as it is for a fairly general population [most Americans believe that certain people will and have poisoned children's trick or treat candy (Best and Horiuchi 1985)]. Comparing the claims of science, which contend that neither satanic ritual murders nor Halloween sadism exist, with typifications that insist they do, as Best has done, demonstrates how powerful a process "worlding" can be.

Where I differ with him and many other contextual constructionists, however, is that evaluating some claims (such as those claiming Halloween sadism is common) against scientific claims (no statistics indicating such sadism has ever harmed a child) should be what constructionism is about. Science is a special kind of typification, in the classic sense, one based on hypothesis testing through consistent observation of the empirical world coupled with careful application of reasoning and logic. As such it has an overwhelming validity to those trained to evaluate such typifications—it is viewed as how things "really" are as opposed to "mere" typifications. But setting up the analytic project of constructionism as an examination of how certain typifications stand up to scientific ones makes constructionism's analytical project into one concerned with demonstrating the validity of scientific (or positivist) ontology instead of examining the human activities that construct and maintain the social world.

The ontology of the social world as I have outlined it above suggests instead that constructionism should have as its primary concern examining how typification processes proceed and why they take the forms they do. As Pollner says more broadly about all postpositivist sociology, constructionism's "phenomenon *par excellence* is not the world *per se* but worlding, the work whereby a world [is] constructed and sustained" (Pollner 1987). One of constructionism's central purposes, in my view, is to investigate epistemological processes. In other words, I am interested in learning how people come to know what they say they do know by examining how the warrants upon which typifications are constructed accumulated over time. In this case, for instance, I am interested in investigating the *process by which* various people came to "know" that homelessness existed and was a serious social problem.

This focus on claimsmaking activities as they occur over time, suggests that typification is best investigated through recounting "how things went" over time. Indeed, strict constructionists Sarbin and Kitsuse maintain that "the underlying structure of constructionist accounts is the narrative" (1994:6) while philosopher Ian Hacking contends that if to construct something means to build it up, then "a history of building" should be a central analytic feature of constructionist analyses (2001:50).[6]

While, potentially, reconstructing the events that typified homelessness as a social problem could have taken place "behind the scenes" and then a summary of what happened presented, I have chosen to pursue instead an "open epistemology." That is, I think that the texture of typification processes and their complexity is better revealed through a public reconstruction of "how things went." Recounting the story in some detail and careful and accessible documentation of the evidence upon which my analysis hinges better allows the reader to see how I claim to know what I know, and from what evidence I reached the conclusions presented. This reconstruction process of course still hinges (as all presentation of evidence does) on an attempt on the investigator's part to present the data honestly and an effort to faithfully reconstruct events. Multiple sources of data from which one can reconstruct the spate of claimsmaking activities of interest seems to me to best enable an analyst to faithfully attempt to reconstruct the very complicated social processes of interest.

Without question, I have reconstructed the myriad events of this era as an organized narrative, rather than the blur of activity that actually occurred. Indeed, I would argue that it is not possible to reconstruct what has already happened in any other form *but* as a narrative. But I do so also because I contend that claimsmaking is persuasive and typification occurs only after people reflect and organize what they know of ongoing events. This interpretive process is how we make sense of the social world. Thus I suggest that my narrative about homelessness during the 1980s is in some sense a reflection of similar reflective processes that audience members engaged in as they confronted and made sense of homelessness-related claimsmaking activities as they experienced them. It is in this sense that Schutz spoke of sociology as "second-order claimsmaking" (1962). I do not make the claim that my narrative is what "really" took place, as there is no way to reclaim ongoing social life in such a precise fashion. But I do claim that reconstructing the multitude of voices that participated in claimsmaking activities can produce the "gist" of the narrative as it unfolded in ways that are close enough for some conclusions to be drawn.

Epistemological considerations in constructionism enter at two levels. The first is the examination of how claimsmakers and their audiences came to know what they know—their grounds for accepting a certain typification of a social problem. This is one epistemological issue central to how I define the constructionist project. The other consideration is over the methods that the investigator employs to examine how a social problem is constructed and how she communicates that to others. To attempt to meet the epistemological demands of constructionism, I have chosen to reconstruct claimsmaking activities as they occurred over time using multiple voices and to make that reconstruction part of the overt analytical process. Analyst epistemology thus becomes part of the constructionist method.

OTHER METHODOLOGICAL CONCERNS

Constructionist ontology, as I have outlined it here presupposes that the world (the universe, reality) *for us,* is comprised of the social, that is, interactive and interpretive, activity of typification. For us, worlding (constructing and sustaining interpretations through interaction) is all we know and all we do. The seemingly obdurate and sedimented social world in which we are embedded, our context, and our current projects (our claimsmaking activities) are comprised of activity, the activity of interpretation and interaction. If all the social world is made of interpretive and interactive activity, then only what Schutz calls "cosmic time," (1962) and what we might call history separates context from claimsmaking activities. Because context and claimsmaking are comprised of the "same stuff" their *interplay* can be reasonably investigated. The central analytic activity in my version of constructionism then becomes examining the interplay of claimsmaking activities particular to the issue at hand with the context in which they are embedded. This requires what Archer has termed analytic dualism (1995, 1996), wherein claimsmaking activities and context are strategically, and of course artificially, segregated for the purpose of analysis.

The narrative aspect of my method has as its center the reconstruction of an analyst-interpreted history of the claimsmaking activities of interest as they emerged and occurred over time. By reconstructing typification processes as they occurred over time, *how* social life proceeds becomes central (Gubrium and Holstein 1997). By embedding claimsmaking activities in their sociocultural milieu, their context, the analytic agenda can be expanded to include consideration of *why* claimsmaking activities unfolded as they did. Examining the interplay of claimsmaking activities and context in a comparative design, though not strictly necessary, allows for better identification of the salient activities and the conditions of action (the specific elements of context) that shaped the way that social life was elaborated around a specific social problem. Examining how claimsmaking activities and the conditions of action in which they occurred elaborate one another is the technique through which I approach the "why" question of constructionism. That is, beyond recounting how the typification narrative unfolded, I closely examine how context and claimsmaking constrained and provided opportunities to one another to attempt to explain why social life was elaborated as it was and not in some other way.

In the exemplar presented here, I distinguish between two features of context, the environmental and the interpretive (see Chapter 1). Again, this is merely an analytic distinction, an aid in examining and presenting relevant aspects of the context and one that relies on the closely related field of social movements scholarship for its definitions. Context is meant to evoke a notion of the "world as it is," the circumstances claimsmakers must confront, use, and change if they are to successfully pursue their projects (Schutz 1962).

Other concepts have been developed by constructionists to use in examining "claimsmaking activities." For example, beyond suggesting a narrative structure for claimsmaking activities, Ibarra and Kitsuse have developed categories for the analysis of "vernacular discourse" (1993). Gubrium has analyzed the relatively "unpublic" actions that often form the initial stages of social problem construction (1991, 1993). Holstein and Miller have delineated varieties of "social problems work" that contribute to social problem construction (1993). Hilgartner and Bosk have argued that competition between social problems shapes their construction (1988). The "iron quadrangle" of types of relevant claimsmakers (government, experts, activists, and media) has been noted by Best (1999). Loseke (1992) has examined the way prospective audiences for social problems claims shape claimsmaking activities and the categories of types of moralities used in claimsmaking (1999). These various analytic categories can help to shape the narrative reconstruction of claimsmaking activities and its interpretation and some of these are employed in this work.

The "end product" of claimsmaking activities is the elaboration of the context in which those activities were embedded (Archer 1995). The relationship between claimsmaking activities and context is reflexive and recursive; context is always in the process of being remade by human action while action is constrained by the context in which it is embedded (Berger and Luckmann 1967). This method, then, focuses on reconstructing "both the artful processes and the substantive conditions of meaning making and social order" (Gubrium and Holstein 2000:497) involved in social problems construction so that their effects on one another can be illuminated. This is, I contend, an effective technique for exploring the construction of a social problem such as homelessness, from its emergence to its ameliorative "outcome."

NOTES

1. While I do not see social constructionism as an "ontological doctrine" (Schwandt 2000), neither do I think constructionism can escape ontology as Potter contends (1996). All social inquiry, including constructionism, confronts its ontological presuppositions at one point or another. Neither theoretical nor empirical work can proceed without ontological presumptions.

2. For example, as Archer says, "Atheists cannot attribute their well being to divine providence" (1995:21).

3. For example, a tree may be viewed by humans as shade, as potential lumber, as an object of beauty, an integral part of an ecosystem, as an object of worship, or in any number of ways that might affect the future of its existence. The tree, once it becomes a part of the human world, through our perceptions and interpretations of it, becomes a social object. If no one ever thought about or saw the tree, however, the tree would still continue to exist, grow, and perish completely independently of human consciousness.

4. I distinguish external realism from "the object constancy presumption," the main ontological position of positivism because merely by using the term "object" one has already represented the world as made of objects and made implicit claims about its likeness to our representations of it. It is perhaps only a semantic distinction, but I want to be clear that the version of realism I am invoking is that there is an external, pre- or uninterpreted reality that is not knowable directly by human beings. Nonetheless, this natural world precedes all our interpretations of it and is the basis for our existence.

5. Typifications can be definitionally opposed to private hallucinations or dreams, which are not promoted as typifications or which, though they are promoted by the person having them, are not persuasive (such as claims by people we have categorized as schizophrenics).

6. See Bogard (2003) for further discussion of this point.

References

American Bar Association. 1986. Section on Individual Rights and Responsibilities, Commission on Legal Problems of the Elderly and Commission on the Mentally Disabled. Report to the House of Delegates. July 26.

Appelbaum, Richard. 1987. "Testimony on A Report to the Secretary on the Homeless and Emergency Shelters." Pp. 156–64 in *Housing the Homeless*, edited by Jon Erickson and Charles Wilhelm. New Brunswick, NJ: Center for Urban Policy Research.

Appelbaum, Richard. 1990. "Counting the Homeless." Pp. 1–16 in *Homelessness in the United States: Data and Issues*, edited by Jamshid Momeni. New York: Praeger.

Archer, Margaret. 1995. *Realist Social Theory: The Morphogenetic Approach*. Cambridge UK: Cambridge University Press.

Archer, Margaret. 1996. *Culture and Agency*, rev. ed. Cambridge UK: Cambridge University Press.

Bahr, Howard M. 1973. *Skid Row: An Introduction to Disaffiliation*. New York: Oxford University Press.

Baxter, Ellen and Kim Hopper. 1981. *Private Lives Public Spaces: Homeless Adults on the Streets of New York City*. Community Service Society Working Papers in Social Policy. New York: Community Service Society Institute for Social Welfare Research.

Becker, Howard S. 1963. *Outsiders: Studies in the Sociology of Deviance*. New York: Free Press.

Benford, Robert D. 1997. "An Insider's Critique of the Social Movement Framing Perspective." *Sociological Inquiry* 67:409–30.

Benford, Robert D. and David A. Snow. 2000. "Framing Processes and Social Movements: An Overview and Assessment." *Annual Review of Sociology* 26: 611–39.

Berger, Peter L. and Luckmann, Thomas. 1967. *The Social Construction of Reality: A Treatise in the Sociology of Knowledge*. New York: Anchor.

Best, Joel. 1990. *Threatened Children: Rhetoric and Concern about Child-Victims*. Chicago: University of Chicago Press.

Best, Joel. 1993. "But Seriously, Folks: The Limitations of the Strict Constructionist Interpretation." Pp. 109–27 in *Constructionist Controversies: Issues in Social Problems Theory*, edited by Gale Miller and James A. Holstein. Hawthorne, NY: Aldine de Gruyter.

Best, Joel. 1999. *Random Violence: How We Talk About New Crimes and New Victims.* Berkeley: University of California Press.

Best, Joel. 2000. "The Apparently Innocuous 'Just,' the Law of Levity, and the Social Problems of Social Construction." *Perspectives on Social Problems* 12:3–14.

Best, Joel. 2001. *Damned Lies and Statistics: Untangling Numbers from the Media, Politicians, and Activists.* Berkeley: University of California Press.

Best, Joel, and Gerald T. Horiuchi. 1985. "The Razor Blade in the Apple: The Social Construction of Urban Legends." *Social Problems* 32:488–99.

Blau, Joel. 1992. *The Visible Poor: Homelessness in the United States.* New York: Oxford University Press.

Bluestone, Barry and Bennett Harrison. 1982. *The Deindustrialization of America.* New York: Basic Books.

Blumer, Herbert. 1971. "Social Problems as Collective Behavior." *Social Problems* 18:298–306.

Bockman, Shel. 1991. "Interest, Ideology, and Claims-Making Activity." *Sociological Inquiry* 61:452–70.

Bogard, Cynthia J. 2001. "Advocacy and Enumeration: Counting Homeless People in a Suburban Community." *American Behavioral Scientist* 45:105–20.

Bogard, Cynthia J. 2003. "Explaining Social Problems: Addressing the Whys of Social Constructionism." Pp 209–35 in *Challenges and Choices: Constructionist Perspectives on Social Problems,* edited by James Holstein and Gale Miller. Hawthorne, NY: Aldine de Gruyter.

Brower, Bonnie. 1989. *Missing the Mark: Subsidizing Housing for the Privileged, Displacing the Poor. An Analysis of the City's 10-Year Plan.* New York: A Joint Report of the Association for Neighborhood and Housing Development, Inc. and the Housing Justice Campaign.

Burt, Martha R. 1992. *Over the Edge: The Growth of Homelessness in the 1980s.* New York: Russell Sage Foundation.

Burt, Martha R. and Barbara Cohen. 1989. *America's Homeless: Numbers, Characteristics, and the Programs that Serve Them.* Washington, DC: Urban Institute Press.

Collins, Randall 1981. "On the Microfoundations of Macrosociology." *American Journal of Sociology* 86:984–1014.

Conrad, Peter and Joseph Schneider. 1980. *Deviance and Medicalization: From Badness to Sickness.* St. Louis: Mosby.

Dyan, Daniel and Elihu Katz. 1992. *Media Events: The Live Broadcasting of History.* Cambridge, MA: Harvard University Press.

Erickson, Jon and Charles Wilhelm (Eds.). 1986. *Housing the Homeless.* New Brunswick, NJ: Center for Urban Policy Research.

Fine, Gary Alan. 1997. "Scandal, Social Conditions, and the Creation of Public Attention: Fatty Arbuckle and the 'Problem of Hollywood.'" *Social Problems* 44(3):297–323.

Freeman, Richard B. and Brian Hall. 1987. "Permanent Homelessness in America?" *Population Research and Policy Review* 6:3–27.

Foucault, Michel. 1972. *The Archaeology of Knowledge.* New York: Pantheon.

Gamson, William A. 1992. *Talking Politics*. Cambridge, MA: Harvard University Press.

Gamson, William and David S. Meyer. 1996. "Framing Political Opportunity." Pp. 275–90 in *Comparative Perspectives on Social Movements*, edited by Doug McAdam, John D. McCarthy, and Mayer N. Zald. Cambridge, MA: Harvard University Press.

Gamson, William and Andre Modigliani. 1987. "The Changing Culture of Affirmative Action." In *Research in Political Sociology*, edited by Richard Braungart. Greenwich, CT: JAI.

Gerstel, Naomi, Cynthia J. Bogard, J. Jeff McConnell, and Michael Schwartz. 1996. "The Therapeutic Incarceration of Homeless Families." *Social Service Review* 70:543–72.

Gitlin, Todd. 2001. *Media Unlimited*. New York: Metropolitan.

Goffman, Erving. 1974. *Frame Analysis*. Boston: Northeastern University Press.

Gubrium, Jaber F. 1991. "Recognizing and Analyzing Local Culture." Pp. 131–41 in *Experiencing Fieldwork*, edited by William B. Shaffir and Robert A. Stebbins. Newbury Park, CA: Sage.

Gubrium, Jaber F. 1993. "For a Cautious Naturalism." Pp. 55–67 in *Constructionist Controversies: Issues in Social Problems Theory*, edited by Gale Miller and James A. Holstein. Hawthorne, NY: Aldine de Gruyter.

Gubrium, Jaber F. and James A. Holstein. 1997. *The New Language of Qualitative Method*. Oxford: Oxford University Press.

Gubrium, Jaber F. and James A. Holstein. 2000. "Analyzing Interpretive Practice." Pp. 487–508 in *Handbook of Qualitative Research*, 2nd ed., edited by Norman K. Denzin and Yvonne S. Lincoln. Thousand Oaks CA: Sage.

Gusfield, Joseph R. 1981. *The Culture of Public Problems: Drinking-Driving and the Symbolic Order*. Chicago: University of Chicago Press.

Hacking, Ian. 1999. *The Social Construction of What?* Cambridge, MA: Harvard University Press.

Hayes, Robert. 1982. "The Problems of the Homeless Confront the City Government." *CBC Quarterly* 2(2):1–4.

Hewitt, Christopher. 1996. "Estimating the Number of Homeless: Media Misrepresentation of an Urban Problem." *Journal of Urban Affairs* 18:431–47.

Hilgartner, Stephen and Charles L. Bosk. 1988. "The Rise and Fall of Social Problems: A Public Arenas Model." *American Journal of Sociology* 94:53–78.

Hoch, Charles and Robert A. Slayton. 1989. *New Homeless and Old: Community and the Skid Row Hotel*. Philadelphia: Temple University Press.

Holstein, James A. and Gale Miller. 1993. "Social Constructionism and Social Problems Work." Pp. 131–52 in *Constructionist Controversies: Issues in Social Problems Theory*, edited by Gale Miller and James A. Holstein. Hawthorne, NY: Aldine de Gruyter.

Hombs, Mary Ellen and Mitch Snyder. 1982. *Homeless in America: A Forced March to Nowhere*. Washington, DC: Community for Creative Non-Violence.

Hopper, Kim. 1991. "A Poor Apart: The Distancing of Homeless Men in New York's History." *Social Research* 58:107–32.

Hopper, Kim and Jim Baumohl. 1994. "Held in Abeyance: Rethinking Homelessness and Advocacy." *American Behavioral Scientist* 37:522–52.

Hopper, Kim, Ellen Baxter, and Stuart Cox. 1982. *One Year Later: The Homeless Poor in New York City, 1982.* Community Service Society Working Papers in Social Policy. New York: Community Service Society Institute for Social Welfare Research.

Hopper, Kim and Jill Hamberg. 1984. The Making of America's Homeless: From Skid Row to New Poor, 1945–1984. Community Service Society Working Papers in Social Policy. Community Service Society Institute for Social Welfare Research, 105 East 22nd Street, New York, NY 10010.

Hopper, Kim, Ezra Susser, and Sarah Conover. 1985. "Economies of Makeshift: Deindustrialization and Homelessness in New York City." *Urban Anthropology* 14:183–236.

Horowitz, C. 1989. "Mitch Snyder's Phony Numbers: The Fiction of Three Million Homeless." *Policy Review* 49:66–69.

Ibarra, Peter, discussant. 2002. "The Future of Social Problems Theory." Thematic Session at the Society for the Study of Social Problems Annual Meeting, Chicago, August 2002.

Ibarra, Peter and John I. Kitsuse. 1993. "Vernacular Constituents of Moral Discourse: An Interactionist Proposal for the Study of Social Problems." Pp. 21–54 in *Constructionist Controversies: Issues in Social Problems Theory,* edited by Gale Miller and James A. Holstein. Hawthorne, NY: Aldine de Gruyter.

Interagency Council on the Homeless, United States Department of Housing and Urban Development. 1994. *Priority Home! The Federal Plan to Break the Cycle of Homelessness.* Washington, DC: U.S. Government Printing Office.

Jenness, Valerie. 1993. *Making It Work.* Hawthorne, NY: Aldine de Gruyter.

Johnson, John M. 1995. "Horror Stories and the Construction of Child Abuse." Pp. 17–31 in *Images of Issues: Typifying Contemporary Social Problems,* edited by Joel Best. Hawthorne, NY: Aldine de Gruyter.

Katz, Michael B. 1989. *The Undeserving Poor: From the War on Poverty to the War on Welfare.* New York: Pantheon.

Kielbowicz, Richard B. and Clifford Scherer. 1986. "The Role of the Press in the Dynamics of Social Movements." Pp. 71–96 in *Research in Social Movements, Conflicts and Change,* edited by Louis Kriesberg, Michael Dobkowski, and Isidor Wallimann, vol. 9. Greenwich, CT: JAI Press.

Kingdon, John. 1984. *Agendas, Alternatives, and Public Policies.* Boston: Little Brown.

Klandermans, Bert and Sjoerd Goslinga. 1996. "Media Discourse, Movement Publicity, and the Generation of Collective Action Frames: Theoretical and Empirical Exercises in Meaning Construction." Pp. 312–37 in *Comparative Perspectives on Social Movements,* edited by Doug McAdam, John McCarthy, and Mayer N. Zald. Cambridge, MA: Harvard University Press.

Knickman, James R. and Beth C. Weitzman. 1989. *A Study of Homeless Families in New York City: Risk Assessment Models and Strategies for Prevention* (Final Report: Volumes 1, 2, and 3). Health Research Program, Urban Research Center, Graduate School of Public Administration, New York University, New York.

Kozol, Jonathan. 1988. *Rachel and Her Children: Homeless Families in America.* New York: Crown.

Kubal, Timothy J. 1998. "The Presentation of Political Self: Cultural Resonance and the Construction of Collective Action Frames." *Sociological Quarterly* 39: 539–54.

Laska, E. M. and M. Meisner. 1993. "A Plant-Capture Method for Estimating the Size of a Population from a Single Sample." *Biometrics* 49:209–20.

Link, Bruce, Jo Phelan, Michaeline Bresnahan, Ann Stueve, Robert Moore, and Ezra Susser. 1995a. "Lifetime and Five-Year Prevalence of Homelessness in the United States: New Evidence on an Old Debate." *American Journal of Orthopsychiatry* 65:347–54.

Link, Bruce, Sharon Schwartz, and Robert Moore. 1995b. "Public Knowledge, Attitudes and Beliefs about Homeless People: Evidence for Compassion Fatigue?" *American Journal of Community Psychology* 23:533–55.

Link, Bruce, Ezra Susser, Ann Stueve, Jo Phelan, Robert Moore, and E. Struening. 1994. "Lifetime and Five-Year Prevalence of Homelessness in the United States." *American Journal of Public Health* 84:1907–12.

Loseke, Donileen R. 1992. *The Battered Woman and Shelters.* Albany: State University of New York Press.

Loseke, Donileen R. 1995. "Writing Rights: The 'Homeless Mentally Ill' and Involuntary Hospitalization." Pp. 261–85 in *Images of Issues: Typifying Contemporary Social Problems,* 2nd ed., edited by Joel Best. Hawthorne, NY: Aldine de Gruyter.

Loseke, Donileen R. 1999. *Thinking about Social Problems: An Introduction to Constructionist Perspectives.* Hawthorne, NY: Aldine de Gruyter.

Lowney, Kathleen S. and Joel Best. 1995. "Stalking Strangers and Lovers: Changing Media Typifications of a New Crime Problem." Pp. 33–57 in *Images of Issues: Typifying Contemporary Social Problems,* 2nd ed., edited by Joel Best. Hawthorne, NY: Aldine de Gruyter.

Margolis, Michael and Gary A. Mauser (Eds.). 1989. *Manipulating Public Opinion: Essays on Public Opinion as a Dependent Variable.* Pacific Grove, CA: Brooks/Cole.

Massey, Douglas S. and Nancy A. Denton. 1993. *American Apartheid: Segregation and the Making of the Underclass.* Cambridge: Harvard University Press.

McAdam, Doug, John D. McCarthy, and Mayer N. Zald. 1996. "Introduction: Opportunities, Mobilizing Structures, and Framing Processes—Toward a Synthetic, Comparative Perspective on Social Movements." Pp. 1–20 in *Comparative Perspectives on Social Movements: Political Opportunities, Mobilizing Structures, and Cultural Framings,* edited by Doug McAdam, John D. McCarthy, and Mayer N. Zald. Cambridge: Cambridge University Press.

McCarthy, John D., Jackie Smith, and Mayer N. Zald. 1996. "Accessing Public, Media, Electoral, and Governmental Agendas." Pp. 291–311 in *Comparative Perspectives on Social Movements: Political Opportunities, Mobilizing Structures, and Cultural Framings,* edited by Doug McAdam, John D. McCarthy, and Mayer N. Zald. Cambridge: Cambridge University Press.

McCombs, Maxwell E. and Donald L. Shaw. 1972. "The Agenda Setting Function of the Mass Media." *Public Opinion Quarterly* 36:176–87.

Miller, Leslie. 1993. "Claims-Making from the Underside: Marginalization and Social Problems Analysis." Pp. 349–76 in *Reconsidering Social Constructionism: Debates in Social Problems Theory*, edited by James A. Holstein and Gale Miller. Hawthorne, NY: Aldine de Gruyter.

Mills, C. Wright. 1959. *The Sociological Imagination*. Oxford: Oxford University Press.

Murray, Harry. 1990. *Do Not Neglect Hospitality: The Catholic Worker and the Homeless*. Philadelphia: Temple University Press.

Nelson, Barbara J. 1984. *Making an Issue of Child Abuse: Political Agenda Setting for Social Problems*. Chicago: University of Chicago Press.

Neuman, W. Russell. 1990. "The Threshold of Public Attention." *Public Opinion Quarterly* 54:159–76.

Nichols, Lawrence T. 2003. "Voices of Social Problems: A Dialogical Constructionist Model." *Studies in Symbolic Interaction* 26(93–123).

Page, Benjamin I. and Robert Y. Shapiro. 1992. "Educating and Manipulating the Public." Pp. 294–320 in *Manipulating Public Opinion: Essays on Public Opinion as a Dependent Variable*, edited by Michael Margolis and Gary A. Mauser. Pacific Grove, CA: Brooks/Cole.

Pollner, Melvin. 1987. *Mundane Reason: Reality in Everyday Sociological Discourse*. Cambridge: Cambridge University Press.

Polsky, Andrew J. 1991. *The Rise of the Therapeutic State*. Princeton, NJ: Princeton University Press.

Potter, J. 1996. *Representing Reality: Discourse, Rhetoric and Social Construction*. London: Sage.

Rader, Victoria. 1986. *Signal Through the Flames: Mitch Snyder and America's Homeless*. Kansas City, MO: Sheed & Ward.

Ropers, Richard. 1985. "The Rise of the New Urban Homeless." *Public Affairs Report* 26(4–5):1–14.

Rossi, Peter H. 1989. *Down and Out in America: The Origins of Homelessness*. Chicago: University of Chicago Press.

Rossi, Peter H., James D. Wright, G. A. Fisher, and G. Willis. 1987. "The Urban Homeless: Estimating Composition and Size." *Science* 235:1336–41.

Ryan, Charlotte. 1991. *Prime Time Activism*. Boston: South End Press.

Salo, M. T. and P. C. Campanelli. 1991. "Ethnographic Methods in the Development of Census Procedures for Enumerating the Homeless." *Urban Anthropology* 20:127–39.

Sarbin, Theodore R. and John I. Kitsuse. 1994. "A Prologue to Constructing the Social." Pp. 1–18 in *Constructing the Social*, edited by Theodore R. Sarbin and John Kitsuse. London: Sage.

Schutz, Alfred. 1962. *Collected Papers*, Volume 1. *The Problem of Social Reality*. The Hague: Martinus Nijhoff.

Schutz, Alfred. 1973. *The Structure of the Life World*. Evanston, IL: Northwestern University Press.

Schwalbe, Michael, Sandra Godwin, Daphne Holden, Douglas Schrock, Shealy Thompson, and Michele Wolkomir. 2000. "Generic Processes in the Reproduction of Inequality: An Interactionist Analysis." *Social Forces* 79:419–52.

Schwandt, Thomas A. 2000. "Three Epistemological Stances for Qualitative Inquiry." Pp. 189–213 in *Handbook of Qualitative Research*, 2nd ed., edited by Norman K. Denzin and Yvonna S. Lincoln. Thousand Oaks CA: Sage.

Searle, John R. 1995. *The Construction of Social Reality.* New York: Free Press.

Shinn, Marybeth and Colleen Gillespie. 1994. "The Roles of Housing and Poverty in the Origins of Homelessness." *American Behavioral Scientist* 37:505–21.

Snow, David, Leon Anderson, and Paul Koegel. 1994. "Distorting Tendencies in Research on the Homeless." *American Behavioral Scientist* 37:461–75.

Snow, David A., Susan G. Baker, and Leon Anderson. 1986. "The Myth of Pervasive Mental Illness among the Homeless." *Social Problems* 33:407–23.

Snow, David A. and Robert D. Benford. 1988. "Ideology, Frame Resonance, and Participant Mobilization." Pp. 197–217 in *From Structure to Action: Social Movement Participation Across Cultures*, edited by Bert Klandermans, Hanspeter Kriesi, and Sidney Tarrow. Greenwich CT: JAI.

Snow, David A. and Robert D. Benford. 1992. "Master Frames and Cycles of Protest." Pp. 133–55 in *Frontiers in Social Movement Theory*, edited by Aldon D. Morris and Carol McClurg Mueller. New Haven, CT: Yale University Press.

Spector, Malcolm and John I. Kitsuse. 1977. *Constructing Social Problems.* Menlo Park, CA: Cummings.

Spencer, J. William. 1996. "From Bums to the Homeless: Media Constructions of Persons without Homes from 1980–1984." *Perspectives on Social Problems* 8: 39–58.

Tarrow, Sidney. 1994. *Power in Movement.* New York: Cambridge University Press.

Trattner, Walter I. [1974] 1989. *From Poor Law to Welfare State: A History of Social Welfare in America.* New York: Free Press.

United States Department of Housing and Urban Development. 1984. *A Report to the Secretary on the Homeless and Emergency Shelters.* Washington, DC: U. S. Government Printing Office.

Wright, James D. (Ed.). 1992. "Counting the Homeless." *Evaluation Review* 16(4) (entire issue).

Wright, James D. and Joel A. Devine. 1992. "Counting the Homeless: The Census Bureau's S-night in United States Cities." *Evaluation Review* 16:355–64.

Wright, James D., Beth A. Rubin, and Joel A. Devine. 1998. *Beside the Golden Door: Policy, Politics and the Homeless.* Hawthorne, NY: Aldine de Gruyter.

Zald, Mayer N. 1996. "Culture, Ideology, and Strategic Framing." Pp. 261–74 in *Comparative Perspectives on Social Movements: Political Opportunities, Mobilizing Structures, and Cultural Framings*, edited by Doug McAdam, John D. McCarthy, and Mayer N. Zald. Cambridge: Cambridge University Press.

NEWSPAPER ARTICLES CITED

Washington Post

1977

Column. McCarthy, Colman. "Night Hospitality." December 21.
D'au Vin, Constance. "Churches Tackle Job of Sheltering Roving Homeless Overnight." December 23.

1978

Editorial. "Night Shelter for the Homeless." January 29.
D'au Vin, Constance. "DHR Opens New Shelter for Homeless." February 10.
Hyer, Marjorie. "One Man's Battle to Build a Shelter for the Homeless." June 2.
Column. McCarthy, Colman. "A Bitter Church Conflict on Help to Poor." August 20.
Column. McKenna, Horace (Rev.). "A Night in a Public Shelter." October 28.
Valentine, Paul W. "Officials Back Visitor Center Use as Shelter." November 30.
Valentine, Paul W. "Officials Impatient with Live-In at Center." December 5.
Valentine, Paul W. "Street People in Visitor Center Vex U.S." December 7.
Valentine, Paul W. "Street People's Benefactors a Diverse Group." December 9.
Editorial. "Help for the Homeless." December 9.
Valentine, Paul W. " 'Street People' Locked Out Of Visitor Center by U.S." December 10.
Lardner, James and Paul W. Valentine. "32 Are Arrested In Protests at Visitor Center." December 11.
Valentine, Paul "10 More Arrested as Protests Continue at Visitor Center." December 12.
Valentine, Paul W. "Group Submits Formal Demand for 'Street People' Shelters." December 14.
Valentine, Paul W. "City Agrees to Provide More Homeless Shelters." December 16.
Valentine, Paul W. "Hunger Strike Against Church: Activist Wants Holy Trinity Building Funds for Poor." December 24.
Valentine, Paul W. "Militant Ends 4th Day of Fast." December 28.
Column. Cohen, Richard. "Exploring the Purpose Behind a Dying Man." December 31.

1979

Hyer, Marjorie and James Lardner. "Anguish Pervades a Georgetown Church: Parishioners React to 'Death Fast.' " January 1.
Valentine, Paul W. "High Catholic Officials Seek to Mediate Snyder Dispute." January 3.

Valentine, Paul W. "Protester on Fast in 'Perilous' State." January 4.
Column. Mann, Judy. "Snyder's Fast Shows Who Values Life Most." January 5.
Valentine, Paul W. "Snyder Ends His Death Fast After Rejection by Church." January 5.
Editorial. "The Act of Mitch Snyder." January 5.
Valentine, Paul W. "Effect of Snyder Fast on Poor Debated." January 6.
Column. McCarthy, Colman. "A Weakness in Christianity." January 8.
Column. Raspberry, William. "Rethinking Our Priorities." January 10.
Column. McCarthy, Colman. January 11.
Valentine, Paul W. "Experiment for D.C. Homeless." January 19.
Valentine, Paul W. "Scattered, Private Shelters Urged." January 20.

1980

Column. Mitchell, Henry. "One Man's Charity, Another Man's Choice." February 8.
Harden, Blaine. "A Man with No Fear of Hard Times: Virginia Hobo Says His Life Is 'the Way to Stay Happy.' " March 19.
"Order Blocks City From Transferring or Closing Shelters." May 5.
Henry, Neil. "Down and Out: Exploring the World of the Urban Derelict." 12-part series (April 27–May 8).

1981

"Barry: Some Public Buildings Will Be Opened to Homeless." January 1.
Janisch, Rick and Robin J. Stein. "Pacifist Fights to Get Help for Homeless." January 8.
Column. McCarthy, Colman. "Shelter for the Poor We Cannot See." January 10.
Editorial. Raspberry, William. "The Homeless Who Want Help." January 12.
Bonner, Allen. "The Drifters' Endless Odyssey: The Homeless Roam in City Powerless to Help." October 23.
Bonner, Alice. "Activist Group Gains Permit to Rebuild Tent Village Here." December 2.
Kiernan, Laura A. "U.S. Judge Rule Group Can Sleep In Federal Park." December 24.
Editorial. McCarthy, Colman. "A Gift to the Hungry and the Homeless." December 27.

1982

"Appeals Court Says Protesters May 'Camp' Near White House." January 23.
Column. Cohen, Richard. "Fatal Policy." February 4.
Letters to the Editor. "Death in a Cardboard Box." February 13.
Editorial. "The Death of Rebecca Smith." February 16.
Column. McCarthy, Colman. "Reaganville: Population Countless, and Growing." February 21.

Bowman, LaBarbara. "Shelter Poor For City's Homeless." June 27.

"Pie-Party Protest." July 2.

Remnick, David. "The Salvage Project: Food for the Poor From What's Thrown Away." July 24.

Richman, Phyllis C. "Second Helpings: CCNV Brings Home the Bacon—& Its Point." July 29.

Engel, Margaret. "1982's Homeless: Americans Adrift in Tents, Autos." August 14.

Column. McCarthy, Colman. "Feeding People Instead of Dumpsters." October 2.

Dobrin, Adam A. "Large Poor Families Face Critical Shortage Of Public Housing." October 6.

Kurtz, Howard. "Cities Stagger Under Needs of 'Newly Poor.' " October 14.

Kamen, Al. " 'Apple Pie Five' Jury Deadlocked." November 2.

Engel, Margaret. "America's Poor Overload Soup Kitchens, Shelters." November 23.

Editorial. "Thanksgiving." November 25.

"Thanksgiving 1982." November 26.

Kamen, Al. "Homeless Can't Sleep In Parks, Judge Rules." December 4.

Sargent, Edward D. "Federal Buildings' Use as Emergency Shelters Urged." December 16.

Column. Mitchell, Henry. "Saints and Cinders: Housing and the Homeless." December 17.

Editorial. "America's Dispossessed: Christmas on the Grates." December 25.

Column. McCarthy, Colman. "The Shocking Truth About the Homeless." December 26.

Editorial. "America's Dispossessed: The New Migrants." December 26.

Editorial. "America's Dispossessed: Searching for Jobs." December 27.

Editorial. "America's Dispossessed: What Needs to Be Done (I)." December 28.

Editorial. "America's Dispossessed: What Needs to Be Done (II)." December 29.

Editorial. "America's Dispossessed: What Needs to Be Done (III)." December 30.

Editorial. "America's Dispossessed: What Needs to Be Done (IV)." December 31.

1983

"Full Court to Hear CCNV Case." January 6.

Kamen, Al. "Appeals Court Weighs Rights of Homeless to Sleep in U.S. Parks." January 15.

Henry, Neil. "Freddie Dies: Streets of Georgetown Were His Home." January 24.

Teeley, Sandra Evans. "Homeless Care Adequate, Senate Hearing Is Told." January 25.

"162 Arrested in Protest for Jobs, Shelter." January 26.

Toth, Robert. "Agencies Explore Plan to House Poor in Unused Federal Facilities." January 29.

Column. McCarthy, Colman. "Out in the Cold with Chicago's Homeless Men." January 30.

Balz, Dan. "Tent City: Jobless Vacate Campsite after Order to Clean Up." February 5.

Column. McCarthy, Colman. "Homeless and Hungry and Headed for a Jail Cell." February 6.

"Judge's Order Shuts Tent City." February 8.

Melton, R. H. "Freddie's Path to the Street." February 9.

Editorial. "Dumb, Mean Budget Cuts." February 17.

Muscatine, Alison. "Suburbs Send Homeless to D.C. Shelters." February 19.

"Army Reserve Centers Considered for Shelters." February 22.

Engel, Margaret. "As Evictions Strike the Middle Class, the List of Homeless Grows Longer." February 23.

"Home Is a Motel." February 23.

"Moving Them Out: A Hurting Thing." February 23.

"Unwitting Victims: Getting Caught in the Hard Times." February 23.

"Middle Class: New Victims of Homelessness." February 23.

Pichirallo, Joe. "U.S. Buildings Available for Shelter." February 26.

Editorial. "The Suburbs' Homeless." February 27.

Valente, Judith and John Mintz. "Street People Win Limited Go-Ahead to Sleep in Park." March 10.

Gregg, Sandra. "Army Offer to Shelter Homeless Rejected." March 16.

"Cities Reject Spaces Offered for Homeless." March 17.

Bredemeier, Kenneth. "Group Barred from Sleeping in Mall Tents." March 18.

Column. Will, George F. "First Amendment Campout." March 20.

"Tents on Mall Taken Down." March 20.

Pianin, Eric. "Coalition Urges Barry to Keep Shelters Open." April 2.

Teeley, Sandra Evans. "New Policy Proposed on Helping Homeless in Freezing Weather." April 5.

Teeley, Sandra Evans. "Emergency Aid on Way for Summer Homeless." April 6.

"Loud Voices on Capitol Hill." April 19.

Column. McCarthy, Colman. "The Government's Go-Slow Shelter Program." April 23.

Column. McCarthy, Colman. "Getting the Food to the Poor." June 5.

Lardner, George. "House Votes Wider Food Aid Program." June 17.

Column. McCarthy, Colman. "The Politics of Cheese." July 10.

Hornblower, Margot. "New York City Is Exporting Its Homeless." July 16.

Column. McCarthy, Colman. "There's Hunger Right in His Neighborhood." August 13.

"New York Taking Back Homeless." August 16.

Hornblower, Margot. "New York Landlords' War on Poor Tenants Adds to Street People." September 9.

Kessler, Ronald. "Demand for Shelter by D.C. Homeless Is Greater Than Supply, Study Finds." October 14.

Editorial. "Homeless in the Cold." November 13.

"Local Groups Report More Needy Families Seeking Food, Shelter." November 21.

Valente, Judith and Leon Wynter. "More Needy Families Seek Aid." November 24.

Marriott, Michel. "Holiday Volunteers Turn out in Droves." November 25.

Column. McCarthy, Colman. "New Neighbors on Cordell Avenue." December 3.

Column. McCarthy, Colman. "The Congressman, and the Poor." December 4.

Kurtz, Howard. "Experts Dispute Answer to Housing Crisis—and Whether It Exists." December 18.

Struck, Myron. "Water Electricity Lack Raises Doubt of UDC Building Becoming Shelter." December 23.

Pichirallo, Joe. "Accord Reached on Homeless Shelter at Old Campus." December 24.

LaFraniere, Sharon and Michael Martinez. "Oliver Carr Opens Hotel Presidential for D.C. Homeless." December 25.

Martinez, Michael and Alison Muscatine. "Area Homeless Find Room at the Inn at Hotel Presidential." December 26.

Rich, Spencer. "Hunger Called Exaggerated." December 28.

1984

Kernan, Michael. "Snyder, the Wayward Shepherd." January 11.

Bruske, Ed. "Cooperation Marks Opening of D.C. Shelter." January 16.

Kurtz, Howard. "In Shelter for Homeless, Mayors Plead for Additional U.S. Aid." January 26.

Williams, Juan. "Homeless Choose to Be, Reagan Says." February 1.

McCarthy, Colman. "Reagan's Grate Society." February 11.

DuBuclet, Linda. "Seeking Out the Homeless." March 8.

Hentoff, Nat. "The Free Sleep Case." March 16.

Perl, Peter. "Supreme Court Hears 'Freedom-to-Sleep' Case Arguments." March 22.

Perl, Peter. "Reagan Orders Shelter Closing Delay." March 31.

Column. McCarthy, Colman. "Power Broker for the Powerless." April 8.

Pianin, Eric. "Some Homeless Denied D.C. Vote." April 10.

Kurtz, Howard. "HUD Says Number of U. S. Homeless Falls Well Below Private Estimates." May 2.

Column. McCarthy, Colman. "Just What the Homeless Needed." May 12.

Pianin, Eric. "Board Rules Homeless May Vote in D.C." June 5.

Guillermoprieto, Alma. "Street People Savor Decision Allowing Them to Vote," June 6.

Editorial. "A Man's Grate Is His Castle." June 12.

Kamen, Al. "Suit Asks Retraction of Study on Homeless." June 22.

Barbash, Fred. "Court Supports Ban on Sleep-ins in U.S. Parks." June 30.

Editorial. "Sleep, Speech and the Parks." July 3.

Letter. Berg, Terrence G. "Sleep and Protest." July 10.

Greene, Marcia S. "Ballot Initiative to Propose D.C. Shelters for Homeless." August 2.

Evans, Sandra. " 'Tent City' Erected to Protest Conditions at Shelter." August 16.

Smith, Philip. "Judge Dismisses Suit Disputing HUD Report." September 7.

Marriot, Michael. "Defense Diverted Funds Congress Appropriated to Shelter the Homeless." October 4.

Editorial. "Army 7, Homeless 1." October 5.

Boodman, Sandra. "D.C. Sues to Bar Shelter Initiative." October 12.

Snyder, Mitch. "Yes. Close to Home. Should We 'Require' Shelter for Homeless?" October 14.

Nahikian, Marie. "No. Close to Home. Should We 'Require' Shelter for Homeless?" October 14.

Anderson, John W. "11 Arrested at D.C. Shelter." October 20.

Anderson, John W. "27 Arrested at White House in Protest of Homelessness." October 25.

Bruske, Ed. "Shelter Issue to Stay on D.C. Ballot." October 30.

Boodman, Sandra. "Mitch Snyder Weakens As Protest Continues." November 1.

Shales, Tom. "On '60 Minutes,' A Somber Profile." November 3.

Boodman, Sandra. "U.S. Official Visits Shelter." November 3.

Barker, Karlyn. "Battle on Homelessness." November 4.

Smith, Phillip. "74 Arrested in Finale of White House Protest." November 4.

"CCNV Members Go to Market." November 4.

Boodman, Sandra. "A Life Style Dedicated to Poverty." November 4.

Boodman, Sandra. "Reagan Agrees to Refurbish Homeless Shelter." November 5.

Editorial. "Mitch Snyder's Victory." November 6.

Boodman, Sandra. "Snyder: Final Hours Hardest." November 6.

Boodman, Sandra. "Voters Approve Homeless' Right to Shelter." November 7.

Boodman, Sandra. "City Softens Opposition to Shelter Initiative." November 8.

Editorial. "What to Do about the Shelter Vote." November 9.

"Reagan's Point Man for the Homeless." November 11.

Berenbaum, Michael and Rosenfeld, Judith. Insight. "Snyder's Suicide Tantrum: What Does He Do for an Encore?" November 11.

Pianin, Eric. "City Forms Unit to Aid Homeless." November 17.

1985

Conconi, Chuck. "Personalities: Mitch Snyder Signs TV Movie Deal." February 21.

Kastor, Elizabeth. "Taking On the Grate Society." February 25.

Rich, Spencer and Jay Mathews. "Emergency Help Urged for Homeless." April 20.

Marriott Michel. "D.C. Shelter Closes Daytime Section." April 23.

Mathews, Jay. "Heritage Group Criticizes U.S. Aid for Homeless." April 28.

Brisbane, Arthur. "Clash Threatens Shelter Project." June 9.

Boodman, Sandra. "Homeless Shelter May Be Shut." June 14.

"2 Homeless Rights Advocates Arrested at White House Sit-in." June 15.

Boodman, Sandra. "Group Sues Over Shelter Renovations." June 18.

Column. Milloy, Courtland. "The Snyder Story." June 20.

Boodman, Sandra. "U.S. to Close Shelter for Homeless." June 22.

Milloy, Courtland. "Mitch Snyder's People, Fighting for Shelter." June 23.

Milloy, Courtland. "Judge Halts Posting of Closure Bills." June 23.

Boodman, Sandra. "U.S. Agrees to Delay Closing of CCNV Shelter for Homeless." June 26.

Boodman, Sandra. "Homeless Protest Shelter Closing." June 28.

Forgey, Benjamin. "Designs for the Homeless." June 29.
Anderson, Jack and Dale Van Atta. "HUD Cooked Statistics on Homeless." July 15.
Boodman, Sandra. "Reconsider Shelter, Judge Says." July 17.
Feinberg, Lawrence. "Ruling Keeps Shelter Open." July 27.
"D.C. Board Appeals Decision on Homeless Shelter Initiative." July 31.
Boodman, Sandra. "House Panels Weigh Shelter Repairs." August 2.
Bredmeier, Kenneth. "Judge Allows Shelter to Close If Homeless Are Relocated." August 20.
"CCNV Claims Harassment." August 26.
Mathews, Jay. "Head-Counting Efforts Complicated by Politics." August 26.
Bredemeier, Kenneth. "NW Shelter to Stay Open." August 30.
Editorial. "Where Is the Mayor?" September 3.
Bredmeier, Kenneth. "U.S. Proposes 40 Temporary Trailers for Homeless." September 7.
Editorial. "A Solution for the Homeless?" September 14.
Brisbane, Arthur. "U.S. Says Shelter Pledge Not Binding." September 20.
Brisbane, Arthur. "Barry Rejects Federal Plan for Homeless." September 21.
Brisbane, Arthur. "SE Shelter Foes Present Petitions at White House." November 5.
Shales, Tom. "Lukewarm Lucy." November 5.
Brisbane, Arthur and Lyle Harris. "Homeless Demonstrate Against Move." November 15.
Brisbane, Arthur. "Population at Anacostia Shelter Rises." November 19.
Feinberg, Lawrence. "Shelter Closing Approved." November 20.
Wheeler, Linda. "Shelter Attacked in Lawsuit." December 24.
Conconi, Chuck. "Personalities." December 24.
Hockstader, Lee and John Mintz. "Reagan Blocks Evictions at Shelter." December 29.

1986

Barker, Karlyn. "$250,000 Pledged for CCNV Shelter." January 4.
Engel, Margaret. "D.C. Allowed to Repair CCNV Shelter." January 8.
Conconi, Chuck. "Personalities." January 8.
Kantor, Elizabeth. "Adding a Sheen to the Shelter." January 13.
Kantor, Elizabeth. "Hollywood Meets the Homeless." January 13.
"Repairs Begin on D.C. Shelter." January 19.
Peterson, Bill. "Hunger, Homelessness Up Steeply, Mayors Say." January 22.
Tholes Cartoon, February 15.
Column. McCarthy, Colman. "The Homeless: Bad Policy, Not Bad Luck." February 23.
Column. McGrory, Mary. "Sheltering a Costly Grudge." February 25.
Jordan, Mary. "Cold Forces Many Homeless Inside." March 9.
Zibart, Eve and David Hoffman. "Reagan Offers City CCNV Shelter, $5 Million." March 16.

Mintz, John and Barbara Carton. "Snyder Agrees to Deal on D.C. Homeless Shelter." March 17.

Barker, Karlyn and Sandra Evans. "Snyder Turns to Hollywood for Funds." March 18.

Editorial. "The Shelter Embarrassment." March 19.

Jordan, Mary. "D.C. Shelter Residents Report Attacks by Staffers." April 12.

Brisbane, Arthur and Joe Pichirallo. "Police, FBI Investigate Spending by D.C. Coalition for Homeless." April 13.

Pichirallo, Joe and Chris Spolar. "Coalition Defends Shelter Operation." April 14.

Pichirallo, Joe and Arthur Brisbane. "U.S. Suspends $2 Million in Funds to Shelter Operator." April 15.

Brisbane, Arthur and Joe Pichirallo. "Homeless Issue Alliance Shift." April 16.

Brisbane, Arthur. "HHS Modifies Suspension of Homeless Coalition Grant." April 17.

Dawson, Victoria. "Snyder's Shelter and the 'Samaritan' Celebrities." May 13.

Column. McCarthy, Colman. "Mitch Snyder's Screen Alter Ego, Smoldering with the Same Anger." May 18.

Shales, Tom. "The Activist, Drearily." May 19.

Walsh, Elsa. "Homeless Initiative Ruled Valid." May 21.

"Mitch Snyder Threatens a New Hunger Strike to Force Fund Release." May 22.

Editorial. "Shelter Yes, Initiative No." May 22.

Barker, Karlyn. "At 3 P.M., Hands Were Linked and Voices Raised." May 26.

Pichirallo, Joe. "Snyder, 26 Followers Start New Hunger Strike." June 2.

Zibart, Eve and Patrice Gaines-Carter. "Reagan Pledges Shelter Funds." June 5.

Anderson, Jack and Dale Van Atta. "Justice Dept. Halts Probe of HUD Official." October 6.

Hirsch, Kathleen. "Who Will Save the Homeless?" *Washington Post Magazine* November 2.

Milloy, Courtland. "Playing Politics with Poor." November 27.

Lewis, Nancy. "Judge Rules for CCNV on Statue." November 29.

1987

"House Leaders Propose $500 Million for Emergency Aid to Homeless." January 9.

Engel, Margaret. "Speaker Pledges Aid for Homeless." January 11.

"No Room at the Capitol." January 15.

Rich, Spencer. "Group Says Aid to Poor May Fall 10%." January 14.

"No Room at the Capitol." January 15.

Column. McCarthy, Colman. "The Speaker for the Homeless." February 8.

Barker, Karlyn. "Refurbished D.C. Shelter for Homeless Opens." February 20.

Conconi, Chuck. "Personalities." February 20.

Mathews, Jay. "Homeless Shelter Officials Differ on Problem's Scope, Nature." February 28.

Barker, Karlyn and Eric Pianin. "The Grate Society." March 4.

Editorial. "Gestures and the Homeless." March 4.

Broder, David. "House Votes Additional Homeless Aid." March 6.
Column. Leland, Mickey. "A Night on the Grates." March 9.
Kenworthy, Tom. "$422 Million Homeless Aid Bill Introduced." March 24.
Jordan, Mary. "18 Million Homeless Seen by 2003." June 3.
Dewar, Helen. "Homeless-Aid Measure Waylaid by Pay Raise." April 9.
Dewar, Helen. "Senate Votes Homeless Aid." April 10.

New York Times

1978

McNeil, Donald G. "Drunks of Times Square Giving Area a Hangover." November 14.

1979

"Judge to Hear Suit on Derelict Shelter." October 27.
Kaiser, Charles. "A State Justice Orders Creation of 750 Beds for Bowery Homeless." December 9.

1980

Herman, Robin. "Some of City's Homeless Gather in Convention's Shadow." August 14.
Bird, David. "Wilted Lives On the Fringe Of the Garden." September 26.
Herman, Robin. "New York City Resists State on Shelters for Homeless in Residential Areas." December 30.
Herman, Robin. "Aide Denies Carey Assailed City Policy." December 31.

1981

Bird, David. "Help Is Urged for 36,000 Homeless in City's Streets." March 8.
Johnston, Laurie. "A Journey into the City's Netherworld." March 11.
Editorial. "Shelter." March 21.
Carmody, Deirdre. "New York Is Facing 'Crisis' on Vagrants." June 28.
Letter. Sakano, Rev. Donald. "Who Will Take New York's 36,000 Outcasts?" August 22.
Column. Schanberg, Sydney. "Ping-Pong for 36,000." August 25.
Editorial. "Hysteria and the Homeless." August 31.
Sulzberger, A. O., Jr. "Mayor Defends City's Handling of Its Homeless." November 20.
Goodwin, Michael. "S.R.O. Hotel: Rare Species." November 20.
" 'Reaganville' Camp Erected to Protest Plight of the Poor." November 27.
"Protest Group Gets a Permit to Put Tents by White House." December 1.

Column. Schanberg, Sydney H. "The Expendable People." December 15.
Herman, Robin. "City to Make a Count of Homeless People." December 30.

1982

Daniels, Lee. "Housing-Aids Cuts Affect Poor Individually and Collectively." January 3.
"Judge Approves New York's Plan to Shelter Men." January 6.
"Lawyer Terms Shelters for Women Inadequate." January 8.
Smothers, Ronald. "3,000 Families in City to Lose Welfare Funds." January 9.
Column. Quindlen, Anna. "About New York: The Priorities of Life by a Fire in the Cold." January 13.
Herman, Robin. "City's Homeless: Story of Bobby Cruz." January 16.
Rule, Sheila. "Many Families in East Harlem Seek Food Aid." January 28.
Waggoner, Walter. "Plight of the Homeless in Cold Stirs Contributors to Neediest." January 28.
Editorial. "A Place of Light, Refreshment and Peace." January 29.
Herman, Robin. "One of City's Homeless Goes Home—in Death." January 31.
Szasz, Thomas. "The Lady in the Box." February 16.
Editorial. "Forced Shelter." February 19.
" 'Reaganville' Folds Up After 4-Month Protest." March 21.
Herman, Robin. "Public Shelters in City Drawing Young and Able." April 26.
Cummings, Judith. "Increase in Homeless People Tests U.S. Cities' Will to Cope." May 3.
Shipp, E. R. "Suit over Homeless Mental Patients in City Asks State for Housing." May 21.
"Jobless Rates for April Set Record in 27 States." June 20.
Rosellini, Lynn. "Unkindly Cut Of a Tax Pie: 4 Leap into It." July 2.
Herman, Robin. "New York Trying to Add Shelters for Its Homeless." July 26.
Bird, David. "Study on Homeless Sees Some Gains on Shelters." July 28.
Editorial. "The Homeless, Revisited." July 30.
Herman, Robin. "More Beds for Homeless Are Needed, Group Says." August 16.
Editorial. "The Homeless Won't Go Away." August 23.
Herman, Robin. "City Is Dropping a Plan to Count Homeless People." September 6.
Shipp, E. R. "Lawsuit That Sought Homes for Homeless Dismissed by a Judge." October 5.
Editorial. "Hand-Wringing and the Homeless." October 15.
Letter. Connell, Sarah. Letter to the Editor. October 27.
Editorial. "Hidden Money for the Homeless." November 15.
"Thousands Give Thanks with Free Holiday Meal." November 26.
Editorial. "Mental Health Is Not a Jobs Program." December 1.
Peterson, Iver. "Homeless Crisscross U.S. Until Their Cars and Their Dreams Break Down." December 15.
Peterson, Iver. "Congress Is Urged to Help Homeless." December 16.
Column. Quindlen, Anna. "About New York: From Overabundance, Sustenance for the Needy." December 22.

Peterson, Iver. "Advent of Holidays Deepens the Scars of Those on the Road Seeking Work." December 24.

Anderson, Susan Heller. "New York Clergy Fault Government for Failures in Housing Homeless." December 25.

Peterson, Iver. "For Homeless, the Cheer Is Gone from Holidays." December 25.

1983

Teltsch, Kathleen. "Donations for Poor Quickly Depleted in Big Cities." January 1.

Navarez, Alfonso. "New Jersey Journal." January 9.

"Homeless to Get Place to Sleep Atop Nob Hill." January 18.

Carroll, Maurice. "Koch Says 'Not a Single Synagogue' Aids City's Program for Homeless." January 20.

Rule, Sheila. "3 Synagogues to Aid City's Homeless." January 21.

Goodwin, Michael. "Koch Shift on Shelters: Target of Criticism, He Becomes Critic." January 22.

Rule, Sheila. "3 State-Owned Buildings Open as Shelters in City." January 22.

"France Comes to the Aid of Its 'New Poor.' " January 27.

Perlez, Jane. "Rangel Seeking U.S. Aid for Sheltering Homeless." January 28.

"Rescind Tax Cut, U.S. Mayors Urge." January 29.

Tolchin, Marin. "All House Democratic Chiefs Ask Emergency Jobs and Aid Program." February 2.

Sheppard, Nathaniel. "Trail of 2 Lives That Disintegrated Led to Lonely Deaths on an Icy Day." February 3.

"Military Seeks Space to Shelter Homeless." February 5.

Goodwin, Michael. "Rabbi Rebutted by Koch in Dispute on Homeless." February 5.

Hoopes, Judith. "Princeton Harbors a Secret World." February 6.

"Equality in Shelters." February 9.

"Koch Visits Synagogue that Helps the Homeless." February 9.

Editorial. "Opening Doors for the Homeless." February 11.

Gaiter, Dorothy. "Cold Drives Record Numbers to Shelters." February 11.

Column. Schanberg, Sydney. "The Depression Army." February 15.

Letter. Sakano, Rev. Donald. "The American Dream at Its Irreducible Minimum." February 19.

Editorial. Koch, Edward. "Homeless: One Place to Turn." February 26.

"Warmth of Gloves, Warmth of Sentiment." March 2.

"Capital Park Sleeping Upheld." March 13.

"High Court Fails to Act on Park Sleep-In Case." March 19.

"Help for Homeless Criticized in Audit." April 1.

Letter. Goldin, Harrison. "Neediest Veterans Without VA Help." April 8.

Melvin, Tessa. "A Haven for the Homeless Extends Its Efforts." April 10.

"Nontraditional Offerings." April 11.

"Drama, Counterdrama." April 15.

Rule, Sheila. "17,000 Families in Public Housing Double Up Illegally, City Believes." April 21.

Parisi, Albert. "Home for Homeless Sought in Bergen." April 24.

Chira, Susan. "17 Groups Await Aid for Homeless." May 15.

Peterson, Iver. "Warm Season Masks but Doesn't End Problem of Homeless." June 3.

Editorial. "Cut Hunger, Not Food Spending." June 17.

Rule, Sheila. "Judge Increases Protection for Homeless Families." June 26.

Pear, Robert. "U.S. Hunger on Rise Despite Swelling of Food Surpluses." July 19.

"Reversal on Remodeling Men's Shelters." July 23.

"Campaign to Assist Homeless." July 28.

Dunlap, David. "Former School Opened by City as 16th Shelter." August 17.

"Welcome and Rejection for the City's Homeless." August 20.

Goodwin, Michael. "New Program in Shelters Stresses Work Ethic." September 7.

"Funds Approved to Aid Homeless." September 16.

"Sleeping Rights." October 4.

Rimer, Sara. "Religious Groups Plan More Shelters for Homeless." October 16.

Rule, Sheila. "3 Synagogues to Aid City's Homeless." October 19.

"A Haven on Verdi Square." October 21.

Rule, Sheila. "2000 More Beds for the Homeless Planned in City." November 24.

Sullivan, Ronald. "The Homeless: Officials Differ on the Causes." November 24.

Peterson, Iver. "Job Upturn Barely Felt in Shelters." November 29.

"More of Hungry Are Seeking Help." December 4.

McFadden, Robert D. "Comments by Meese on Hunger Produce a Storm of Controversy." December 10.

" 'New Homeless.' " December 11.

Schmidt, William. "Atlanta's Lack of Public Toilets Spurs Debate." December 19.

"Diversion for the Homeless." December 20.

Goodwin, Michael. "State Is Penalizing City Over Shelter Conditions." December 21.

1984

"Congress Is Asked to Help the Homeless." January 26.

Editorial. "Homeless by Choice? Some Choice." February 7.

Editorial. "Sound Investment for the Homeless." February 28.

Letter. Moynihan, Senator Daniel Patrick (D-New York). "Desperate Homeless Need Federal Attention." March 6.

Robbins, William. "11-Year-Old Ministers to Needs of Homeless." March 12.

Boyd, Gerald M. "Reagan Intervenes to Spare Shelter in Capital." April 2.

"Gimme Shelter Overnight." May 1.

Pear, Robert. "Homeless in U.S. Put at 250,000, Far Less Than Previous Estimates." May 2.

"Nonviolence in Action." May 18.

"Homeless Get Vote in District of Columbia." June 6.

"Demand for Housing Aid for the Poor Soaring, Report Says." June 15.

McQuiston, John. "Homelessness Spreading to Bedroom Communities." July 15.

Molotsky, Irvin. "Lafayette Park: Not Just Another Pretty Postcard." September 7.
Robbins, William. "A Boy Provides a Home for the Homeless." September 12.
"Fasting Wins Concessions on Shelter for Homeless." November 5.

1985

"Suit to Renovate Shelter for Homeless Is Lost." August 20.
"Aid for Homeless in Capital Sought." November 5.
"Federal Court Halts Eviction of 600 in Washington Shelter." November 21.

1986

"A Curt Exchange." January 17.
Shipp, E. R. "Do More for Homeless, Say Half of Those Polled." February 3.
Fuerbringer, Jonathan. "Homeless Are Not Duty of U.S., Reagan Aide Says." February 19.
"The Nation's Housing: An Affordability Crisis." March 16.
"Agreement Ends Dispute Over Capital Shelter." March 17.
O'Conner, John. "Sheen's 'Samaritan' and Robard's in 'Johnny Bull.' " May 19.
Shipp, E. R. "Budget Cutbacks Seen Leading to Wider Crisis of Homeless in U.S." May 22.
Kerr, Peter. "Millions Join Hands Across U.S. to Aid the Homeless and Hungry." May 26.
"Activist for Homeless Begins Hunger Strike." June 2.
"Hands-Across-America Pledges Unkept." August 31.

1987

"The Homeless Become an Issue." February 7.
"Chilly Night on a Sidewalk Grate Teaches Lesson about Homeless." March 5.
Fuerbringer, Jonathan. "Aid for Homeless Passed by House." March 6.
Pear, Robert. "President Signs $1 Billion Bill in Homeless Aid." July 24.

2003

Lueck, Thomas J. "Volunteers Gather to Count City's Homeless." February 25.

Other News Sources

1976

Sabath, Bob. "Community with the Poor in Washington, D.C." *Sojourners*, March: 30–33.

Colter, Stephan E. "CCNV Still Fighting for Evicted." *Washington Afro-American,* August 13.

1978

Ferris, Nancy. "Religious Group Bucks the Trend to Save Housing for the Urban Poor." *Washington Star,* February 12.
"CCNV Plans Action to Aid Homeless." *Rock Creek Monitor,* November 30.
Murray, Laura. "Interior: Nomads Disrupt Visitor Center." *District Star,* December 8.
Editorial. WHLA Channel 7, December 10.
Murray, Laura. "If Activist Dies, Who Is to Blame?" *District Star,* December 29.

1979

Spencer, Duncan and John Tierney. "Snyder Lives But What Did Fast Achieve?" *Washington Star,* January 5.
Editorial. "Mitch Snyder's Fast." *Washington Star,* January 6.
Interview. "Christian Radical Snyder Hasn't Finished." *Washington Star,* January 10.
Healey, Anne. "Value of Snyder's Fast Is Hotly Debated." *Catholic Standard,* January 11.
Column. Roll, V. Lynn. "A Sixties Child Reflects on Snyder." *Washington Star,* January 12.
Column. Du Vall, Jack. "Holy Trinity Was Not Callous." *Washington Star,* January 15.
Comment. "Mitch Snyder's Side of the Story." *Washington Star,* January 21.

1980

Gettlin, Bob. " 'Street People' Die Cold and Lonely." *Washington Star,* December 27.
Murry, Laura. "Barry Opens City Buildings to Homeless." *District Star,* December 31.

1981

Muth, Mark. "The Homeless: 'They Are Not Irrecoverable.' " *Christian Science Monitor,* February 6.
"Homeless People: 36,000 without Shelter in NYC." *Guardian,* March 18.
" 'Sleeping Rough' in the Big City." *Newsweek,* March 23.
Kates, Brian and Marcia Kramer. "The Buck Passing Business." *Daily News,* March 27.
Abrams, Arnold. "Below the Bottom Rung." *Newsday,* October 15.

Herbert, Bob. "Orders City to Open Armory for Homeless." *Daily News*, October 21.

"Protest Group Sets Up Tents Across from White House." *Boston Globe*, November 27.

"Thanksgiving on the Bench." *San Francisco Chronicle*, November 27.

" 'Reaganville' Protest Group Arrested Near White House." *Seattle Post-Intelligencer*, November 28.

"D.C. Protesters Arrested: Police Dismantle 'Reaganville.' " *San Diego Union*, November 28.

"Police Close 'Reaganville,' Arrest Protesters." *Philadelphia Inquirer*, November 28.

" 'Reaganville' Dismantled." *Baltimore Sun*, November 28.

Channel 4 NYC. "The Homeless: Shame of a City." *News*, December 7–14.

"A Tent City of the Dead, Dubbed 'Reaganville.' " *National Catholic Reporter*, December 11.

PBS. *McNeil-Lehrer News Hour*, December 25.

Brown, Frank D. "Homelessness Among Blacks Now Epidemic." *Amsterdam News*, December 26.

"Members of the Community of Creative Non-Violence Place Markers in Lafayette Park." *Baltimore Evening Sun*, December 29.

"Mock Cemetery To Protest Cuts." *Bremerton Sun (WA)*, December 29.

"Mute Protest." *Springfield Daily News*, December 29.

1982

Brown, Frank D. "Homeless Shelter Sparks Fear, Spite." *Amsterdam News*, January 2.

CBS. *60 Minutes*, January 10.

Muth, Mark. "Public, Private Sectors Unite to Find Housing for New York's Homeless." *Christian Science Monitor*, January 12.

Bell, Bill. "Into the Heart of Darkness." *Daily News*, January 26.

"Victims of Reaganomics: RIP." *Guardian*, February 3.

English, Bella. "Should We Seize Homeless People against Their Will?" *Daily News*, February 14.

"And the Long-Term Problem Remains: Homes." *Daily News*, February 14.

"Hungry So Angry." *New York Rocker*, March.

Walsh, Celeste. "Tent City to Rise Again, Some Say." *Philadelphia Inquirer*, March 24.

English, Bella. "Shelter Program Still a Bummer." *Daily News*, May 4.

"One Man's (Apple) Pie Is Another Man's Protest." *Washington Times*, June 30.

"Pie-In." *News American*, July 2.

"Apple Pie Slip-Up." *Dayton Daily News*, July 2.

"Slice of Life." *Los Angeles Times*, July 2.

"Applesauce." *Philadelphia Daily News*, July 2.

"Some Folks Have a Lot of Crust." *Seattle Times*, July 2.

"Giveaway Spoiled." *Houston Chronicle*, July 2.

Grande, Judy. "Scavenging Against Waste." *Cleveland Plain Dealer*, July 25.

Hume, Ellen. "Lawmakers to Dine on 'Garbage' to Dramatize Food Waste." *Los Angeles Times*, July 25.

Mezzacappa, Dale. "A Beggar's Banquet Set before Congress." *Philadelphia Inquirer,* July 29.

"Beggar's Banquet." *Time,* August 9.

"A Dumpster Quiche." *Newsweek,* August 9.

English, Bella. "More Homeless Expected." *Daily News,* August 16.

Langway, Lynn, Rick Rutz, and Mary Hager. "Here's the Throwaway Line." *Newsweek,* August 23.

" 'Reagan Ranches' in Over 15 Cities." *Washington Afro-American,* November 2.

"Crisis on Our Streets." *Boston Herald American,* December 16.

Sellars, David. "Deaths of Homeless Protested." *Washington Times,* December 29.

"Homeless Protest." *Baltimore Sun,* December 29.

"10 Vital Problems for the New Year." *USA Today,* December 30.

1983

"Senators Ask for Surplus Food." *Richmond-Times Dispatch,* January 1.

Acquaviva, Donna. "Federal Aid Asked for Homeless." *Washington Times,* January 25.

Van Riper, Frank. "2 Styles in Rapping Prez." *Daily News,* January 26.

Mezzacappa, Dale. "Poor See Different State of the Union." *Philadelphia Inquirer,* January 26.

Kramer, Marcia. "Cuomo Will Aid Drifters." *Daily News,* February 16.

Coalition for the Homeless. "On the Street." *NewsLetter,* Issue #2, February/ March.

"Appeals Court's Decision Upholds Capitol Tent City." *Idaho Statesman,* March 10.

Acquaviva, Donna. "Sleeping in Tents OK as Protest, Court Says." *Washington Times,* March 10.

"Court Lets Protesters 'Sleep' in Park." *Waterbury Republican (CT),* March 10.

Acquaviva, Donna. "No Tenting, Just Tents, in Park, Mall Last Night." *Washington Times,* March 18.

"They're Tenting But Not Sleeping." *Daily News,* March 18.

Denniston, Lyle. "Sleeping on Mall, Even as a Protest, Barred by Burger." *Baltimore Sun,* March 18.

"At Home in Reaganville." *Philadelphia Inquirer,* March 18.

Nadler, Eric. "Dorothy Day Meets Groucho." *Mother Jones,* May.

Neuman, Johanna. "Giveaway of Food Stashes Urged." *Pacific Daily News,* May 3.

Birnbaum, Jeffrey. "Congress at a Cattle Crossing." *Wall Street Journal,* June 14.

Goodman, Howard. "Protest to Seek Increased U.S. Food Giveaways." *Kansas City Times,* June 16.

Berg, Melissa. "Park Panel Lukewarm to Protest." *Kansas City Star,* June 22.

Purnell, Florestine. "Release More Food, Groups Say." *Kansas City Star,* June 26.

Purnell, Florestine. "Congressmen Urge Release of More Surplus U.S. Food." *Kansas City Star,* June 27.

"Subterropolis." *Time,* July 4.

Gemperlein, Joyce. "Fasters Aim to Free Surplus Food to Feed Nation's Hungry." *Philadelphia Inquirer,* July 4.

Martin, Vivian. "Crisis Foreseen unless Surplus Food for Needy Is Increased." *Hartford Courant*, July 5.

Shepherd, Marquis. "Fast to Protest Hunger in U.S. Begins in Kansas City." *Kansas City Times*, July 5.

"Fast Continues by Surplus Food Activists." *USA Today*, July 6.

Gibeau, Dawn. "Tons and Tons of Surplus." *National Catholic Reporter*, July 15.

"Giveaways for Needy Only, Official Tells Protesters." *Post-Dispatch*, July 24.

"Gregory Joins Hunger Strike." *Chicago Tribune*, July 19.

CBS. *Sunday Morning with Charles Kurault*, July.

"Two Groups from Area Back Fasters." *Post-Dispatch*, July 25.

Editorial. "Hunger: The Paradox of Bulging Storehouses and Empty Bellies Continues." *Detroit Free Press*, July 27.

"Speaker Backs Surplus Food Release." *Kansas City Kansan*, July 29.

Fehr, Stephen. "Dole Pushes Food Giveaway Plan through a Congress Hungry for Break." *Kansas City Times*, August 6.

Gibeau, Dawn. "Month-Long Missouri Fast Ends with Feast." *National Catholic Reporter*, August 12.

"Tabling Hunger." *New Republic*, September 5.

Evans, Rowland and Robert Novak. "Growing Scandal of Food Surplus as Millions of Poor Go Hungry." *Star (Washington)*, October 4.

Overend, William. "Homelessness Groups Plan a Political Thrust." *Los Angeles Times*, October 27.

"Americans Give Thanks at Home, Abroad." *Dallas Morning News*, November 25.

"Federal Move to House and Feed Homeless in U.S." *Daily News (Los Angeles)*, November 25.

"Meese Is Invited to Dine With Poor." *Richmond Times-Dispatch*, December 10.

"Hunger Issue Kept Alive." *Richmond News Leader*, December 15.

Quinn John, Editor. "Too Many Homeless for a Caring Nation." *USA Today*, December 21.

Main, Thomas. "Number of 'Homeless' Has Been Exaggerated." *USA Today*, December 21.

"Miracle on I Street Warms Capitol Needy." *Richmond Times-Dispatch*, December 26.

"Death Count Grows as Storms Hit USA." *USA Today*, December 27.

"Word Spread About Shelter." *Washington Times*, December 27.

"New Shelter Being Prepared." *Washington Times*, December 30.

1984

"Diana Hears." *Washington Times*, January 2.

Alter, Jonathan. "Homeless in America." *Newsweek*, January 2.

Cunningham, Dwight. "HUD Study Defining Homeless Problem." *Washington Times*, January 12.

Mezzacappa, Dale. "Red Tape Unraveled, Shelter Opens." *Philadelphia Inquirer*, January 16.

"Heckler Helps Out." *USA Today*, January 16.

"Secretary in a Soup Kitchen." *Baltimore Sun,* January 16.

Janisch, Rick. "The Feds Help Build Shelters." *Washington Tribune,* January 19.

Feinsilber, Mike. "Congressional Panel Told On-Scene about Plight of Homeless." *Richmond-Times Dispatch,* January 26.

Kramer, Marcia. "Gov Rips Ron on Lost and Homeless." *Daily News,* January 26.

"Mayors' Hands Out for Nation's Hungry." *USA Today,* January 26.

Mezzacappa, Dale. "For Those Without a Home, the Union's State Is Desperate." *Philadelphia Inquirer,* January 26.

"More Homeless Shelters Sought." *Middesex News (NJ),* January 26.

"Panel Goes to D.C. Shelter to Hear Testimony from the Homeless." *Baltimore Sun,* January 26.

Rothberg, Donald. "Mayors' Hunger Study Chief Says U.S. Failing Urban Poor." *Minneapolis Tribune,* January 26.

Shanker, Thom. "Mayor Urges Congress to Fund Shelters." *Chicago Tribune,* January 26.

"Seeking Shelter." *Richmond Times-Dispatch,* January 26.

Fustero, Steven. "Home on the Street." *Psychology Today,* February.

Askin, Steve. "Skeptical, Homeless Listen as Politicians Plead for Aid." *National Catholic Reporter,* February 3.

Column. Payne, Ethel. "Homeless by Choice or by Circumstances?" *Washington Afro-American,* February 7.

Ridgeway, James. "The Administration's Attack on the Homeless." *Village Voice,* February 14.

Kaplan, Janice. "Homeless, Hungry and Jewish." *Washington Jewish Weekly,* February 16.

"Young and Homeless." *Philadelphia Inquirer Magazine,* February 19.

Mezzacappa, Dale. "A Little Bit of Heaven for Many Homeless." *Philadelphia Inquirer,* March 3.

"Enfranchise the Poor—A Goal for '84." *Nation,* April 21.

"Mayor Barry Signs Petition for Homeless." *USA Today,* May 2.

"Barry Backs Shelter Referendum." *Washington Times,* May 2.

O'Leary, Timothy. "Street People Allowed to Register." *Washington Times,* June 5.

McGregor, James. "Dicklich, Paymar Join Suit to Discredit Homeless Report." *Minnesota News-Tribune and Herald,* June 22.

Bassuk, Ellen. "The Homeless Problem." *Scientific American,* July.

"Initiative 17: How Many Homeless Can D.C. House?" *City Paper,* July 27.

"Homeless Initiative on Ballot." *Washington Times,* August 2.

Farnsworth, Steve. "Homeless Systematically Undercounted by HUD to Minimize Issue, Critics Claim." *Los Angeles Times,* August 11.

"Group Rebuts Report on Homeless." *Kansas City Times,* August 16.

Bates, Leslie. "CCNV's Steve O'Neil Calls On D.C. to House Its Homeless." *City Paper,* August 24.

"Fight for D.C. Shelter Escalates." *Guardian,* September 5.

Dwyer, Jim. "Judge: Let the Homeless Vote." *Newsday,* September 27.

Harvey, Miles. "Capital to Vote on 'Right to Shelter.' " *Washington Times,* September 30.

"Washington Protest." *Associated Press,* October 19.

"Arrests at White House." *Daily News*, October 20.

"Arrests at the White House." *USA Today*, October 25.

"White House Protest." *Houston Chronicle*, October 25.

Lewis, Dennis. "Activists' Hunger Strike for Homeless Continues." *Washington Times*, November 1.

"Lobbyist Starves to Help Homeless." *USA Today*, November 1.

Gemperlein, Joyce. "White House Is the Target of Struggle to Help Needy." *Philadelphia Inquirer*, November 2.

"Carried from Protest." *Hartford Courant*, November 4.

"Hunger Strike Enters 51st Day." *Seattle Times/Seattle Post-Intelligencer*, November 4.

"Marchers Arrested at White House." *Cleveland Plain Dealer*, November 4.

Mezzacappa, Dale. "61 Demonstrators Arrested in Front of White House." *Philadelphia Inquirer*, November 4.

"61 Arrested in White House Protest." *State Journal-Register (Springfield, IL)*, November 4.

"61 'Harvest of Shame' Protesters Arrested Outside White House." *Miami Herald*, November 4.

"Activist's Fast Forces Renovations." *Winnipeg Free Press*, November 5.

Allegar, Bill. "Snyder's Fast Ends in Success." *Washington Times*, November 5.

"Champion of Homeless Ends Fast After Reagan Orders Renovation." *Dallas Morning News*, November 5.

Coppola, Michele. "51-Day Fast for Homeless Wins Demand from U.S." *Detroit Free Press*, November 5.

"Fast Ended." *Pittsburgh Press*, November 5.

"Fast Ends after Reagan Agrees to Aid Shelter." *Boston Globe*, November 5.

"Fast Ends; Reagan Agrees to Renovate Shelter." *Chicago Tribune*, November 5.

"Fast Ends With Agreement to Fix Shelter." *Kansas City Times*, November 5.

"Fast for the Homeless Ends." *San Francisco Chronicle*, November 5.

"51-Day Fast Helps Homeless." *USA Today*, November 5.

"Helping the Homeless." *Los Angeles Herald Examiner*, November 5.

"Hunger Strikers Tastes Success." *Milwaukee Journal*, November 5.

Irwin, Don and Doyle McManus. "Activist Gets Home for Poor; Ends Fast." *Los Angeles Times*, November 5.

McGinty, Derek. "Protester Ends 51-Day Fast after Pledge from Reagan." *Philadelphia Inquirer*, November 5.

Myre, Greg. "Fast for Homeless Is Ended." *Gardner Massachusetts News*, November 5.

"Reagan Officials Meet Faster's Demands." *Baltimore Sun*, November 5.

"Shelter: Citizens Fight for Home, Security." *Commercial Appeal (Memphis, TN)*, November 5.

"Snyder in Serious Condition: Ends Hunger Strike." *Washington Afro-American*, November 6.

"D.C. Backs Homeless Shelter; Hundreds of Issues on Ballots." *Baltimore Sun*, November 7.

"New City Unit for Homeless Starts Work this Week." *Washington Afro-American*, November 20.

1985

Chaze, William. "Helping the Homeless: A Fight Against Despair." *U.S. News and World Report*, January 14.

Thomas, Evan. "Coming in from the Cold." *Time*, February 4.

Hartman, Chester. "Why They Have No Homes." *Progressive*, March.

Dowling, Carrie. "Separate Dorms Divide Shelter Planners." *Washington Times*, June 12.

Mezzacappa, Dale. "Dispute Stalling Work on Capital's Shelter for Homeless." *Philadelphia Inquirer*, June 14.

"A Slide from Grace." *Washington Times*, June 19.

" 'Holiday Inn' for the Homeless?" *Newsweek*, July 8.

Hedges, Michael. "Federal Officials File Plan for Closing Homeless Shelter." *Washington Times*, August 1.

Hedges, Michael. "U.S. Can Close Shelter after Planning for Displaced." *Washington Times*, August 20.

Hedges, Michael and Peter Baker. "U.S. Delays Closing Homeless Shelter for Lack of Housing." *Washington Times*, August 30.

Hedges, Michael. "Attorneys Say Agreement Signed for D.C. Shelter for Homeless." *Washington Times*, September 27.

Adams, Jacqueline. "Protesters Drive to White House about Shelter Site." *Washington Times*, November 5.

Jacob, John. "Poverty Still at Record Level: Reagan Administration Thinks It's Best to Ignore Problem." *Washington Afro-American*, November 5.

Adams, Jacqueline. "Barnes Raps Reagan for Homeless Policy." *Washington Times*, November 8.

"Doonesbury." *D.C. Home News*, November 15.

Hanna, Ronald. "Feds Hint Metro Delays Possible Unless City Moves on Homeless." *Washington Afro-American*, November 16.

"Anacostia Neighborhood Coalition Official Files Complaint Against Florida Ave. Shelter." *Washington Afro-American*, November 26.

"Festivities, Sharing Mark Thanksgiving." *Los Angeles Times*, November 29.

"Parades, Reminders of Famine Mark Thanksgiving." *Baltimore Sun*, November 29.

"Reagans Spend Holiday at Ranch; Volunteers Feed Poor in D.C." *Philadelphia Inquirer*, November 29.

Conason, Joe. "Body Count: How the Reagan Administration Hides the Homeless." *Village Voice*, December 3.

"Homeless Remain in CCNV Shelter Despite Eviction Notice." *Washington Afro-American*, December 17.

Campbell, Gail. "Clake Urges Mayor to End Court Fight, House Homeless." *Washington Times*, December 30.

Dowling, Carrie. "New Influx at Shelter Is Forecast by Snyder." *Washington Times*, December 30.

1986

"Official Blame." *Des Moines Register*, January 6.

Gemperlein, Joyce. "Homeless to Mark Film about Them in High Style." *Philadelphia Inquirer*, January 12.

"Hollywood's Homeless." *Wall Street Journal*, January 13.

"Hollywood Stars Share Street People's Scene." *Richmond Times-Dispatch*, January 13.

Lynch, Lorrie. "Homeless Host Hollywood." *USA Today*, January 13.

"Hosts of a chic catered affair." *Los Angeles Times*, January 15.

McDougal, Dennis. "Comic Relief Will Give Aid to Homeless in U.S." *Washington Times*, January 15.

Moss, Desda. "Hollywood on Heat Grates." *USA Today*, January 17.

"Television's Good Samaritans." *Newsweek*, January 27.

"I Never Imagined That I'd Be Homeless." *People*, January 27.

Blair, Joann. "Mitch Snyder: 'Part Saint and Part Publicity Hound.' " *Cleveland Plain Dealer*, January 28.

Hansen, Susan. "Hollywood Discovers the Homeless." *National Catholic Reporter*, January 31.

"Not Mentioned in Reagan's Message." *Washington Afro-American*, February 8.

"Bringing the Hunger Fight Home." *Newsweek*, February 10.

"Making of a Bag Lady." *Globe*, February 11.

Kaufman, Marc. "More Homeless but Less Money." *Philadelphia Inquirer*, February 15.

Letter. Grant, Donald. "CBS's Role." *Wall Street Journal*, February 18.

"CCNV Fasts for Homeless; Administration to Pull Net." *National Catholic Reporter*, February 28.

National Coalition for the Homeless. "Opinions on Homelessness Subject of New York Times Poll." *Safety Network*, March.

Devereaux, Kathleen. "Snyder Still Fasts Despite Public Apathy." *Washington Times*, March 7.

"Fasting Snyder Hospitalized." *Washington Times*, March 12.

"HBO Provides 'Comic Relief.' " *Newsday*, March 12.

"These Comics Have a Cause—No Fooling." *USA Today*, March 13.

Wright, Tyra. "Union for Homeless to Focus on Housing, Jobs, Health." *Washington Times*, March 20.

Commentary. Kondratas, S. Anna. *Washington Times*, March 28.

Adams, Jacqueline. "Shelter Worker Fired After Assault Charge Revealed." *Washington Times*, April 14.

Dowling, Carrie. "Shelter Money Needed Now or It's Too Late, Snyder Says." *Washington Times*, April 15.

"Man Who Starved 33 Days Joins Hands Across America." *Globe*, April 15.

Roush, Matt. "Sheen Makes a Good 'Samaritan.' " *USA Today*, May 19.

Dowling, Carrie. "Snyder Threatens Another Hunger Protest for Shelter." *Washington Times*, May 22.

Drake, Bruce. "Hungry Out to Lunch: Ron." *Daily News*, May 22.

Minzesheimer, Bob. "Cicely Tyson Makes Plea for the Hungry in the USA." *USA Today*, May 22.

"President's Thought for Food." *Philadelphia Inquirer,* May 22.

"Actress Valerie Harper Spoke." *National Catholic Reporter,* May 23.

Belcher, Mary. "Reagans Join Chain in 'Hands' Campaign." *Washington Times,* May 26.

"Hunger Strike for Homeless." *USA Today,* June 2.

Wright, Tyra. "Snyder Swears Off Food, Water Until Shelter Is Funded." *Washington Times,* June 2.

Dowling, Carrie. "House Urges Hill to Act on Shelter Repairs." *Washington Times,* June 3.

"Renovations Begin Today." *USA Today,* June 23.

"Persistence Pays Off." *Washington Times,* June 24.

"Hands Across America: Too Little 'Commitment.' " *Washington Times,* August 26.

Malone, M. E. "Activists Say Estimate of 350,000 Homeless in U.S. Is Too Low." *Boston Globe,* September 6.

Mallin, Jay. "Activist Asks Jury to Probe HUD's Count of Homeless." *Washington Times,* October 15.

Gay, Lance. "New Federal Problem: Bringing Benefits to the Homeless." *Washington Times,* November 27.

Clardy, Jim. "Snyder Hosts Dinner on Capitol Lawn." *Washington Times,* November 28.

Blair, Gwenda. "Saint Mitch." *Esquire,* December.

"Homeless Coalition Plans National Strategy." *Sojourners,* December.

1987

Marin, Peter. "Helping and Hating the Homeless." *Harper's,* January.

"$70 Million Allocated to Feed, Shelter Poor." *USA Today,* January 15.

"Sheen Asks Aid for Homeless." *Baltimore Sun,* January 15.

Speers, W. "A Homeless Night." *Philadelphia Inquirer,* January 15.

"NAACP to Defend Tent City Leader Ted Hayes in LA." *Washington Afro-American,* January 20.

"Slow Descent into Hell." *Time,* February 2.

McManus, Jim. "Congress Begins Debate on New Homeless Relief Bill." *National Catholic Reporter,* February 6.

Dowling, Carrie. "CCNV Shelter Gets A New Wing; Snyder Asks for $5 Million More." *Washington Times,* February 20.

Moss, Desda. "Shelters Count on More Federal Aid." *USA Today,* March 3.

"Actors, Politicians Take to the Streets." *Baltimore Evening Sun,* March 4.

"Bedding Down." *USA Today,* March 4.

Boyle, Patrick. "Big Names Trade Beds for Grates—1 Night." *Washington Times,* March 4.

Robinson, John. "Camp-out for the Homeless." *Boston Globe,* March 4.

" 'Sleep-Out' for Homeless by Congressmen, Actors." *Philadelphia Inquirer,* March 4.

"Celebrities Turn Out for 'Sleep-Out.' " *Philadelphia Inquirer,* March 5.

"Sleep-Out." *New York Post,* March 5.

"Some Lawmakers Go Homeless for a Night, Don't Like It Much." *Wall Street Journal,* March 5.

"The Debate: Street People." *USA Today,* March 5.

Birnbaum, Jeffrey. "House Sends Senate $500 Million Bill to Aid Homeless." *Wall Street Journal,* March 6.

Aeppel, Timothy. "Shelters for Homeless on the Increase, but Most Longterm, Individual Needs Neglected." *Christian Science Monitor,* March 9.

Minzesheimer, Bob. "Pay Raise Foe Gives In; Homeless Bill Ok'd." *USA Today,* April 10.

Sirica, Jack. "Senate Oks $423 Million in Homeless Aid." *Newsday,* April 10.

First, Richard and Debra Roth. "Study Finds High Number of Blacks Homeless." *Washington Afro-American,* June 9.

Brown, Frank. "Where's the Help for the Homeless?" *Black Enterprise,* August.

Other News Sources

2002

National Coalition for the Homeless. *Safety Net,* Autumn.

Internet References

Homelessness: Programs and the People They Serve. http://www.huduser.org/publications/homelessness/ch_2h.html. December 13, 2002.

Interagency Council on Homelessness. About the Interagency Council on Homelessness. http://www.ich.gov/about/index.html. July 16, 2002.

National Alliance to End Homelessness. Homelessness Provisions in Final Fiscal Year 2002 VA/HUD Appropriations Bill and Accompanying Committee Report. http://www.naeh.org/pol/papers/2002VAHUDBill.htm. December 13, 2002.

National Alliance to End Homelessness. Highlights of the "Community Partnership to End Homelessness Act of 2002." http://www.naeh.org/pol/congress/CPEHAhighlights.htm. December 13, 2002.

National Association to Restore Pride in America's Capitol. History of the District of Columbia. http://www.narpac.org. March 15, 2003.

Urban Institute. Millions Still Face Homelessness in a Booming Economy. http://www.urban.org. February 1, 2000.

Index